I GAVE YOU LIFE TWICE

A STORY OF SURVIVAL, DREAMS, BETRAYALS AND ACCOMPLISHMENTS

An autobiographical memoir by

Henry Fribourg

The events and characters in this memoir are the product of the author's recollection of actual events, supplemented after the fact by research. Although the author strove to recount the factual basis of the writing as accurately as possible, inadvertent errors may have crept in unknowingly, and the author apologizes for any untruths or inaccuracies. At times, the author has presented his opinions on a number of topics; readers may disagree, and that is their privilege.

© 2003, 2004 by Henry Fribourg.
All rights reserved.

No part of this book may be reproduced, stored in a retrieval system, or transmitted by any means, electronic, mechanical, photocopying, recording, or otherwise, without written permission from the author.

ISBN: 1-4140-1090-7 (e-book)
ISBN: 1-4140-1091-5 (Paperback)

Library of Congress Control Number: 2003099144

This book is printed on acid free paper.

Printed in the United States of America
Bloomington, IN

A Rocking FB production

1stBooks - rev. 01/29/04

My deepest appreciation and love to
my wife Claude,
who has borne with me all these years
and who helped me edit this document.

My thanks to my sister Rosette
and to my brother Sylvain,
who reviewed this manuscript and
suggested needed clarifications and
corrections, and to my son Dan
for his careful editing, especially
of colloquial and cultural references.

Profound thanks to Rabbi Beth Schwartz
for her perceptive and thought-provoking review,
and to Nancy Waller
for her professional and valuable
editorial suggestions. Many thanks to
my colleague John Reynolds and to Bill Cleveland
for their invaluable comments and corrections,
and to my bibliophilic friends of the
Knoxville Morning Readers Book Club.

DEDICATION

*This document is addressed and dedicated to
my children, Daniel and Renée,
my grandson Bryan,
my nephews, nieces, grandnephews
and grandnieces Marc, Pascal, David,
Naomi, Aimée, Jonathan, Chris, Lauren,
Nastasia and Oliver, their current or
future spouses, and any descendants and
relatives who may be born into or join the
family through marriage or adoption,
and to the memory of
my grandparents,
my mother whose premonitions and tenacity
saved her family's life, and
my father whose intellect and investment
acumen made it possible.*

CONTENTS

Growing up—1929 to 1939 1
Fontainebleau 15
Winter Holidays and Truck Gardening 29
My Grandparents —and their Parents 33
Rumbles of Disaster—1939 46
The Retreat—1940 51
My Father's Walk through France 62
Living under the French Quislings—1940 to 1942 71
The Escape—Winter 1942 86
Cuba—1942 to 1945 94
Becoming a North American - 1945 to 1951 116
Becoming a Professional Agronomist 133
From Ph.D. to Pfc. 144
Finding my Love and Founding a Family 152
Claude and her Family's Escape 159
A Satisfying Career 164
In Search of our Beliefs and Ancestors 172
Henry's Ancestors 177
Claude's Ancestors 184
May their Memories be a Blessing 192
Traveling the World for Agronomy and for Me 195
Our Cabin on the Lake 220
Family Inheritances— Past and Future 223
Appendix I—Notes on the Descendants of Bernard Diedisheim
    and the Nordmanns 227
Appendix II—Speech Given by Charles Wolff on the
    Centennial of the Maison Wolff on September 19, 1948 230
Appendix III—Selected Professional Publications 237

PREFACE TO FIRST EDITION

As some of you may know, I have had an interest in our family's genealogy for some time, actually going back to before 1955, at which time I obtained information primarily from my maternal grandmother Renée Samuel Oury and from my father Jean Fribourg. I then used this information to develop genealogical trees which I composed during periods of free time when I was in the Army stationed at Fort Detrick near Frederick, Maryland. Later on, I transferred this information, plus many additions, to a computer program which is much more flexible, readable and useful than large rolls of unwieldy paper. My primary motivation for doing this is my conviction that if I, a person of the New World who still has vivid memories of the Old World, did not do it, it might never be done within our family, or be done only with much greater difficulty in later times.

Consider that I was born before television, penicillin, the polio vaccine, frozen dinners, regularly-scheduled commercial airline crossings of the Atlantic Ocean, before photocopying, plastic contact lenses, frisbees and The Pill. I was before radar, cellular telephones, credit cards, split atoms, laser beams and ballpoint pens; before pantyhose, dishwashers, clothes dryers, electric blankets, air conditioners, drip-dry clothes—and before humans had walked on the moon.

How quaint could I be? I was raised to think that closets were for clothes, not for coming out of. When I started to learn English in Cuba at the age of twelve, bunnies were small rabbits, not young women working for a magazine company, and rabbits were small furry animals, not German-made small cars. I was before househusbands, gay rights, computer dating, dual careers, and commuter marriages; before daycare centers, group therapy, and nursing homes. I had never heard of FM radio, tape decks, electric typewriters, artificial hearts, rock concerts, word processors, and males (other than pirates) wearing earrings. Before the War (World War II to me), "made in Japan" meant junk, and "McDonald's" and instant coffee did not exist.

When I first arrived in the United States in 1945, there were 5 & 10 stores where you actually could buy things for five or ten cents. For one nickel, you could ride a streetcar or a New York subway, make a phone call, and buy enough stamps to mail one letter and two postcards. Cigarette smoking was fashionable, and I almost achieved manhood when my parents allowed me to smoke my pipe in public at the age of sixteen. In 1945, grass was mowed, coke was a cold drink, and pot was something in which you cooked.

I do want it to be clearly understood that I am not, and never have claimed to be, a survivor of the Holocaust, that period during the 1940s when some human beings, mostly but not exclusively of Germanic heritage, demonstrated conclusively to the world that they did not belong to humanity. The millions who were murdered, and the few who survived to tell the tale, suffered indescribable hardships and tortures that stand as a monument to human endurance. It will become clear, during the recounting of this tale, that my parents, my sister Rosette, my brother Sylvain, and I, escaped from Europe just in time to survive, and before we could become either Holocaust survivors or Holocaust victims, at least in the traditional meaning of the words. Many of our relatives and friends, including two of my grandparents, were not so fortunate.

We escaped because our parents presciently felt the coming storms and were able to get us out of harm's way, to live another day in a new country. We were to live in a new country, not in our native France, but in the United States of America, land of freedom, opportunity and tolerance, where we could strive to fulfill our dreams and expectations. This we were able to do, surmounting governmental obstacles on both sides of the Atlantic and the perfidy of authorities in many lands, and in some instances we were helped by friends of all kinds of ethnicity and religion.

To all my relatives, those I have met and those I never knew before the Holocaust, all those whose traces I have been able to document in my genealogy, and those whose traces were lost to me, to all of them I dedicate this tale, and commend their memory to my descendants.

REMEMBER, DO NOT FORGET!

Knoxville, Tennessee, 1997

PREFACE TO SECOND EDITION

I did not realize, when I first wrote this tale, that there would be as great a demand for copies as there turned out to be. I had printed only a few dozens, distributing them to relatives in the US and abroad, and to a few intimate friends. Within a short while, my supply was exhausted, even as friends urged me to make this tale more readily available to the general public. I wrote the first edition while recovering from knee surgery, a convalescence that took many months.

Many readers of my early drafts marveled at the multiple details which I included, to which I respond that I have been endowed with a good memory which I was able to supplement with information from documents salvaged by my parents, by friends in France who turned them over to my family after the war, and by research into historical literature. Since the writing of the early drafts, I have gotten involved in digitizing my photographs and some of those inherited from my parents, in order to preserve them better for future generations, and thus I shall be able to include in this edition a number of illustrations. I have also had additional recollections of past events and have retired from my professorship at the University of Tennessee.

With more time available, I decided to revise and amplify my previous effort. I shall also be better able to afford to print several hundred copies, using some of the reparations money that the French government recently decided to award to my siblings and me in partial token compensation for the thefts that the predecessor governments committed against our family in 1942-1945. Finally, I have renamed this edition to "I Gave You Life Twice," a much more appropriate and less egocentric title than the "Fox-trot" of the first edition. The meaning of these phrases will become clear to the readers as they progress through this tale.

REMEMBER, DO NOT FORGET!

Knoxville, Tennessee, August 2003

GROWING UP—1929 TO 1939

Maybe I have your attention now, with these irrelevant and irreverent comments. So, let me start at the beginning, that is, on the tenth of March 1929, a Sunday, very early in the morning, when I was born in my parents' bedroom, in an apartment on the third floor (French numbering, where the first floor is one floor above the ground floor) of number 25, boulevard Bonne Nouvelle, in the Second *Arrondissement* (district) in Paris. The building probably dated from the house constructions that followed the creation of the boulevards on the sites of the former walls of the city by Baron Georges Haussman during Napoléon III's Empire. Although my mother always said I was born very early in the morning the birth certificate (HY 76823, 141/53) states I was born at 1540h; I have no explanation for the discrepancy. You may marvel at the extent of my memory, but in fact although I must admit I do not remember my birth, I do remember being brought into the same room on the 30th of May 1932 when my sister Rosette was born. I do recall that in my three-year-old's eyes, the room was very large, and overlooked the interior courtyard. In fact, the entrance to the building was through a large "*porte cochère*," *i.e.*, a door large enough for a horse-drawn coach, and the cobblestoned interior courtyard had been for the storage of these coaches. I remember vaguely playing in this courtyard, but I do not remember what was stored there, if anything. Certainly not our automobile, because we did not own one. In addition to my parents and my new sister, all four of my grandparents were there, and perhaps other relatives.

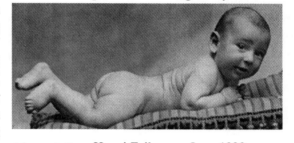

Henri Fribourg, June 1929

Besides the above description of my parents' bedroom, the earliest recollection I have is of towering waves, perhaps 60 to 90 cm (2 to 3 ft) high breaking over my head when my parents took me to the beach in Holland in the summer of 1931. I was also reminded numerous times in later years of how much of an embarrassment I had been to my parents, or at least to my mother, when I persisted in crying loudly, for no apparent reason, when they took me with them to visit an art museum in Amsterdam.

We moved from Boulevard Bonne Nouvelle to a third-floor apartment at 3, rue Paul Escudier not too long after Rosette's birth; I do not know exactly when, but certainly before I was old enough to go to kindergarten. The building had six stories, plus naturally the ground floor, and a small elevator with waist-high brass-framed large windows running up inside the spirally winding stairs.

3, rue Paul Escudier, Paris, June 2002 (the X marks my bedroom window in 1932-1938)

As I recall, when I was older, it was an easy walk up the stairs to beat the elevator to the third floor. I found out later, in 2002, that the building had been bought by my paternal grandfather, and my father had bought the third floor for our residence. All floors had two apartments, one on each side of the elevator landing. On the third floor, however, remodeling had taken place to join the two sides, because I recall some construction / renovation before we moved in to make the whole floor into one apartment.

When one entered the apartment and turned right in the hall, the kitchen was first on the left, and then the main bathroom. On the right were the living room and the dining room, which had no partition wall between them, only the grand piano on which I was later to spend many hours of practice. As I recall, there were four windows overlooking the street below from this combined large room, and there were red velvet drapes as well as sheer white lace curtains. Upon entering the apartment and turning left, the bedrooms were on the street side. First, my parents had a bedroom that had one or two windows looking out to the street. Then, my bedroom had a window overlooking the street, and my sister's bedroom was next to mine.

At the other end of the apartment, the last two rooms beyond the living room were my father's office, where he kept his business records. Often my grandfather Albert Fribourg also would work there with my father. One of the fascinating things they would do would be to make copies of hand-written letters and order forms, using a wet process of some sort, whereby the original on white paper, and paper suitable for the copies, which were made on thin yellow sheets, were placed flat into a press, and a large screw had to be turned on top to squeeze the sheets together, in a manner similar to that used by Gutenberg when he printed his first bibles. In later years, it used to be a thrill for me to be allowed to turn that big screw down, wait the requisite time, and then back it off. The wet copies had to be laid on flat shiny (aluminum or galvanized) metal sheets to dry.

I later learned that my father was carrying on the sales practice which his father had founded in Paris. They were the sales representatives in Paris for textile and clothes manufacturers, many of whom were out of town, primarily in the Lyon, Villefranche, and St. Etienne areas. A large portion of the business was for men's work clothes, but there must have been many other kinds also, because I remember my father explaining to me that the quality of woolen and cotton cloth was dependent on how many strands there were per centimeter, and how thick the cloth felt between the thumb and index finger, and whether the strands were regular when looked at closely. He knew about cotton, flannel, wool, and other kinds of fabrics, some of which would have been used in clothing other than men's work clothes. The feel of wool clothing also was very different from that of cotton, and many other things had to be considered to establish the worth of a cloth. In later years, much of the work was conducted from the office, using an upright black desk telephone. Often, though, my father had suitcases of clothing samples, as well as many books of swatches that he would personally take to the customers. I guess that I was considered too young to be asked whether I would care to accompany him, although I would have been interested. As I recall, the major customers were the *grands magasins*, department stores such as La Samaritaine and Les Galleries Lafayette, where he met with their purchasing agents. I do not know whether he also visited small or specialty men's clothing stores.

This business apparently was lucrative, having been started by my grandfather some time before World War I, and expanded by my father. In fact, my grandfather Albert had a taxicab business at the turn of the 20th century. This business was run from a house at 120 *bis*

Avenue de Neuilly, on the right-hand side, about half-way down from the Arc de Triomphe down to the river, on the other side of which now is La Défense. I know that because my father often alluded to the fact that he had been born in 1901 in the bedroom above the stables where the horses were housed. Since my paternal and my maternal great-grandparents and my paternal grandmother had been born in Lorraine, and my grandfather Albert had served in the French Army and was a reserve officer, I have deduced that my great-grandparents had left eastern France following the forced annexation of Alsace and Lorraine by Germany after the Franco-Prussian War of 1870-71 (the Prussian von Bismarck's war). This departure occurred prior to my grandparents getting married at La-Ferté-sous-Jouarre (Seine-et-Marne) on 26 January 1897, when Albert was 31 and lived at 23, rue de Berne (23rd arrondissement in Paris) and Lucie was 24 and lived with her parents at 43, rue d'Ussy at La-Ferté-sous-Jouarre. My grandfather apparently was slow in recognizing the advent of automobiles and that horse-drawn *fiacres* could not compete with gasoline-powered cabs. So, sometime after my father was born, my grandfather had probably gone bankrupt, and then started the clothing representative agency. As noted earlier, this agency was doing very well by the time I recognized its existence in the late 1930's.

When my father was a young man and registered for military service in 1922, as required by law, he lived with his parents at 14, rue Damrémont (Paris 18e). This major thoroughfare runs along the northern lower edge of the hill of Montmartre. I have no idea as to how long they lived there. My father excelled in mathematics, both when he received his *baccalauréat* on July 10, 1918 after attending the Lycée Chaptal and, after several years of study at the Académie de Paris (La Sorbonne), when he obtained a Certificat d'Etudes Supérieures (equivalent to an M.S. degree) in Mathematics on July 7, 1922 at the young age of 21. I am sure that it was a matter of considerable disappointment to my father, for his entire life, that he was not able to continue a career in mathematics, physical sciences, or engineering. He was an only child, and he undoubtedly recognized, or was pressured by his parents to recognize, that his obligation to earn a living to take care of a future family mandated that he associate himself with his father in the clothing representation business. I suspect that this attitude may not have been unusual among emancipated urban Jews in France, removed from the villages of Alsace-Lorraine by only two generations. In a way, it is very fortunate that he did and was successful at it. Otherwise, he would never have accumulated the financial resources that enabled our family to escape from Europe during the war and survive for several years when he was not allowed to work and so could not earn a living.

He loved mathematics all his life, and I know he was disappointed that I did not share his enthusiasm and ability as a youngster. He did try to tutor me in algebra, helped me learn to do simple arithmetic in my head, and attempted, with little success, to teach me some calculus. After I started teaching statistics at the University of Tennessee, however, he did recognize that I had followed in his footsteps to some extent, although a practical pedestrian use of mathematics such as statistics was not quite in the same league as learning and proving abstract theorems!

My mother often recalled fondly having attended the Lycée Lamartine. My sister Rosette remembers that our mother had a degree from the Ecole des Beaux-Arts in Paris. I do not know how many years of study this represented. Since the Ecole des Beaux-Arts did not admit female students until 1900, it was a real accomplishment for her to have been admitted right after the end of World War I. I suspect that this educational background was considered by my mother, and by her parents, as an appropriate prelude to her becoming a wife and mother, and never as a means of preparing her for a business vocation. On the other hand, both my parents revealed, after their financial condition had improved after several years of living in New York, that they liked antique furniture, original paintings, and objets d'art of all kinds. It is clear to me, however, that our mother had unusual common sense, and was a resolute, and some might say, an obstinate, realist. It is thanks to that characteristic that our family escaped the Holocaust.

In early October 1934, I believe, I was taken to the kindergarten at the Lycée Jules Ferry, which was not too far from our home, near the Place Clichy. I recall discussions as to whether this was too early for me, but because my birthday is in March, I was old enough to be entitled to start in school the following October. An early start in the school process was judged to be to my competitive advantage by my parents. The Rue Paul Escudier runs into the Rue

Blanche, about half-way up the hill, as the Rue Blanche climbs the hill from the Eglise de la Trinité to the Place Clichy. The Lycée Jules Ferry was then, and still was in 1986, at the top of the hill, just one block off to the right from the Place Clichy on the boulevard. The kindergarten was either in the first or the second room off to the right when you entered the Lycée from the corner main entrance. My mother would walk me to school in the morning, and would come to walk me back in the early afternoon.

A year later, I started elementary school at the Ecole Communale de Garçons, 32, rue de Bruxelles, a school that was still there in 1986, although it appeared that the very large inner courtyard used as a playground, visible from the street through the grilled gate, had "shrunk" considerably during the years since I left there in 1939. I have found this shrinking to have occurred in all the buildings I remember from my youth, as I have gone back to see them later as an adult—a phenomenon which afflicts most human beings.

Henri in school uniform, 1936

The walk to school was not too long, about four or five blocks, but I remember not liking it in winter, because the woolen underwear shorts I was made to wear, in order not to catch cold, were scratchy and irritating. Just like all the other boys (yes, it was a boys-only school, a normal situation in those days) I wore a black smock over my clothes and under my overcoat, so that everybody looked the same in school. However, that did not stop the other kids from finding out that I was Jewish and therefore an appropriate target to be picked on by some at recess, although the abuse was not severe at that time. The probable way that they found out I was Jewish was by having some taller older boys examine me over the partitions when we used the urinals that were off to the right hand side of the entrance gate to the asphalt playground/courtyard, since circumcision in France in those years was essentially limited to religious ones. I recall that this topic was of considerable interest to the younger male teacher of the beginning grades of *Sixième* (Grade 6, the first school year after kindergarten) and/or *Cinquième* (Grade 5), who was quite athletic and did not shrink from using his feet on the backside of boys who had displeased him.

I recall that the teacher of *Deuxième* (Grade 2 - the fifth year of elementary school) was M. Boucher, who had a long commute from the suburb of Le Vésinet. He was tall, fairly heavy but not fat, wore tortoise-shell-framed eyeglasses, and was always dressed in a brown suit. His classroom was on the first floor, right above the principal's office, whereas all the other classrooms had doors that opened right on the interior courtyard, on the ground floor. I liked him a lot. A major extracurricular accomplishment of that year was my earning the first diploma I ever received. It certifies that on April 13, 1938, I became a school swimmer, having swum in deep water, and without any help, for a distance of 25 meters (80 ft).

The teacher of *Première* (Grade 1), M. LeMaitre, was feared because he was extremely demanding. This fear was somehow reinforced by his appearance, since he wore rimless spectacles, somewhat unusual in those days. The 2nd of June 1939 report card which survives from this class is signed by M. Lacombe, the principal. In any case, M. LeMaitre did his job well, because at some time during the 1939 spring I took the all-day written competitive examination (separating the goats from the sheep!) for admission to secondary school at the very high caliber Lycée Rollin. This was the lycée where my late uncle Robert, my mother's younger brother, had gone to school, before dying of a ruptured appendix followed by peritonitis about four years before I was born. It had been made clear by my parents that this was where I was expected to be admitted to go to school. The expectation from my parents reinforced my own motivation to excel in school. I remember well being overjoyed several long weeks later when written notice was received that I had been accepted to enter the Sixth Class, Section B (mathematics and science, not Latin and Greek which were Section A) at the Lycée Rollin in the fall (first Monday of October) of 1939. This admission was considered quite an achievement, since it implied I would not have to earn my living in the future by being a blue-collar worker earning his bread with the sweat of his brow and the calluses of his hands. Rather, I was being ushered into the more privileged antechamber of the intellectual world.

Yvonne and Jean Fribourg, Jardin du Luxembourg, Paris, winter 1938

We celebrated this achievement with a many-course "*dîner*" (starting about 1400 h) at one of the better Parisian restaurants, Restaurant Drouaut. All of us were there, my parents, my sister, and my four grandparents. It was a memorable lunch, lasting several hours, with langouste (European lobster, looks like a giant shrimp or crayfish) and white wine, roast leg of lamb and red wine, salad, several cheeses, and dessert. That meal started with "Père" (Father = old man) Binet's radishes and vegetable salad, followed by bass from Brittany served with a 1926 Viersteiner, a German Rhine wine bottled by Hoch Söhne, from Maïnz. Following a dish of mixed beans, a roast side of Sussex lamb was served with a Burgundy wine, Beaune des Hospices, first 1923 pressing. The romaine salad then preceded the Brie cheese from Melun, which was followed by ice cream served with chocolate-covered oak-leaf cookies, accompanied by a 1930 Pol Roger champagne. A basket of assorted fruits was then brought out, following which coffee was served. Armagnac and Cointreau were made available to the men, my father and my grandfathers; I had to be satisfied with a *canard*, a lump of sugar soaked in my father's glass of liqueur. The menu bears the caption written by me *"Un repas sans vin, c'est comme un jour sans soleil"* (a meal without wine is like a day without sunshine).

I remember a few events from Thursdays, the day off from school. Yes, school was on Mondays, Tuesdays, Wednesdays, Fridays, and Saturday mornings. I do not know when or why this particular schedule was initiated, but I believe it was changed after World War II to provide the longer weekends that the urban dwellers demanded. Actually, even before I started school, our mother on Thursdays took my sister Rosette and me to the Parc Monceau (one time I left the baby carriage to walk around a grove of trees, got lost, and boy, did I get reprimanded when I either re-appeared or mother found me), to the Jardin du Luxembourg, and to the Jardin des Tuileries. Sometimes we also went, usually as a family, to the Jardin des Plantes or to the newer Jardin Zoölogique in Vincennes, which really interested me at that time. It was much later in life that I began to consider zoos as fancy, and sometimes not so fancy, prisons for helpless animals—even in spite of the current justification for perpetuating biological diversity. I know one of my greatest regrets was that I never did get a toy sailboat with which to play at the Tuileries, where the fortunate kids would sail theirs from one side to the other of the circular ponds. The greatest tragedy was when a boat capsized in the middle of the pond and could not be retrieved, for no one, to this day, has ever been allowed to wade in these ponds for any reason.

After I started school, of course, Thursdays were not just days during which to play, but were the days when mother would take me to recreational/educational activities. We went to the Théatre du Châtelet at least twice, but I have no recollection of the plays presented. Some Thursdays we would go to the Musée de l'Homme at the Palais de Chaillot (the Trocadéro was brand-new then, but already had many hominid skulls) or to the Louvre to see masterpieces. A World's Fair took place between the Palais de Chaillot and the Tour Eiffel in 1937. Our family went there at least a couple of times, and I remember hearing synthetic music there for the first time, and seeing a working television. These were then marvels of the scientific age, but their integration into everyday life was not even suspected by my parents. On the other hand, I remember that my grandfather Albert anticipated the advent of laser beams when he speculated that future wars would be conducted long-distance with "killer rays."

We went to the Musée de Cluny for medieval education, and to the Cité to visit Notre Dame and the Sainte Chapelle. We also went to Versailles to marvel at the Great Sun King's accomplishments

(Louis XIV), and to the Petit and the Grand Trianon. It was whispered that some of the great rulers of the past used the smaller palaces for their mistresses!! I remember my mother taking just me to the Champs Elysées in spring, probably in 1937, to a great cinéma (two-thirds of the way up to the Arc de Triomphe from the Rond-Point, on the left side) to see the first color movie I ever saw, Blanche-Neige (Snow White) with her little friends coming back home from the *boulot* ("*Hayo, hayo, on rentre du boulo* "goes the song, *boulot* being a slangy word for work). Rosette remembers going there too, and crying so hard after Blanche-Neige had eaten the poisoned apple that we all three had to leave. It is probable my mother took me back so I could see the whole film, but my memory is hazy on that subject. That excursion had been promised for a long time, and it was a great thrill. In late autumns, we did some window shopping at the Grands Magasins to see the Noël decorations and the toys. A toy that I always had wanted, but never got, was an electric train. However, Jean Pasdeloup, who lived on the fourth floor right above us at Rue Paul Escudier, had a monster of an electric train, the track ran all over the living room, and he and his father Lucien sometimes would invite me to play with the two of them—that was a rare but wonderful treat.

My closest friend in school was a Jewish boy one year older than I, and therefore one year ahead of me in school. Since he was pretty big, he would protect me and, since he lived on the Rue Blanche less than a full block away from the Rue Paul Escudier, we almost always walked together to and back from school. His name was Gert Rothschild, known in French as Gérard. His father was a refugee German Jew, and his mother was Swiss. His father did not survive the war, but Gert and his mother were able to use her Swiss passport to spend the war, and later remain, in Switzerland. Many years later, and through connections with my wife Claude's family, we were reunited by mail in the 1970's. Our family met him, his wife Marlyse and their two daughters Dominique and Muriel on our return from Turkey in 1974. We all went hiking in the mountains around Sion where Gert had a vacation home. Claude and I also visited Gert and Marlyse at their home in Basel during a long weekend in 1986 when I was teaching in Lille, France. Later on, Dominique and Muriel married two Batteguay brothers, who are sixth cousins, once removed, of my wife's. So, after all, Gert and I turned out to be related, some sixty years after we first met.

It was Gert who got me interested in joining the *Louveteaux* (Cub Scouts) where he had been a member for maybe a year before I was judged old enough to join. I did join the *Meute* (Pack) Hillel of the Groupe Crémieux of the Eclaireurs Israëlites de France (EIF) on 28 April 1938. After a suitable learning period, I took the oath of allegiance on 26 June 1938. My identification card for 1939 (Hebrew year 5699), number 5770-D, states that I obtained my First Star (first advancement beyond tenderfoot) in January 1939 and my Second Star (fully-qualified *Louveteau*) on 4 March 1939. A gorgeous strawberry blonde in her early twenties was Pack Leader; her name was Hélène Salomon.

At this point, I should explain that the scouting movement in France is organized differently than in the US, where there are two organizations, the Boy Scouts and the Girl Scouts, differing only in the gender of their adherents. In France, there were several organizations, independent of each other, and based on religious inclination and, within that, on gender. There was a Jewish association (EIF), a Catholic movement (Scouts de France), and a lay group (Eclaireurs de France, EDF). I do not recall whether there was a movement associated with Protestants who, after all, consisted a minority group almost as small as the Jews. Individuals joined whichever group they and their parents decided, there was no discrimination or compulsion dictating affiliation. Before World War II, I belonged to the EIF; after we left Paris and lived in Vichy France, I joined the EDF. Jewish holidays and the Sabbath were observed in the EIF, whereas only state holidays were of consequence in the EDF.

I remember that, for the first several outings of the Cub Scouts group, my mother took me to the gathering place, at the end of a bus line at the Porte de Meudon in April and May 1938. After a few times, however, I was instructed in minute details by my parents on how to proceed to get there on my own, and admonished about whom to talk to and whom to avoid. I was then permitted to go, in my uniform, by myself, to the meetings each Thursday. My mother insisted on verifying that all my school homework was completed before I could leave. I still feel the wind blowing around me as I went to and returned from these meetings, riding in the rear standing-room-only entry/egress platform of the Parisian buses of the day. I also remember my disappointment at not being allowed to go once or twice when there were labor strikes and demonstrations in some areas traversed by the bus route, when my parents decided I should not be exposed to this potential danger of street demonstrations by the C.G.T. (*Confédération Générale du Travail*, the very large, reputedly communist-tainted labor union).

Occasionally, perhaps once a month, there also were outings on Sunday, when several packs got together for all-day long outings and competitions. In winter, there also were indoor competitions, perhaps at the headquarters building on the Avenue de Ségur. It was at such a Purim competition (*kermesse*) that I won one of the few things I have ever won at a game of chance (a raffle), a floating bath thermometer, a red-tinted spirit thermometer mounted in a brown, unpainted wooden floating frame about 15 cm (6 in) long. It was used many times thereafter to ensure that my bath water would not scald me—showers were unknown to us in those days—as far as I know, they did not exist.

As a recompense for the rapid advances I had been able to make in the Cub Scouts, and as a special favor, in some way that I never learned, I was allowed to join the troop of Boy Scouts with which my Cub Scout pack was affiliated in its summer camping outing. I suspect that the fact that two of my cousins, Pierre and Paul Guthman, were leaders of that troop, was related to my being permitted to join the group. Pierre's *totem* (presumed American Indian name by which a scout was known—see the chapter "Living under the French Quislings "for more detailed explanation) was *Condor* because he was tall and had been born in Argentina, and Paul's was *Fourmi agile* (nimble ant), a reference to his smaller frame and high energy level. In any case, this was a great adventure, to go with the troop by train to somewhere near Annecy (Haute-Savoie), hike several km up the mountain on a packed-dirt road, and set up camp in the Praz-de-Lys near Annemasse (Haute-Savoie). At that time, there were a few dairy farms in that high valley surrounded by towering mountains, although now it is covered with vacation homes. We thirty or so Scouts lived in tents up there for 3 or 4 weeks, taking a couple of strenuous (for me particularly, the youngest of the group) hikes each week. On Fridays, we had to cook twice as much as normal, and then half of the hot food was buried in stone-lined pits with glowing coals so that we could have hot food on the Sabbath, since a fire was not to be lit and cooking was not to occur on the Sabbath. I remember sneaking up on some huge Brown Swiss cows wearing bells, and sometimes squeezing some warm milk straight into my mouth. During a particularly rainy spell, the tents were leaking so much that at least some of us younger ones were allowed to ask for and get permission to sleep in some hay lofts. I can still smell the wonderful smell of that hay.

At one point, we took a long-anticipated day climb of the tallest peak surrounding our valley. I remember struggling on all fours toward the peak, because the rocky slopes were so steep, and our delight at finding a small pocket where there was snow in July. There, I took a photograph of some of my friends with my little box camera. The peak of the mountain was actually a flat top of rock with sheer straight walls, and I was roped up to climb and partly to be hauled up to the top. At the summit, there was a concrete monument with a metal plaque to the memory of several persons who had perished there after being struck by lightning. After gloating at our accomplishment of having climbed this highest of the mountains in sight, we clambered down the other side to reach a highly touted mountain lake where we were to take a swim. It was a rude awakening to find out that the water was absolutely frigid. Those fellows who proved their manhood by total immersion and swimming came out of the water covered with leeches. This event has remained in my memory all these years, and may explain my reluctance at swimming in unfamiliar places.

I do not remember anything else from this overall very happy period, even though we were all, children as well as our parents, much aware of the approaching war storms, since this camp took place ten months after Prime Ministers Neville Chamberlain's and Edouard Daladier's surrender of Czechoslovakia at München (Munich, 29-30 September 1938), 15 months after the Germans invaded and annexed Austria (*Anschluss* of March 1938) and a short three months after they marched into Prague (March 15, 1939). We did go one time into Annemasse with a bus, and on into Switzerland, on a one-day trip. I did purchase one of those special wooden-handled folding knives typical of the Alpine region of France and Switzerland. My last recollection of that summer camp is walking the three blocks from the church on the Rue Grande in Fontainebleau along Rue de la Paroisse to my parents' house at 97, rue St. Honoré. Apparently, by pre-arrangement, I had been left off the train returning from Annecy to Paris at the Avon station, and had taken the streetcar from Avon to Fontainebleau, getting off at the church. I was carrying a huge (to me) knapsack with a metal frame against my back, a large sleeping bag and blanket roll strapped on the outside of the pack, with all the dirty clothes and gear used for camping, and I had not had a decent bath in four weeks. When I finally arrived at home, my mother barely greeted me before demanding that I take a bath immediately. I must have smelled something awful.

FONTAINEBLEAU

The Château de Fontainebleau, started by François 1st in the 16th century, is known for its Cour des Adieux, where Napoléon bid goodbye to his troops in 1814. Our home was much smaller!

Let me tell you now about Fontainebleau, a small town about 62 km (38 miles) southeast of Paris (see page 54) where we spent many weekends during the school year, from early October to late June, and the summer vacations.

The first house that I recall was at 16 *bis* rue Royale, the street that runs from the main gate of the Cour des Adieux of the Château de Fontainebleau to the Forest of Fontainebleau. The Rue Royale house was on the right when walking toward the forest, not too far after crossing the Rue St. Merry, and before the Boulevard André Maginot took off to the right toward a big traffic circle, renamed after World War II as Carrefour de la Libération. This was a relatively narrow attached house, with a basement, ground floor, first floor and probably an attic. The basement I distinctly remember because it had a musty root cellar, where potatoes and onions were stored all year round, and a wood storage room.

The firewood was essential, because the stove in the narrow, often steamy, very nice-smelling kitchen, was fueled by wood. There was a compartment for boiling water, from where it was drawn as needed for making coffee, tea, soup, and for dish-washing. The various sections of the top were moved about by means of metal lever handles, and had to be handled with care and with special quilted rags because the whole stove was made of breakable cast-iron.

My paternal grand-parents' house at 16 rue Royale in Fontainebleau

It was in the Rue Royale, in front of this house, and going north toward the forest, that I learned to ride a bicycle. It was bright yellow and brown, and my father would run by my side, holding on to the bottom of the saddle.

There was another house at 137, rue St. Merry, four or five long blocks away, where my great-grandmother "Nounoute" (pronounced *noo-noot*—Ernestine Rosenwald Ach, my grandmother Lucie Ach Fribourg's mother) resided. My father was very fond of her, for apparently she had been greatly instrumental in bringing him up. I do not know why, but it seems that my father thought his grandmother had brought him up much more than his mother. I remember Nounoute rather well and that she liked to spoil me with hard candy, but I have no memories of any stories she might have told me.

However, my sister Rosette remembers that Nounoute was endowed with a strong will and made many decisions for her daughter's household. On one occasion, she told my mother that she should brush her husband's felt hat, to which my mother responded she had a baby to take care of, and her husband was perfectly capable of brushing his own hat. That response apparently stopped the attempted take-over of another household!

Nounoute seemed to be tall (to me) and had many wrinkles. I can now understand why that should be: she was born 25 May 1848 in Sarre-Union, and died on 10 February 1935, so she was 87 when I was six. She fell and broke her hip (osteoporosis?) and died in a hospital in Paris. I remember visiting her in that hospital room, probably the first time I had been in a hospital.

This house at Rue St. Merry must have been where my father and his parents lived in 1928, because that is the address given by my father, *Représentant de Commerce* (Sales Representative) on his 22 June 1928 marriage certificate, issued in the 9e arrondissement in Paris. At that time, my mother's address was 34, rue Baudin in Paris, and she was listed as *s.pr. = sans profession* (without profession). The Paris notary who executed the marriage contract on June 1, 1928, was Maître Pineau, a person whom I never met, but whose name I heard often, after World War II, which he survived, for he helped my father with some real estate transactions and other legal matters after the war.

My parents' civil wedding certificate

In some respects, there is a greater separation between state and church in France, since the 1789 Révolution, than there is in the United States. In the US, clergy persons not only consecrate marriages, but also are licensed by the state to join persons in marriage legally. That was not the case in France in 1922, and probably still is not. So, after my parents were married legally at the 9e Arrondissement City Hall on June 22, 1928, they were married religiously at the Synagogue on Rue de la Victoire in Paris two days later, according to their *ketubah* written in Hebrew and French and signed by Rabbi Dreyfuss, the *Grand Rabbin* of Paris.

I GAVE YOU LIFE TWICE

ASSOCIATION CONSISTORIALE ISRAÉLITE DE PARIS

Temple de la rue _de la Victoire (Oratoire)_
3039

כתובה

[Hebrew ketubah text with handwritten names: Jean Fribourg, Yvonne Juliette Owry]

KETOUBA OU ACTE DU MARIAGE RELIGIEUX

Aujourd'hui, _Sixième_ jour du mois de _Tamouz_ de l'année 5688 de la création du monde (_24 Juin 1928_), les époux _Jean Fribourg et Yvonne Juliette Owry_ se sont présentés devant nous, à l'effet d'obtenir pour leur union la consécration religieuse et la bénédiction de Dieu.

En présence de Dieu, et dans le temple consacré à son culte, après la récitation des prières d'usage, après avoir indiqué aux deux époux les devoirs qu'ils auront à remplir dans leur nouvelle carrière, après les avoir bénis au nom de la Religion et avoir appelé sur eux les faveurs du Ciel, nous les déclarons unis par les liens du mariage, CONFORMÉMENT A LA LOI DE MOÏSE ET D'ISRAËL.

LE GRAND RABBIN DE PARIS

J. H. Dreyfuss
grand rabbin de Paris

My parents' religious wedding certificate (ketubah)

I suspect that my father probably purchased the house at 97, rue St. Honoré in Fontainebleau after Nounoute died in 1935 and the house where she had lived was sold. In the meantime, my paternal grandparents had moved to the house on Rue Royale. Perhaps before that time, in the late 1930s, another property was sold. This was a garden at Bois-le-Roi, which I recall vaguely. I cannot be sure as to whether it had a dwelling on it, but I remember my father's delight at getting fruits and vegetables (I think, grown or tended by a hired gardener) from the property for our personal use in Fontainebleau and in Paris. This property must have belonged for some time to my grandparents when my father was a young man, because it is from there that he went to the nearby Seine River to exercise in his one-man scull, a feat of which he used to be very proud when he mentioned it to me later on. In any case, I never saw him in a scull. I think perhaps he had been persuaded to give up this activity upon or shortly after marriage. Bois-le-Roi is the local train station just before that of Avon-Fontainebleau, and I suspect that the move to Fontainebleau from Bois-le-Roi was a normal progression to a less isolated but still semi-rural forest-surrounded environment.

In front of 97, rue St. Honoré in Fontainebleau, 1986

The house at 97, rue St. Honoré I remember rather well. Next to the sidewalk was a solid wall about one meter (3 ft) high, on top of which a black metal fence rose another meter and a half (4.5 ft) to pointed spikes. The entrance gate at the street was metal, and opened onto a 3- to 4-m (9- to 12-ft) walk leading to about four stone steps to the front stoop and door. Upon entering into a hallway, the door to the front parlor, used for entertaining honored non-family guests, was on the left. In that parlor was the upright piano where I was supposed to practice, although my practice sessions were not as rigidly scheduled as those in Paris had been. On the right of the hallway was a clothes closet for outerwear, and then the stairways, first the one to the first floor, then the door to the stairs going to the basement. At the end of the hallway was a large room, double the size of the parlor, which was used as a family room and also as a dining room. On the left wall was a huge (to me) grandfather clock which always fascinated me. That is one of the reasons why I built a walnut case for a grandfather clock of my own in 1976 for my home in Knoxville.

To the right of the dining room was a narrow, longish sitting room. It was entered only through a door in the middle of the dining room wall. It was in this room that my mother sewed and knitted, and where we had a radio. This radio was a large piece of furniture, 80 cm (32 in) wide and almost that deep, and perhaps 120 cm (4 ft) high, on top of which was a square coil antenna that could be rotated on its base to capture broadcast transmissions more easily. It is in that room that I first heard the guttural ravings of the maniacal Leader of the Third Reich (*der Führer*), as his discourses were acclaimed by tens of thousands of his countrymen. My uncontrollable profound dislike for the German language goes back to those days, because of course we knew he was raving against us Jews, with the support of millions of Germans when he first became *Kanzler* (Chancellor) of the Third Reich. We had translations of these speeches in the newspapers and from radio commentators, and also my mother understood German quite well. It was in this room, in the fall of 1938, that I heard of the abject abandonment of Czechoslovakia by the weaklings Neville Chamberlain and Edouard Daladier, and where we heard of the destruction and depredations of *Kristallnacht* on November 9, 1938. The revulsion felt at these happenings by my parents and grandparents, and the fear they engendered, were clear to me.

Beyond the dining room, a door opened onto the veranda, perhaps 2.5 to 3 m (7 to 9 ft) wide and stretching from one sidewall of the property to the other, where my parents and grandparents enjoyed sitting in summer. It was shaded by an overhanging trellis roof, and wisteria (*lilas*) climbed the roof supports, enveloping the area with blue flowers and fragrance for several weeks each spring. The garden was reached by climbing down about five or six steps, leading to a meandering pebble walk that soon forked to enclose a small island of vegetation. My sister and I often played hopscotch on the gravelly area, and also frequently in a skittle-like game: a narrow table had holes on its top surface, with one of them adorned with a green metal frog. When a thrown tennis ball disappeared into a hole, a certain number of points were awarded the thrower; a hit through the frog was a jackpot. At the back of the garden was a small *"buanderie"* (laundry shed) where garden tools were kept, and there was a large laundry-tub with washboard that the once- or twice-a-week maid could use.

Later in the fall of 1939, as air-raids were being predicted, a trench was dug in the garden, close to the steps leading down to it. I do not know whether a bomb shelter was recommended to all inhabitants, or whether the decision to build one was a consequence of my parents' protective nature toward their family. I do remember them discussing the pros and cons of various plans for this shelter. The trench was lined on the two long sides with reinforced concrete, a 12-cm (4.5-in) thick slab of reinforced concrete was placed on top of these two walls, and soil excavated from the trench piled on top of the roof to a depth of 70 cm (28 in). There were steps leading down and up from each end of the trench, which was deep enough for my 180-cm-tall (6-ft) father to stand in, and a narrow wooden bench was arranged along one side. I do not remember with pleasure getting up in the middle of the night, donning our ski suits in winter to try to keep warm when the sirens had sounded an air-raid alert, and then going down to the shelter and being made to rehearse getting on our rubbery gas masks with the huge filtering canisters at the bottom, especially when I understood that these canisters were ineffective against several of the nastier gases that the *Boches* (World War I insulting word descriptive of Germans) might use, such as mustard gas. All these preparations were in vain, fortunately, since Fontainebleau was never bombed as long as we were there in 1939 or 1940.

The house on Rue St. Honoré was two long blocks away from its intersection with the Rue de France. At the corner was one of the main town attractions, of which I never tired: a farrier. I just loved to go there, watch him fashion horseshoes in his red-hot forge, and then smell the burnt hooves as he hammered the shoes into place. Both riding horses and huge draft horses were served there. Another block and a half beyond the farrier, before reaching Rue Royale, was a military barracks, a huge 4-sided 3-story building surrounding a large inner courtyard. It was also a thrill to watch the close-order drills and, even more so, see a mounted troop clatter by as they left the barracks or returned in impeccable order after having ridden in front of our house. If that occurred when my grandfather Albert was present, he never failed to remark on the good order of the troop, and to remind me that he had a commission as a mounted reserve lieutenant in the army.

During the school year, we often went to Fontainebleau for the weekend. It was not an easy trip. We had a long taxicab ride from Rue Paul Escudier to the Gare de Lyon, close to an hour, and then close to an hour by train to Avon, where we would get off and ride the electric streetcar for half an hour to the corner of Rue Grande and Rue de La Paroisse, and walk the final three blocks. In summer, the train ride was very uncomfortable because we had to keep the windows closed in order to exclude the cinders from the coal-fired locomotive from entering the compartment. In winter, the house was cold, and the coal furnace in the basement had to be fired up to heat the water for the radiators in each room, a process that took several hours. If we were going to be in Fontainebleau over a Friday evening/Saturday morning, we would walk down the Rue de la Paroisse, cross Rue Grande, and go down about three more blocks down the hill of Rue du Parc on a narrow sidewalk. At the end of this street, the Place de Bois-d'Yver was on the left, a small door entrance to the Parterre (formal garden behind the Château) was in front, and the synagogue was on the right, up against the 2-m (6.5-ft) high garden wall. It was a small structure, with room for about 40 men on the ground floor, and about 20 women on the balcony in the rear. The segregation of men and women was normal practice even in liberal European congregations in those days, and still is in orthodox congregations all over the world. Reform congregations eliminated this practice many decades ago, allowing families to sit together, and were followed by the Conservative movement.

My father was vice president and treasurer of the congregation, the only one in town. He served in this position with pride, although he was embarrassed by the fact that he had had no religious education, could not read Hebrew, and had not had a *Bar-Mitzvah*. The services were 80 to 90 percent in Hebrew, and half of that was mumbled by old men who knew the text by heart, perhaps without understanding it, and had never had any diction lessons. There was no rabbi, since the congregation was too small to be able to afford one, but there was a *chassen* (cantor), M. Hollander. I received some religious instruction at home from M. Hollander, and most of that consisted of learning how to read Hebrew and the most common prayers. He would tell me what those texts meant, using his somewhat accented French. I do not know from what country he was a refugee. I do remember, however, that he had never been informed that his body odor was not pleasant when he was in the same room with me. On the other hand, when he chanted the prayers, I could understand what he said and follow in my prayer book, which was 99 percent in Hebrew.

I recall also that, at some time, perhaps when I was six years old, there was a ceremony when my father and I gave a *wimpel* to the congregation, a long narrow cloth that had been embroidered by my mother, had presumably been used as my swaddling cloth, and would now be used to wrap one of the Torah scrolls. I recall the Rosh Hoshanah and Yom Kippur services in 1939, and the many men dressed in their finest white robes, to be used eventually as their shrouds, as they prayed and prostrated themselves flat on the floor during the *Aleynu* (Adoration prayer). For *Succoth*, the Feast of Booths and Fall Harvest, a tent was erected outside in the front and side yards. I made a terrible mistake once when I accepted to drink some wine from the *Kiddush* cup which had already been tainted by some men's lips, my father yanked me out of there in a hurry to disinfect my mouth so that I would not catch some horrible unspeakable disease. We heard after the war that father was the first Jew for whom the Germans looked when they got to Fontainebleau, because he had been the treasurer of the congregation. He was not there, of course, and I have no idea if there were any congregational funds in his care and what happened to them.

My father wrote about the Fontainebleau congregation in the Central Synagogue (Manhattan, New York City) newsletter, after being urged to do so in the late 1960s by his friend Rabbi David Seligson. My father's was the first in a Series of Recollections. I shall quote extensively from his article:

> "One of these gardens [in association with the Château of Fontainebleau] known as '*Le Parc*' was created in the 16th century; it represents the pure classical garden architecture close to an iron gate with a small exit door on its side there was the Synagogue of the Fontainebleau community. Nothing now reveals that the Synagogue [once] stood there. The Synagogue was burned down with all its contents by the Germans in 1942, then razed by their tanks."
>
> "The synagogue was erected *circa* 1810 on a plot taken from *Le Parc* and granted by Napoléon I to the then recently organized Jewish community created under the statute published by Napoléon after the '*Grand Sanhedrin*' of 1807 [whereby] the civil rights and duties of the French Jews were the same as those of all other French citizens. Under the statute French Jews were entitled to practice their religion in Synagogues. The Third Republic severed relationship between the State and all religious creeds."
>
> "The Community prospered in the 19th century In 1910 there were about 200 Jewish families living in Fontainebleau. After World War I, during which several members of the Community were killed in France's service, a migration to Paris took place. At the start of World War II, there were no more than 40 Jewish families. The services have always been performed along the Orthodox rite. In front of the altar stood an important [meaning: large] 8-light candelabra in Sèvres porcelain presented in 1861 by Napoléon III. I, personally, as Vice-President and Secretary, was in

charge of the accounting and had custody of an extra folio book on which were kept the names of the members with dues and donations since 1855 to 1940."

"Fontainebleau was occupied by the German Army on June 14, 1940. In the second part of 1942 all Jews who remained in Fontainebleau at that time were arrested by the *Gestapo* and all died in deportation. The accounting and archives book left by me with a Catholic neighbor were burned by him in June 1940 for his safety and the safety of the members of the Community. Now the Jewish Community no longer exists in Fontainebleau. For me, the Synagogue is still living, in my memory only."

Persons interested in the early history of the Jewish community in Fontainebleau may wish to consult the book by Rosine Alexandre "Fontainebleau—Naissance d'une Communauté Juive à l'Epoque de la Révolution—1788 - 1808" [Fontainebleau—Birth of a Jewish Community at the Time of the Révolution—1788 - 1808]. The book, in French, was published by the author in 1991, and carries the ISBN number 2-9504973-1-4.

When my wife Claude, our children and I stopped in Fontainebleau on our return from Turkey in July 1974, we went to visit the Château. We started in the Cour des Adieux, in front of the double winding staircase built by François 1st in the 16th century, where Napoléon bid farewell to his *grognards* (grumbling soldiers) before leaving for his exile on the Isle of Elbe. We then entered the Château for a guided visit through the gilded rooms. As we exited from the visit, we went through a gate guarded by two stone lions which had impressed me greatly as a youngster, and observed the carps swimming in the Etang des Carpes. After going through another gate, we arrived at Le Parc, or Le Parterre, a large square formal garden with a square pool in the middle. Along one side, lined with buckeyes, is a sandy wide alley where I used to be thrilled when riding a cart pulled by a donkey. Later on, I also greatly enjoyed pushing my scooter there. On July 14 (Bastille Day), and also on August 15, I believe, the Feast of the Assumption, fireworks were set off in this area, with people sitting all around the parterre. In winter, we ice skated on the pond; once I went through the ice, but fortunately I was still close to the edge and my father was able to grab my hand and pull me out.

To return to our 1974 visit, we went through the small door in the masonry wall at the end of the donkey cart alley. I had told my children Daniel (age 14) and Renée (age 12) that, after we went though the door, I would show them the place where the synagogue, burned by the Germans, had stood. Imagine my amazement when we found that there was a new synagogue there, on the same spot. Since this was a Friday, we went back there that evening and attended the service. There were more people there than I remembered from pre-war. Most of them were Algerian Jews who had migrated to France after Algeria won its independence on July 1, 1962. We also met a M. Louis Guthman (no relation), president of the congregation, judge at the *Cour de Cassation* (the highest Appeals Tribunal in France) in Paris, who invited us to his home for some cookies and coffee. He had no information whatsoever about any of the pre-World War II Jewish residents of Fontainebleau. Unfortunately, my father had suffered a severe stroke by the time we returned to the US and, although I did visit him in the clinic in Los Angeles where he spent the last six months of his life, I was unable to communicate to him that the Synagogue in Fontainebleau had been reborn and rebuilt in 1965.

When we were in Paris before World War II, we occasionally went to services at the very large synagogue on Rue de la Victoire, where my parents had been married. As I recall, these visits were principally with my mother and her parents. I would go downstairs with my grandfather Lucien, and my mother, her mother and Rosette would go upstairs in the balcony, usually on the left side. My sister recalls envying her grandmother's elderly status, which allowed her, because of leg pains, to not have to get up like everybody else for some of the prayers. The sanctuary was very impressive, and even more so when the *Grand Rabbin de France* would give a sermon on Saturday morning. Seating and order were controlled by uniformed *shamess* who wore Horatio Hornblower-type hats and a huge gold watch chain across their vest-coated chests. They had coats with tails, and were very impressive. There would be no whisperings during prayers when they were around! The rite was *Ashkenazi*, and presumably was "*libéral*" (progressive in today's parlance). In US terms, this would be known now as "conservative," with a small amount of the vernacular language of the country used during the service. I recall my grandfather walking up to the foot of the *bimah* (platform) to say *Kaddish* in unison with all the other men mourners, I think every time we went there, for his dead son Robert and other relatives. Since I was under age 13, I was not allowed to accompany him.

WINTER HOLIDAYS AND TRUCK GARDENING

Other memories that I have belong to the end-of-year winter holidays. My mother often reminded me that, as a very young boy, up until age 4, I was small and was not eating what was considered enough. I remember our physician (but not his name) visiting our home to tend to my needs during a childhood disease, maybe mumps or chickenpox, counseling my parents that I would grow better if "exposed to a change of air." Consequently, arrangements were made for the family to go spend some time, a week, perhaps two, at the winter vacation spot of Villars-sur-Bex, in western francophone Switzerland. I remember a large outdoor skating rink, next to our hotel, where I started stumbling around on ice-skates. When we returned to Paris, and each year until the war, my mother would take us to the Palais de Glace, near the Rond-Point des Champs-Elysées, to ice-skate on Thursday or Saturday afternoons. There was uninterrupted recorded music for the skaters. I particularly remember the most popular music of the day, the Lambeth Walk. It was not until many years later that I recognized that this was not French music, but rather a popular British melody, dance and song. While we were in Paris, my father was generally too busy with his business to take me out, but he made up for it when we spent the weekend or vacations in Fontainebleau. Then, we would go for day-long hikes in the forest or bicycle tours in the region. When hiking in the forest, he would invariably carry a pair of espadrilles (canvas footwear with rope soles) into which he would change each time large sandstone rocks stimulated him to a climb. If the climb was not too dangerous, he would allow my sister and me to climb also.

I was greatly impressed in Switzerland by huge metal rails sticking out of the mountain above the hotel, and a little to the left when looking up; they were supposed to protect us from those terrifying catastrophes called avalanches, although I did not understand how they did that for many years, and no one would tell me. This first winter sports expedition did somehow awaken my appetite, and from that 1934 spring on, I have usually been hungrier than is good for me. We went to Villars only one year, and in the two succeeding years, we spent our winter holidays in Zeefeld, near Innsbruck in the Austrian Tyrol. I recall being bundled under huge mounds of blankets in a horse-drawn sleigh that took us from the railroad station up to the hotel. It is in Zeefeld that I had my first skiing lessons, which I enjoyed, using the standard wooden skis and leather straps. I also remember several occasions when we hiked up a mountain all morning through the spruce forests, with each of my parents pulling a sleigh. After lunch at a chalet on the mountaintop, I sat on one of the sleighs in front of my seated father, and Rosette in the same way with mother, and we sleighed down that humongous mountain in less than an hour, braking and steering with our heels.

In 1937, we stayed in France for winter holidays, at Les Rousses in the Jura mountains. In 1938, undoubtedly because of the conditions in annexed Austria prior to the *Anschluss*, we went for several days to rainy, rainy Bergen, Norway. We were in a hotel right on the harbor, and I recognized it when Claude and I visited that city in 1994. In 1938, from Bergen, we took a ship across the North Sea to Newcastle. As I recall, it took three days going through what I thought was a violent storm, and my mother was seasick from the moment she got on the ship until she stepped ashore. I was a little scared, but enjoyed the thrill of the pitching ship. From Newcastle, the four of us took a train to London, staying at a large hotel on the Strand. We stayed several days in London, and I remember seeing Buckingham Palace, the mounted Life or Horse Guards in the Admiralty courtyard, visiting the Tower and the flower market near Covent Garden, and going to Hampton Court. The return to France naturally was by ferry across *la Manche* (in French, the "Sleeve," from its shape, arrogantly named by others as the "English" Channel), a trip dreaded by my mother, so susceptible to seasickness before the advent of dramamine.

Upon returning from the Praz-de-Lys camp-out in July 1939, I quickly reverted to my two or three days a week of work with our "Père" Binet, the person from whose stall my mother had been purchasing vegetables for many years in Fontainebleau. The open air market took place on the cobblestones of the 'old' entrance to the Château, the same area where some outdoor sequences for the Louis Jouvet film *"Si Versailles m'était conté"* (If Versailles was told me) on the French Révolution were photographed, as I recall, in the summer of 1938. I remember sneaking off several times to watch the mob scenes as the people, singing the revolutionary song *La Carmagnole*, were storming the doors to the Château. Anyway, as a special favor to a good customer, M. Binet would allow me to go to his home and farm in Avon several days a week, because even then I maintained I was interested in agriculture. I would take the street car to his place, a ride of some 25 or 30 minutes, and work all day for my lunch. Since I was working, I was entitled also to one or two glasses of red wine, diluted by half with water. I would judge the farm was about 1.5 hectare (3.8 acres), surrounded by a high wall, with the home in one corner above the horse stable. The horse was used daily to pull implements and, every afternoon, to run the well pump in the center of the property. There were some sections that were not in reach of the irrigation ditches, and my daily late afternoon chore was to carry a watering can in each hand to irrigate these areas. That was fine, except for the celery area, the smell of which I loathed. To this day, I turn away from the smell of raw celery and refuse to eat any. But overall the experience was excellent. I did this in the summers of both 1938 and 1939.

My desire to become involved in agriculture arose early, in Fontainebleau, as my parents, my sister and I took some of our many bicycle trips in the countryside. Most of these were in the Forest of Fontainebleau, a large forest which, in some areas at least, may have been original vegetation. Much of the forest, however, was second- or third- or whatever growth, or burned over. Since much of the area is quite sandy, and I expect rather acid and shallow, it had been spared from clearing. Once, on our way back from Franchard (a distant section of the forest), we had to traverse very rapidly an area where a fire had just started. I remember the fear in my father's voice as he urged us to pedal even more swiftly when the fire jumped to the crowns of the trees. The forest was a considerable contrast with the surrounding countryside of La Beauce, a rich small grains-growing area. Although many of our bicycle trips were on the narrow sandy roads or trails in the forest, sometimes we would go into the more open agricultural areas bordering on the forest, on trips to Barbizon and other villages. It was then that, in a perverse manner, my interest in agriculture was awakened, because I loved the odors that assailed us as we pedaled past a working barnyard! I must admit that, in later years, as I became involved in beef cattle research, I have left to others activities that would place me in very close working proximity to the sources of the olfactory pleasures that first attracted me to agriculture.

Sometimes, in July and August, we would go as a family to Avon, which borders the Seine, to go swimming. The pool was a wooden enclosure open to the sky, anchored to the bank and floating on the river. The decks were always wet and slippery. This is where I learned to swim, as well as in Paris at an indoor pool which I loathed, because of the pungent chlorine odor. My first lessons were in that pool, where a canvas belt was strapped around my waist. This belt was attached to a davit that the instructor would then use to swing me out over the water. I was taught the breast stroke exclusively, which was considered safer, more useful, and more gentlemanly than the Australian crawl. At Avon, there was a good restaurant next to the pool, so we would have a good meal after all that exercise. The main thing I remember about that place was the contempt with which my parents referred to a white-haired man who was there often and dressed in salmon-colored clothes. Many years later such attire would be called a leisure suit. In my parents' opinion, although the cut of the clothes or their color were marginally acceptable for wear at the pool or at the beach, they were clearly inappropriate for wear in the restaurant.

MY GRANDPARENTS —AND THEIR PARENTS

Another activity which I remember with considerable pleasure are the walks that my grandfather Albert and I took together in the Fontainebleau forest. He was a great storyteller, and we would go along the trails toward Franchard. He always carried one of his several walking sticks, although I am not aware that he needed one to walk. However, when he was a young man, a gentleman would not have been properly dressed to go out without a walking stick.

Albert Fribourg, 1939

Periodically, when we stopped for a minute, he would pull out of his vest pocket a small oval silver box from which we would each partake of a black licorice soft candy, a real treat. He was very proud of being a reserve lieutenant in the French Cavalry; I may be wrong in my recollection, however, since the *lettre de service* shows that he was promoted from reserve second lieutenant to reserve lieutenant in the 116th Infantry regiment on 14 March 1895, when he was 29.

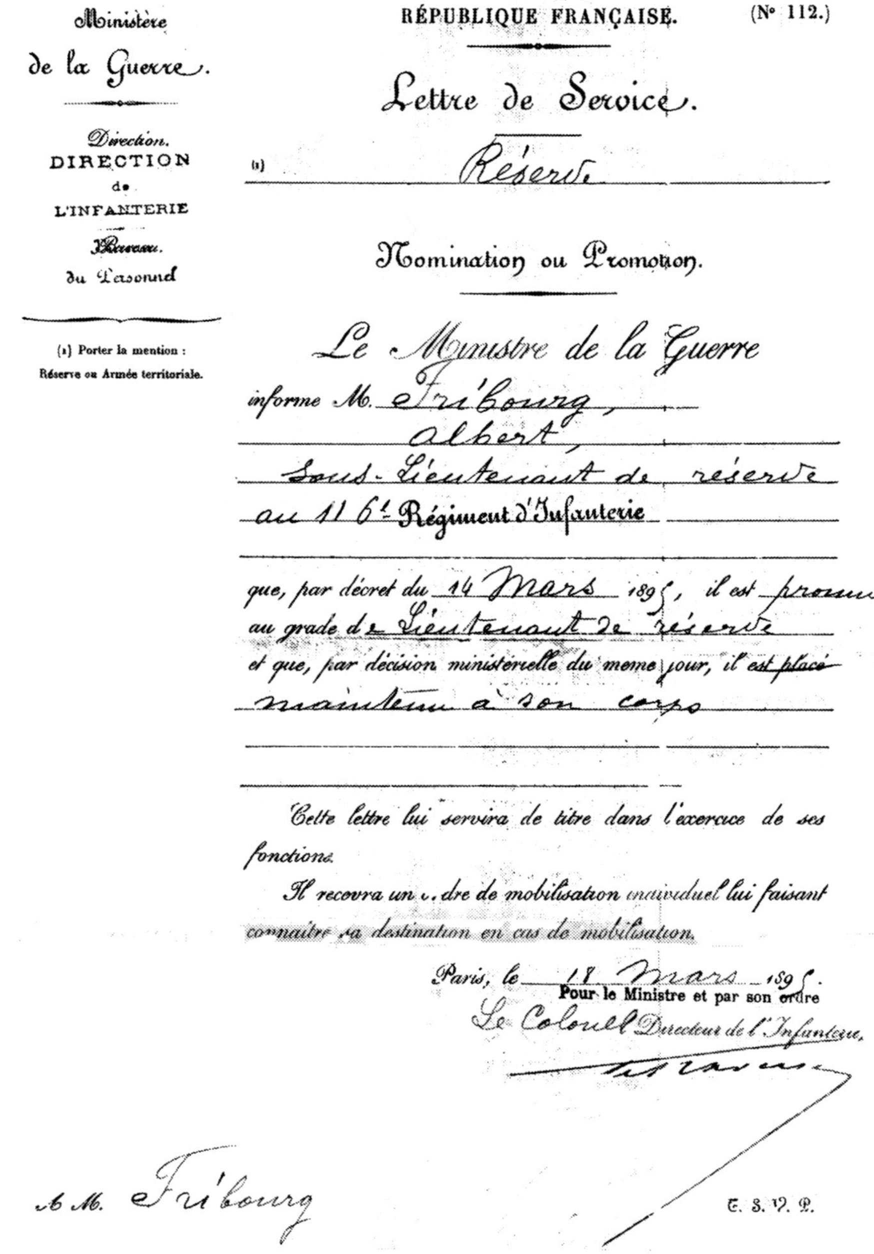

Henry Fribourg

Ministère de la Guerre.

Direction
DIRECTION
de
L'INFANTERIE

Bureau
du Personnel

(1) Porter la mention :
Réserve ou Armée territoriale.

RÉPUBLIQUE FRANÇAISE.   (N° 112.)

Lettre de Service.

(1) Réserve

Nomination ou Promotion.

Le Ministre de la Guerre informe M. Fribourg, Albert, Sous-Lieutenant de réserve au 116ᵉ Régiment d'Infanterie que, par décret du 14 Mars 1895, il est promu au grade de Lieutenant de réserve et que, par décision ministérielle du même jour, il est placé maintenu à son corps

Cette lettre lui servira de titre dans l'exercice de ses fonctions.

Il recevra un ordre de mobilisation individuel lui faisant connaître sa destination en cas de mobilisation.

Paris, le 18 Mars 1895.
Pour le Ministre et par son ordre
Le Colonel Directeur de l'Infanterie,

À M. Fribourg

E. S. V. P.

Albert Fribourg's commission as officer in French Army

At the time of his promotion, he lived with his parents at 23, rue de Berne, Eighth Arrondissement in Paris. Perhaps my recollection is due to the fact that officers in an infantry regiment in those days rode horseback. His age would explain why he was not called to serve in 1914, since he then would have been 48 years old. He was born in the First Arrondissement in Paris on April 24, 1865. He was 72 in 1938, but he walked very straight, and was meticulously dressed every single day, a very dapper and perfect gentleman.

My father's family in 1902 (from left to right): Ernestine Rosenwald Ach, Auguste Ach, Jean Fribourg, Lucie Ach Fribourg, Albert Fribourg, Henri Caïn Fribourg, Anna Ségnitz Fribourg

I never knew my paternal grandfather's parents, but I was named after Henri Caïn Fribourg, his father. At the time of Albert's marriage in 1897, Henri was sixty years old. He was retired from his shoe manufacturing at 11, rue Grenetat in Paris. Henri's wife was Anna Ségnitz Fribourg, who was fifty-four years old in 1897. My sister Rosette Annie Marguerite is named after her great-grandmother Anna Fribourg. Albert was married on January 26, 1897, at La Ferté-sous-Jouarre (Seine-et-Marne) to a very beautiful girl, Lucie Ach, my grandmother. She lived with her parents in that town, at 43, rue d'Ussy, but had been born in Boulay (Moselle) on July 17, 1863.

Her father, after whom I received my middle name, was Auguste Ach, a horse trader, who was fifty-six at the time of the wedding. He was married to Ernestine Rosenwald Ach (Nounoute), forty-six years old in 1897. Auguste Ach's military record book has survived, indicating six years of service as an enlisted man in the French Army. He was a *Grenadier* in the 26th Infantry Regiment in the 6th Division stationed in Strasbourg in 1864, when he was awarded a Good Conduct Certificate. A *grenadier* was an elite soldier skilled in the handling and launching of grenades. He had been promoted to this rank on May 11, 1862 from his rank of *Fusilier* (rifleman) achieved on June 24, 1859.

Lucie Ach Fribourg, "Mort pour la France", in 1939

My grandmother Lucie also was well dressed every day, thin and elegant. She was 66 in 1939. Two years before her birth, Lorraine had fallen under German occupation. Her birthplace of Boulay was renamed by the occupiers as Bolchen. We have documents that show the reintegration of Lucie and her parents into French citizenship on January 23, 1891. These were some of the documents that my father had to gather in order to force the post-war French Government to recognize that my grandmother indeed was French when she was murdered by the Germans in 1944 at age 71 and that her son, my father, was entitled to receive a *Carte de Déporté Politique* in her name. Such a card, No. 217508284, was issued on December 14, 1955. In addition, at my father's dogged insistence, the Commune de Bugeat, Département de la Corrèze, declared that my grandmother had given her life for her country and awarded her the official designation *"Mort pour la France"*.

I GAVE YOU LIFE TWICE

FX 49359

Département de la Corrèze

Commune de Bugeat

Extrait du registre des actes de Décès

Le quinze Mai mil neuf cent quarante quatre, Lucie ACH née à Boulay (Moselle) le dix sept Juillet mil huit cent soixante treize, fille de Auguste Ach, marchand de chevaux et de Ernestine Rosenwald, son épouse _____
Veuve de Albert Fribourg - est décédée "Mort pour la France" à Auschwitz (Pologne) _____
Dédé le deux Juillet mil neuf cent quarante Six ___
Transcrit le huit Juillet mil neuf cent quarante Six

Pour copie certifiée conforme au registre deposé en Mairie à Bugeat le dix sept Juillet mil neuf cent quarante Six _____

P/ Le Maire
l'Officier de l'État civil

Lucie Ach Fribourg's death certificate

In June 2001, Claude and I had attended the annual meeting of the European Grassland Federation (EGF) in La Rochelle, on the Atlantic coast. After the meeting, we drove from La Rochelle to Avignon, where our daughter Renée was going to meet us prior to taking a vacation in Corsica with us. During our leisurely trip through the Massif Central, we stopped for a while in Bugeat, hoping that we might be able to talk to an elderly person who might remember my grandparents from the time when they took refuge in that small town during the war.

There was no one who could help us at City Hall, but the baker's wife, on Rue de la Liberté, Madame Elisabeth Fournet, was most helpful. Although she was much too young to have known my grandparents, she offered to make inquiries after our departure. Later that summer, we received a letter from Madame Pierre Capodanno, who remembered having met my grandparents when she was a young girl, because her uncle and aunt were my grandparents' landlords.

> Je souhaite vous adresser cette lettre, pour vous parler de vos grands parents.
>
> Je suis, Manchon Germaine, âgée de 93 ans, avec mon mari, Roger, avions loué un petit studio à vos grands parents, Lucie et Albert Tribourg (au 1er étage de la maison, dont vous avez eu la photo et où nous exercions un commerce de vins) (environ 1944)
>
> Ma mémoire des dates est à présent un peu défaillante, mais vos grands parents sont restés environ deux ans dans la maison. Se côtoyant journellement, nous avons pu sympathiser avec vite et nos relations étaient devenues amicales et confiantes : En cette période trouble où la vigilance était de mise ...
>
> Votre grand père est décédé dans la maison et inhumé au cimetière de Bugeat
>
> Votre grand mère ne lui a pas survécu longtemps puisque les nazis sont venus (avec des renseignements précis, dont je ne connais pas l'origine) la chercher avec un comportement brutal ---
>
> Ils ont fouillé totalement le logement et ont emmené votre grand mère avec un minimum de bagage ---
>
> Une cachette recelait des objets et de l'argent que mon mari a remis à M. Goumain, dont il avait l'adresse _
>
> Reste des lettres, photos, carnet d'adresses, que j'ai conservés jusqu'à ce jour, leur attribuant une valeur sentimentale ---

Excerpts from 2003 letter to me from Me. Germaine Manchon

Subsequently, I received a most touching letter from Madame Germaine Manchon, that landlord. When she wrote that letter, Madame Manchon was a widow living in an assisted living home in Paris. In her letter, reproduced here in part, she said: "I wish in this letter to talk to you about your grandparents. I am Germaine Manchon, 93 years old. With my husband Roger, we had rented a small apartment to your grandparents, Lucie and Albert Fribourg, on the first floor of the house where we conducted our wine business. My memory of dates is not exact anymore, but your grandparents stayed with us for about two years. Living side by side, we daily talked and rapidly became friends and confided in each other. Your grandfather died in our home and was buried in the Bugeat cemetery *[Author's note: after the war, his body was exhumed and re-interred next to his parents in Neuilly-sur-Seine]*. Your grandmother did not survive him for long since the Nazis (with precise information about her, the source of which I do not know) came to take her in a brutal manner. They searched the apartment from top to bottom and allowed your grandmother practically no luggage. There were several objects and some money in a hiding place, and my husband later turned these over to Madame Gramain (a friend of my grandparents) whose address he had. There remain several letters, photographs, and an address book, that I have kept to this day, because of their sentimental value." Needless to say, this letter touched me profoundly. Madame Manchon offered to return these objects of sentimental value and, since then, I have received them. They will be cherished by me, my children, and other descendants of my martyred grandparents.

In Paris, Lucie and Albert had lived in a sixth-floor apartment at 111, rue de la Folie Méricourt. The balconies of black-painted forged iron ran all around the apartment, which had a generally triangular floor plan, with the apex pointing to the monument in the center of the Place de la République, two blocks away. One of the thrills of going to visit my grandparents, beside the good meal and a few vertiginous minutes on the balcony, was going with my grandfather to the Quai de Jemmapes, right below their apartment building. At that place, there was a lock in the canal used by barges that were taking a shortcut through Paris, rather than following the Seine River. We used to watch barges being lifted up or down in the lock for hours. I wanted to see this lock again in 1996, but could not locate it. Excusing myself for my lack of manners and my effrontery, I asked an elderly man sitting on a bench about the canal. He advised me that we were on top of it, as it had been roofed over some years earlier.

Renée Samuel Oury and Lucien Oury, 1939

My other grandparents were Renée Oury, née Samuel, and Lucien Oury. As I recall, when we were in Paris during the school year, visits to the apartments of both sets of grandparents were fairly regular. They would be for a lunch during the weekend, perhaps on Sundays, about once a month. My grandparents Oury lived at 2, rue Thimonnier, not far from the Gare de l'Est. I remember the apartment well, perhaps from the days in summer 1948 when Rosette and I went for a visit with them in Paris, just before the Berlin airlift started. One of my proudest possessions is the little marble-topped Louis XVI-style *guéridon* (small round table on high legs) which is now in my living room and used to be in their entryway, where the mail was placed. One of the sweetest memories I have from pre-war is being taken by Grandmère Renée on Thursday afternoon for the *goûter* (afternoon tea), at about four in the afternoon, at a special coffee shop on the east side of the Rue de la Chaussée d'Antin, about half-way between the Eglise de la Trinité and the Opéra, for a hot chocolate, sometimes with my mother, sometimes just the two of us. I did not realize until much later that my grandmother never wore any color other than black. Apparently she never stopped mourning for her son Robert, who died of peritonitis in 1925 at age 17.

My grandfather Lucien was born in 1872 in Château-Salins, in occupied Alsace-Lorraine, the son of Léon Oury and Juliette Daltroff Oury. He left home in 1888, spending several years in England as a young man, working in London with and for his cousins in the Daltroff branch of the family. I have a leather-bound 5-volume Hebrew/English Pentateuch that he obtained there at the time. Some time after he returned to France, he married my grandmother Renée, daughter of Adolphe Samuel and Mathilde Roubach Samuel, on July 6, 1903 (Tamuz 12, 5663). The photographs that I have show that she was a beautiful and young (13 years his junior) bride.

Four generations in 1904 (left to right): Renée Samuel Oury, her grandmother Caroline Lévy Roubach, her mother Mathilde Roubach Samuel, and her daughter (my mother) Yvonne Oury

Soon thereafter, they went to Wien (Vienna, Austria) where my mother was born in 1904 at 11, Unteraugarten Strasse where she resided until 1908. The family returned to Paris in 1912. When my family traveled from Zagreb (then in Yugoslavia, now in Croatia) to Vienna in February 1974, we lodged on the fifth floor of a bed-and-breakfast *Gasthaus* in an apartment building in the pedestrian historical downtown area. In the morning, I asked the hostess for directions to find the building where my mother had resided between

1908 and 1912, at 17, Dominicaner Bastei. The hostess pointed to one of the walls. In other words, the building abutting on the one where we had spent the night!

My grandfather had gone to Vienna for business reasons. He was a sales representative for one or more Swiss manufacturers of lace and organdy, used for frilly and starched ornate dresses, located in St. Gallen. I remember his showing me samples of these materials, bound in large and thick swatch-books. Apparently, he traveled all over France and other countries by train for many years. He talked often about hotels in various cities near the train stations and had a battered leather duffle bag which Grandmère gave me after he died. Unfortunately, the metal closure slide was a little bent, and the empty bag was very heavy, so I did not use it much. Both before and after World War II, my grandfather Lucien always wore long-sleeved collarless dress shirts at home, to which he attached very stiff celluloid white collars when he put on a tie to go out.

My mother was eight years old when the Oury family left Austria in 1912, two years before the start of World War I. She remembered the war in Paris, especially after Big Bertha, the German long-range monster cannon, started to shell the city indiscriminately, when her family moved to Bordeaux. Her birth in Vienna, of French parents, haunted my mother all her life. She certainly wished she had been born elsewhere. Every time she was ever asked where she had been born, she would always insist that the location was an accident, because both of her parents were French. Repeatedly, she had to show documents attesting to the facts that both of her parents were French and that her father had registered her birth in France on July 8, 1919, as soon as he could after the end of the war, when the Treaty of Paris of June 28, 1919, automatically reinstated French citizenship to all persons born under German occupation of Alsace-Lorraine.

Henry Fribourg

RÉPUBLIQUE FRANÇAISE

Extrait du Registre

des personnes réintégrées de plein droit dans la qualité de Français en exécution du Traité de Paix du 28 JUIN 1919.

Commune de Château-Salins

No 1604.
Mademoiselle Oury, Yvonne Juliette
Née à Vienne (Autriche)
le deux Juillet mil neuf cent quatre
Le 6 Juillet 1920

LE MAIRE:

Cachet de la Mairie

Reintegration of my mother into French citizenship

My great-grandfather Léon Oury's military record is still available in my family archives. He started his service in Metz on July 17, 1842, and was given the serial number 13302 in the 54th Infantry Regiment. He was issued a rifle and a saber. On April 21, 1844, in Mézieres, he received a *Brevet de Pointe* (Fencing Certificate) which we still have. He was promoted to Corporal on January 14, 1845. On November 12, 1846, he contracted to pay 420 francs to Corporal Stanislas Aloyse Kuntz to take his place for the remainder of his military service, scheduled to last until December 31, 1848.

The reader may wonder why I have recounted the known and documented details about my ancestors' military service. Shortly after the start of the *Révolution* on July 14, 1789, all citizens of France were expected to serve their country in the army. In 1791, Jews were recognized as French citizens. On July 20, 1808, all Jews who had not yet adopted definite first and family names were obliged to do so within three months. This was a consequence of the emancipation of the Jewish citizens which was legalized by the *Assemblée Générale* and codified by Napoléon. Before 1789, the French monarchy, like the other European powers, did not allow many, if any Jews, to serve in the military. On the other hand, after 1792, Jews were not only permitted and encouraged to serve, but were allowed to become officers in the army of France. In contrast to this situation, German Jews were not allowed to serve in the German army until some 75 or 80 years later, and could not become officers until they were allowed to accept battlefield promotions during World War I. Thus, military service by French Jews was a coveted privilege and considered an honorable ratification of the citizenship which had been withheld in earlier days.

RUMBLES OF DISASTER—1939

Earlier in this account, I mentioned the sitting room where we listened to the radio in Fontainebleau. Soon after I returned from that summer Boy Scout camp in the Alps, it was there, in that room, in late August - early September 1939, in the company of my parents, my sister, and my four grandparents, that I heard about the invasion of Poland and the ensuing inevitable declarations of war by England and France. It took France and England a shamefully long three days to decide that they were going to honor their treaties to defend Poland against aggression. Later that fall, we heard there that the *fascisti* jackals of Italy, egged on by the vainglorious *Il Duce*, had joined Germany to get their share, betraying their cowardice in attacking France from the rear. You cannot accuse me of mincing my words, or not trying to reflect the feelings of the day!

After war was declared at the beginning of September, my parents decided that my mother, my sister and I would stay in Fontainebleau after the end of summer school vacation (due to end as usual on the first Monday of October) rather than return to Paris, and that my father would commute on weekends from his work in the capital city. My credentials of admission to the Lycée Rollin in Paris were accepted without question by the only boys' lycée in Fontainebleau, Lycée Carnot. This lycée was about four long blocks up the hill from our house toward the monument dedicated to the memory of those who had died in World War I. It was at this monument, on what is now known as Boulevard du Maréchal de Lattre de Tassigny, a World War II hero, that on November 11, 1939, I saw my first-ever general, with his one star in the middle on the front of his *képi*. Why I was impressed I cannot tell you, but I have ever since believed my father's comment "do not ever trust a *culotte de peau*," which refers to the custom of officers of pre-World War II days to wear leather riding breeches, thus facilitating horseback riding. An equivalent expression in the US would refer to "brass hats." He would urge me many times since then to not ever trust most military leaders, whose primary motivations are often promotions and medals, to the detriment of the victims, who are not only the civilians but also the fighting men and women on both sides of the conflicts.

My father was a very well-read individual, a habit he got into early while in school as an adolescent. I never did appreciate this as much as I should have, because his education had been developed under the French system, meaning he had become familiar with most of the French authors and philosophers throughout French history, whereas my development involved primarily British, and some American, authors and thinkers. In particular, I remember him citing the writings of Michel de Montaigne (1533 - 1592) known for his wisdom encompassing both stoic and sceptic aspects, of Charles de Montesquieu (1689 - 1755) who was one of the first to recognize the interdependence of religious, moral, political and economic aspects of society, of Jean-Jacques Rousseau (1712 - 1778) who was one of the intellectual fathers of the environmental movement, and most particularly of Blaise Pascal (1623 - 1662). He admired Pascal both for his mathematical discoveries, which he had studied in school, and for his philosophical writings summarized in his *Pensées*, a copy of which he kept at his bedside.

My mother's literary tastes were different from my father's. She liked particularly the poetry of Victor Hugo and of Alphonse de Lamartine. She often hummed the Viennese waltzes of Johann Strauss, and enjoyed the French romantic operas. She had a thorough knowledge of French history and appreciated romantic novels. Later in life, she actually read romantic novels in English, especially those of Barbara Cartland. She was skilled with knitting needles and crochets, and made many embroidered and cross-stitched cushion and pillow covers for her family.

I would imagine that many of the attitudes and thoughts I have acquired over the years were influenced by the considerable mistrust my father expressed many times to me about military and political leaders. The wholesale butchery that results too often from the motivations of the military to obtain promotions and budgets, and acquire medals, not only happened on both sides and throughout both World Wars, but in many other situations such as the war conducted by Lyndon Johnson in Vietnam, and in numerous other conflicts throughout the ages, up to the present. This diatribe does not intend to persuade you to prefer non-military leaders, because it has been demonstrated over and over again that most politicians are self-serving, and often mendacious, liars. Even those whom we thought we could admire, nay, revere, have been shown decades after their deaths to have been hateful, vindictive, bigoted, guilty of acts of disgraceful action or of spiteful omission. Examples abound throughout history, but let me look not too far in the past to mention the names of Franklin Roosevelt, Lyndon Johnson, Robert McNamara, the Duke of Windsor, Richard Nixon, the French Prime Ministers, the Swiss bankers, Henry Kissinger, even Winston Churchill and George Bush. At the same time, it would be unfair to not mention that FDR and Churchill did lead the Allies in defeating the Axis Powers, that Jacques Chirac belatedly recognized the injustices committed by previous French governments against Jews, and that Lyndon Johnson did initiate the War on Poverty.

So, the first week of October 1939, I entered Lycée Carnot in *Sixième* (sixth grade, the lowest), in a B section, meaning I would not take classical Latin and Greek taught in the A sections, but instead would be exposed to more science, math, and a modern foreign language (English). This choice had been urged on me by my father, who felt that a science/mathematics orientation would be better for life preparation than a classical/literary orientation. I concurred in his recommendation.

One class of which I was fond was geography. I recall learning the various ecological zones of North America in particular, not knowing then how much more I would learn about them later during my university studies and professional life in the US. I also had to memorize the names of many countries and their capital cities, including which ones were French colonies or mandates, and which ones were part of the British Empire. History was also very interesting, and covered in detail all important aspects of civilization in Egypt, the Middle East, Greece, Rome, and western Europe. As I recall, there were five main classes each day (French, English, Math, History/Geography, and Science) with two to three hours of homework each day, and other classes such as geometric drawing and gymnastics that alternated with study halls. Another demanding class was French grammar. We essentially memorized a whole book of rules, with examples, written by Bloch and Georgin. My grades were pretty good in most subjects, except for the "minor" class of drawing, which accounted for a minute portion of the overall ranking. I was in the top fourth or better (no ranking or grades for physical education, in which my performance was only mediocre) of the class, a competitive edge which was highly encouraged both by the teachers and my parents.

All during this time, the *drôle de guerre* (*Sitzkrieg*, a derisive term for the phony or funny war) was going on, with the French ensconced in the highly touted Maginot Line, so much more advanced than the Siegfried Line, then under construction, we were told, while the Germans were building their tank corps and the Luftwaffe. We were among the overwhelming majority that had been deluded into believing in the invincibility of the French Army—little did we know how mistaken we were!

There was a peculiar event which I never learned much about. It seems that in late 1939 - early 1940, my father was gone for several weeks, but he had not been mobilized in the uniformed army. What he did then, I do not know, and he never spoke about it. However, he came back with a very heavy canvas coat lined with a solid sheepskin. I used that sheepskin coat to weather several blizzards when I was a student at Wisconsin, Cornell and Iowa State. It was also at about that time that there were engagements between the Allies and the Germans in Narvik, Norway. I do not know if there was a relationship between the events, the coat, and my father's absence. Nonetheless, when he came back in late January or February, my mother clearly demonstrated she was very happy that he had come back—my brother Sylvain was born the sixteenth of October next!

On May 10, the Germans invaded "neutral" Holland and Belgium, and went around the Maginot Line. It was apparent right from the start that the French armies, with their Belgian, Dutch and British allies, were unable to contain the German *Blitzkrieg*. I can still hear Prime Minister Paul Reynaud (or maybe it was the general-in-charge, Gamelin, insisting on the radio that the breakthroughs were being contained (the word he used was *"colmater,"* which refers to the waterproof chinking of planks in a wooden-hulled boat). He was clearly proven wrong each succeeding day when we heard about the further advances of the Panzers. On May 30, my 39-year old father was mobilized with his age class, and left by train to rejoin the horse-drawn 75-mm cannon artillery unit to which he had been assigned. Yes, indeed, the French Army and its generals were going to fight the German tanks with horses and out-dated small-caliber cannons, in spite of the written warnings published earlier, to no one's notice, by an obscure one-star general named Charles de Gaulle!

THE RETREAT—1940

On May 20, my mother, my sister and I took the train to Grandris (Rhône) near Villefranche where one of the primary manufacturers for whom my father worked had his factory and home. His name was Louis Chanfray, and they were devout Catholics. I remember sitting in the Chanfrays' living room during conversations among the adults, while Madame Chanfray did two things of which my mother disapproved greatly: drinking whisky neat, and smoking cigarettes, while talking in a husky, and I suppose I thought sexy, voice. However, my mother never said a word about it to her, because Mme. Chanfray had to be pitied, since she had lost her only son, in his twenties, to a relatively recent fatal motorcycle accident, in which he had been thrown over the handlebars, and had landed on his head. Thus, there was an excuse for this wanton behavior of which mother disapproved, as well as for the speed with which Mme. Chanfray drove her car, boasting that she could go from Grandris to Paris at an average speed of over 100 km/hr (65 mph), having done it many times over two-lane narrow curving roads, thus endangering herself and many others. My mother never failed to remind me of this accident whenever I had the temerity to indicate an interest in a motorized bicycle or a motorcycle. It was very sternly emphasized to me that permission for a motorcycle would never be granted.

The Chanfrays arranged rooms for us at a nearby inn, in the middle of the hilly countryside at a deserted road intersection. There was a small creek in the garden behind the inn. Rosette and I played there for many hours, sometimes in the creek, sometimes playing hopscotch on the highway. I remember envying my sister her initials RF, which I just knew stood for République Française. It is only in 1997 that I learned she considered her initials to be RAF, for Rosette Annie Fribourg, and were shared with her by the Royal Air Force. The road was fairly steep not far from the inn, and this is where I first observed a man cutting hay with a scythe. I talked him into showing me how it was done, I really enjoyed it—my first hands-on experience with forage crops, subject of my future profession.

We stayed at the inn until June 17, when we left early in the morning to drive to Pau (then in Basses-Pyrénées, now in Pyrénées-

Atlantique), where my grandparents Oury had moved for the duration. In fact, my mother had been getting more and more anxious about the southward progress of the German armies, and thought that we should go rejoin her parents, since Pau is not far from the Spanish border. That proximity held the hope that escape from the *Boches* might be possible. She borrowed a car from the Chanfrays: a 13-year old Panhard, a car with the same kind of reputation that Cadillac has in this country. Not many women drove cars in those days in France, and my mother did not know how. It was not until 1950, in New York City, that she got her first driver's permit. There had been no need to learn to drive in France since we had never owned a car. So the Chanfrays' car came with a driver, a short, thin, timid, white-mustached, World War I veteran of about 60, who must have been a driver or butler for the Chanfrays. My mother had to keep reminding him constantly of the vital necessity of keeping on going, and to do so as quickly as possible, because often, in the days to come, he would want to quit and turn back, rather than drive us to Pau, as had been agreed.

> Voyage à travers la France
> en Juin 1940
>
> 17 — Grandris → Tarare (déjeuner)
> Tarare → Bon.
> Bon → Noirétable (bobine à changer
> coucher dans l'auto)
>
> 18 — Noirétable → Vallore-Montagne
> (déjeuner — faux — contact dans l'auto)
> Vallore-Montagne → Ambert
> Ambert → Arlanc (bombardement)
> Arlanc → La Chaise-Dieu
> (coucher sur un matelas)
>
> 19 — La Chaise-Dieu → Siaugues
> Siaugues → Le Charret par Chan-
> teugues (coucher dans lit — crevaison
> du réservoir — pas d'essence
>
> 20 — Le Charret → Langeac (essence)
> Langeac → Saugues (côte de 8 km)
> Saugues → Aumont (coucher dans lit)
>
> 21   Aumont → Espallion
> Espallion → Rodez (déjeuner)
> Rodez → Carmaux (pneu crevé)
>
> Carmaux → Albi (coucher dans lit)
> 22 — Albi → Montauban (déjeuner)
> Montauban → Castelnau-Magnoac
> (coucher dans lit)
>
> 23 — Castelnau-Magnoac → Ibos (déjeu-
> ner — brigadier de papa).
> Ibos → Pau

Portion of the journal I kept during the Retreat

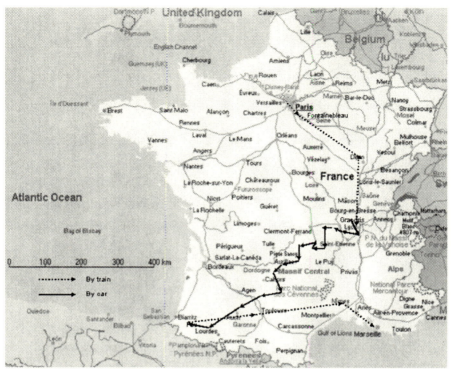

Escape of my mother and her two children by train from Fontainebleau to Grandris near Lyon (April 20, 1940), by car from Grandris to Pau (June 17 - 23, 1940), and again by train from Pau to Nîmes (late July). Later, the whole family went from Nîmes to Marseille and then Alger

A few days after the end of our trip, I wrote down our daily itinerary, and this 2-page diary survives to this day. On June 17, we left quite early in the morning. I recall our driver grumbling about the early hour when we loaded the luggage in the boot and lashed some more on the roof. We stopped for lunch in Tarare (Rhône). We then drove to Boën (Loire) and to Noirétable (Loire). While we were eating some supper, having parked the car next to many others in a vacant lot, someone helped himself to our spark plugs. My mother asked me to see if I could get some, and I did, using a monkey wrench to extract them from the cars of people who, I thought, needed them less than we did. I also was convinced, like my mother, that this was a matter of survival. Never again would we leave our car unattended.

Since we could not find a place to rent for the night, we slept in the car.

This spark plug incident was not my first major sin, it was the second. The first one occurred in Fontainebleau at l'Hôtel de l'Aigle Noir, where we had had that great lunch of which I wrote earlier. From a tray in the entry hall, I had removed and kept some pretty postcards that were for sale, although I thought they were free. Some days later, my mother found out about my theft. I was made to return all the postcards and deliver a tearful verbal apology to the hotel manager.

Both the newspapers and the car radio kept us advised of the rout of the French Army. The gendarmes had received orders to keep civilians off the highways, so that the nonexistent reinforcements could reach the battle fronts. During this Retreat (*"La Retraite"*) there were continuous streams of people from further north and east walking on the highways to get away from the German troops. People carried suitcases, bundles of clothes, knapsacks, babies; pushed wheelbarrows loaded with grandmas or possessions; rode carts heaped high with furniture, mattresses, and household goods, pulled by oxen, mules, horses, or donkeys; and rode in cars and trucks of all kinds. The pace was set by the slowest pedestrian and, once caught in such a stream, it was impossible to get out of it. Certainly overtaking could not occur. If you reached a police roadblock, you were ordered off the highway into an adjoining field, and you could not proceed any further except by furtive escape. People verged on panic, although outwardly calm, but certainly most were afraid of the aerial bombardments they could hear from time to time. Mixed in with this fear was disbelief at the rout of the "invincible" French Army.

Consequently, my mother decided that we would not travel on any national (main) road, or even on roads of second or third category. Instead, we headed across country using country roads: some paved, some with gravel surfaces, and some dirt roads. Sometimes, these roads were marked on the maps we had, and sometimes we had to guess and use dead reckoning to get through the rough topography of the Massif Central. Occasionally, she made exceptions to the rule, so that we could get food, lodging, or even more difficult, gasoline for the car. Gasoline supplies were scarce because of large military and civilian demands and uncertain or non-existent deliveries. Consequently, each purchaser was limited to a few liters, usually five or ten (1.2 or 2.4 gal) at each purchase.

The scarcity of essential supplies, the need to travel along narrow, poorly-maintained roads, and the desirability of avoiding crowds, undoubtedly increased the stress under which my mother was functioning. She kept control of herself very well, but she did everything she could to communicate her sense of urgency to our driver and to me, insisting that we had to reach Pau and its proximity to the Spanish frontier, as rapidly as possible and before the German armies overtook us.

On June 18, we left Noirétable early in the morning, driving to Vallore-Montagne near St. Etienne for lunch. When we were ready to leave, there was a short circuit in the car ignition system. My mother was quite put out that the driver did not have the faintest idea about how to fix it. Fortunately, we were able to find a mechanic who took care of it in a minute by re-wrapping a wire with frayed insulation. We then drove to Ambert (Puy-de-Dôme) and to Arlanc in the same département. In Arlanc, we waited in line about half-an-hour to get our car tank filled up, a difficult feat that my mother was able to achieve by flouting her pregnant status. In addition, my mother had a dark-blue cape that looked like the cape normally worn by nurses.

The gasoline attendant disregarded the limit that supposedly applied to all other customers, judging that a pregnant woman and nurse should get all the fuel she needed so as not to have to wait again in line. We had driven only a very few km when we heard planes overhead. They dropped bombs on Arlanc and got a direct hit on the gas station where we had been just a few minutes earlier. The noise and the smoke column will remain etched in my memory. The Germans bombed civilian towns and villages, and strafed highways populated shoulder to shoulder by refugees, adding to the panic and blocking highways to French military traffic. We arrived at La-Chaise-Dieu (Haute-Loire) very late that afternoon, but it was still light. Mother was able to find a room for us in a house that had an interior courtyard with a lockable door, so that our car would be safe. Unfortunately, the gate opening was barely wide enough for the car and, while my mother was guiding the driver as he backed in, a wheel ran over her foot. In order that her swelling foot would not prevent her from traveling the next day, she kept her shoes on all night while we tried to sleep on mattresses laid out on the floor.

June 19 found us driving from La-Chaise-Dieu to Saugues, and then to Le Charret-par-Chanteugues (both in Haute-Loire). The inn where we coasted to a stop was at the bottom of a very long steep hill. The engine of our car had quit half-way down the hill. We did not know why, until my mother asked me to check on our gasoline supply status. This chore was mine at every stop because the fuel gauge in the car did not function properly. As I drew out the notched calibrated stick that I had carved from a meter-long switch, we realized, to our horror, the magnitude of the catastrophe that had befallen us. In order to bypass the police roadblocks, we had earlier that day traveled over a gravel road with very large rock fragments. One of these had bounced up and punched a hole in the bottom of our 13-year old, rusted gasoline tank, and an almost full tank of gas had leaked out. We were able to get private accommodations at the inn, and I was assigned an attic closet all to myself.

My mother found out that there was a smithy about 5 km (3 miles) or so down the road. After lunch, I set out on foot to find the smith, on the chance that he would be able to fix the hole in the bottom of our gas tank. It was early afternoon of a clear, sunny day. I had walked about 2 or 3 km and reached a fairly level stretch when I attracted the attention of a German Messerschmitt fighter pilot. I was the only person in view, so I know I had his undivided attention as he strafed me with his machine guns. As I had been taught, I threw myself in the ditch when I realized what he was up to. He missed me the first time, so he went around for a second pass, and then a third. I must really have been menacing to this great Teutonic warrior, who felt he had to try three times to get an aggressive eleven-year old solitary boy on a narrow rural road.

After the plane had broken off the engagement, and after I had stopped shaking, I resumed my walk to the smithy. The smith was very nice, gave me some red wine after he heard about the plane incident, and proceeded to build a device with two metal plates joined by a bolt. The smaller plate was to be introduced through the hole into the gas tank, and the larger one would be on the outside to prevent leaks. He saddled his horse, and I rode behind him to return to our car. He fixed the problem in a few minutes, and the tank never did leak after that.

I slept rather well that night in my attic closet. I was a little concerned, though, about being alone for the first time since our departure from Grandris. I was concerned because my mother had entrusted me for the duration with a piece of luggage from which I was never, ever to be separated, for any reason, unless she relieved me of the duty, as she had when I had gone searching for the smith that afternoon. This luggage appeared to be a bedroll, with a Scotch plaid blanket on the outside tied with two leather straps that passed through a leather handle (I still have the leather handle and straps, inherited from my parents). However, inside the blanket was a locked metal box, about 60 cm wide, 15 cm thick, and 40 cm deep (24 x 6 x 16 in). It contained jewelry, stock certificates, and other important documents. I appreciated later on that our family was able to escape from Europe and survive for several years from the contents of this box. Even then I understood that it was extremely important I be careful with this innocuous-looking blanket roll. It was my pillow, rested between my legs during meals, and accompanied me everywhere, including the bathroom.

On June 20, the biggest problem we faced was the need for gasoline. We had a number of 5-liter (1.2 -gal) gasoline cans, about 50 or so cm (20 in) high, with a square 15-cm (6-in) or so cross-section and a metal handle at the top. We had heard a rumor that gasoline was to be had at Langeac (Haute-Loire), 8 km (5 miles) away, near Saugues. My mother successfully begged somebody for a couple of liters of gasoline, just barely enough so we could drive there. So, we left Le Charret to go to Saugues and then Langeac, which were opposite to the direction of our trip, so as to find gasoline. My sister, my mother, the driver, and I each took two 5-liter gas cans and joined the queue at a gasoline station. After we had established our position in the line, however, my mother decided it was going much too slowly, and the station might run out of fuel before we arrived at the pumps. So, using her pregnancy, her nurse's coat, and her status of mother with two small children, she was able to get permission from the gas station owner to jump with the other three of us to the head of the line, fill up all our cans, empty them into our car, and return for a second shot! As soon as we had refilled the tank, we high-tailed it out of there, ending up sleeping that night in beds in Aumont-Aubrac (Lozère).

June 21 was the day when we finally drove out of the mountains, getting to easier, straighter, flatter and less crowded roads, going from Aumont-Aubrac through Espalion (Aveyron) and on to Rodez (Aveyron) for lunch. In the afternoon, we pushed on to Carmaux (Aveyron) where we had to have a flat tire repaired, and on to Albi (Tarn) where again we were able to sleep in decent beds. The next day saw us motoring from Albi to Montauban (Tarn-et-Garonne) for lunch and on to Castelnau-Magnoac (Hautes-Pyrénées) for the night.

As you have read this account, you may have wondered why we stopped for lunch every day while fleeing for our lives. The fact is that our driver, whose name I cannot recall, insisted on having three meals a day, and both lunch and supper had to be accompanied by a bottle of red wine and normally lasted an hour and a half or two. The driving that his employer had demanded of him was indeed a terrible inconvenience. My mother found his insistence on normal lunch hours extremely exasperating. Nonetheless, he was essential to our continued travel and she had little choice but to humor him.

On June 23, we left Castelnau-Magnoac for Ibos, the home of our father's *"brigadier"* (corporal), where we had lunch, and finally achieved our original goal, Pau (Basses-Pyrénées) where we were reunited with my grandparents Oury. They had left Paris in early May, while the trains were still running unimpeded. We lodged with them, in their apartment at 1, rue Valéry Meunier, until mid-July 1940. My grandparents remained in this apartment during the entire war. They survived several searches by Germans looking for Jewish jewelry and other valuables. Fortunately, they had honest Christian neighbors with a daughter employed at City Hall, and were warned of the raids ahead of time. The neighbors hid the valuables during the searches, and returned them afterward.

In early June, the *"Héro de Verdun"* (surviving soldiers might call him the Butcher of Verdun), Maréchal Pétain, had been named, more or less by default, since no one else wanted the job, to be head of what later became known officially as *l'Etat Français* (the French State) and unofficially as Vichy France, from the name of the resort town to which the seat of government had fallen back. On June 17,

Pétain begged the Germans for an armistice; it was granted on June 21 and signed at Compiègne (Oise) the next day, in the same railroad car where the November 11, 1918 armistice had been agreed. This explained in part why we had been able to travel more easily the last two or three days of our automobile trip, because the fear pervading the fleeing population had decreased. The city of Pau was close to the Pyrénées, which on a clear day could be seen from the street overlooking the gorge of the Gave River tumbling tumultuously deep down below the observer. It is there that I saw my first uniformed German soldiers, three officers in their *feldgrau* uniforms and peaked caps chatting on the other side of the street from me. Since I was alone at the time, I hurriedly walked back toward Rue Valéry Meunier, which was not far from there.

During July, we kept hoping to hear from my father. In the extreme confusion which overshadowed the country, communications were in a shambles. Mail was neither picked up nor delivered, and telephones did not function. We had no idea where he was. Had he survived or not? Perhaps he had been taken prisoner. Under such circumstances, my mother decided that the proximity of Pau to the Spanish border was of no consequence to us. She would not leave France with her children without knowing about her husband's fate. Rather, it seemed appropriate to get as far away as possible from the Germans, whose armies were very close to Pau, occupying a strip all along the Atlantic coast down to the Spanish border. So, in mid-July, we got on the train to Toulouse (Haute-Garonne), where we spent a few days in the home of a friend of my father's, M.le Professeur René Morquer. I should say here that the Chanfray car and its driver had left us immediately after our arrival in Pau, with the driver planning to return to Grandris and his home.

M. Morquer lived with his wife and his son Jean in a relatively small apartment at 1, rue du Paradis, not too far from the St. Etienne Cathedral or the older St. Sernin church. Professor Morquer was a mycology professor at the University of Toulouse, a devout Catholic, and a good friend of my father's. They had met when both were students at the Sorbonne after the first World War. In any case, my mother had deduced that he would be a possible contact person through whom my father would try to re-establish contact with us. If he had survived the retreat and was in the non-occupied zone, he would not know where we were either. My paternal grandparents had had the same thoughts, and we met them at the Morquer's. After about a week in Toulouse, during which Jean, one year older than I, showed me the sights, my mother, Rosette, and I took the train to Nîmes (Gard), equidistant from the Germans and their allies the Italians. My grandparents Fribourg followed us a few weeks later.

In the late 1970s, after my father had died, I continued his correspondence with René Morquer. At his instigation, I received an invitation to join the Faculty of Sciences of the University of Toulouse for several months. Unfortunately, neither he nor I could secure any financing to render the visit feasible. When I was teaching in Lille in 1986, I located Jean Morquer with the help of the Minitel, the ubiquitous French national electronic telephone directory and digital information system. Jean was teaching Latin at a lycée in Laon (Aisne). We talked over the telephone for a while, and he told me both his parents had died and he was unmarried. He spoke French with a marked southwestern accent. Since he showed no interest in a meeting, even if I drove to the town where he lived, we soon terminated the conversation.

We arrived in Nîmes on July 20, 1940. My mother found a small apartment on the first floor of a very old dingy house just two blocks from the Maison Carrée, at 17, rue Littré. It was rather amazing that she was able to find these lodgings, for the city was overrun by thousands of refugees, but her pregnancy condition was very helpful in eliciting sympathy from prospective landlords. One afternoon shortly after our arrival, walking on the street across from the Maison Carrée, we ran into a cousin of my mother's, Germaine Schneeberger, and I recall that the conversation was very lengthy, on the hot sidewalk. The two cousins exchanged news and commiserations about the whereabouts of dozens of family members, but I did not know most of the people they were talking about, and I have no memories of the specific bits of information which they exchanged.

MY FATHER'S WALK THROUGH FRANCE

During the last week of July, we finally received a telegram from my father, in which he told us he was alive and about to be mustered out at Rochechouart (Haute-Vienne), to the east of Limoges.

He had found out our whereabouts from his friend René Morquer. Later, my father was able to travel by train and advised us by another telegram of the time when he thought he would arrive at the railroad station in Nîmes. My mother had difficulty walking long distances at that time, being almost seven months pregnant, so I set out on the Boulevard Victor Hugo, from the Maison Carrée, past the Lycée de Garçons on my right, then going around the right of the *Arènes* (Roman Coliseum), continuing down the very wide tree-shaded avenue leading to the railroad station. I was about one-fourth of the way down when I saw and ran to my father.

Jean Fribourg (right) and his buddy Lefebvre at Videix (Indre) in July 1940

He was dressed in a bedraggled khaki soldier's uniform, with his legs wrapped in *molletières* (puttees). He had lost much weight. He also sported a huge black moustache, protective coloration since many French enlisted men had such a moustache. It was somewhat incongruous, in view of the almost-total baldness with which he had been afflicted since his mid-twenties.

Over the next several days, we learned about the ordeal our father had undergone. He had come close to being taken prisoner by the Germans several times, a fate which would probably have insured his death if found by his captors to be a Jew. Upon being called to the colors in early May, he had rejoined his assigned regiment of horse-drawn artillery armed with 75-mm cannons, a weapon that had been extremely effective in World War I. Unfortunately, when these obsolete cannons fired point-blank at German panzers, the shells bounced off the armor. After a few tries that ended in such a manner, my father's regiment stopped using their cannons, and eventually abandoned them. My father wrote a diary of his peregrinations during the retreat, and I have here transcribed his hand-written notes.

According to his *Carnet Militaire* (military record book), Jean Fribourg was classified in the 5th Part of the List in 1922, and then in the 7th Part, reflecting a delayed call to arms, according to Article 21, because he was a university student. He was reclassified as *"bon pour le service"* (acceptable for military service) on May 30, 1940, called by individual notice, and incorporated into the *Dépôt d'Artillerie Hippomobile* (Horse-drawn artillery depot) number 21, 101st Battery, on June 10, 1940.

Henry Fribourg

Portion of the journal kept by my father during his Retreat

I GAVE YOU LIFE TWICE

The following represent transcriptions of his notes during and shortly after his retreat:

> June 10, 1700h: arrive at Fort de Charenton (Val-de-Marne), near Créteil, southeast of Paris.
> June 12, 1100h: leave for Fort de Vaujours (now in Seine-St.-Denis) near Meaux; 2200h: start retreat from Vaujours; 2230h: partial abandonment of equipment [Author's note: I imagine this refers to the 75-mm cannons].
> June 13, 0730h: arrive (again, after fruitless effort at stopping the Germans) at Fort de Charenton; 1100h: leave Fort de Charenton, destination Longjumeau (Essonne); 1300h: arrive at Choisy-le-Roi (Val-de-Marne), at M. Lavigne's, 15 av. Victor Hugo; 2000h: arrive at Longjumeau.

As I recall my father's recountings, it was about at this time that the horses were let go, and the soldiers continued walking individually south, with the hope of being able to cross the Loire River before the Germans overtook them and the bridges, rigged with explosives, were blown up.

The diary notes continue:

> June 14, 0400h: leave Longjumeau; 0930h: arrive at Augervilliers.
> June 15, 0230h: leave Augervilliers; 0930h: arrive Sainville (Eure-et-Loir); 1600h: leave Sainville.
> June 16, 0700h: arrive Orgères-en-Beauce (Eure-et-Loir); 1530h: leave.
> June 17, 1100h: arrive Pont-de-Mer (on the Loire River).

I remember my father emphasizing that the only reason he was able to rejoin us was that he had kept on and on, pushing himself to continue walking, knowing that capture was to be avoided at all costs if he wanted to ever see his family again. Many of his comrades did lie down by the side of the road for a few winks; if they slept too long, they woke up as prisoners of war! From the times he jotted down in his diary, it is obvious that my father slept little, but when he did sleep, it was in homes or barns where he could be awakened at pre-arranged times.

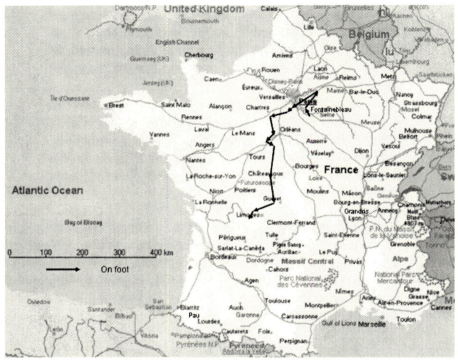

My father's walk, June 10 - 24, 1940

Upon reaching the Loire River, the first bridge he had intended to use had been blown up by the French *"sapeurs"* (engineers). He turned west, going downstream, and found that the next bridge also had been blown up. The third bridge was still standing, the one south of Pont-de- Mer. He started walking across it, not knowing if and when it would blow up. In fact, he heard the explosions after having walked about half-a-kilometer (a quarter of a mile) beyond the bridge. So, on June 17, after having left Pont-de-Mer, he crossed the river at noon and arrived at Chambord (Loir-et-Cher) at 1600h; later that day, at 1800h, he arrived at the military depot Lafont, at Nihou, close by Bracieux (Loir-et-Cher) near Blois.

On June 18, the day after the armistice had been sought, he left Nihou at 1600h, arriving June 19, 0100h at St. Aignan (Loir-et-Cher), probably not knowing about the impending armistice.

Leaving at 1030h, he rested briefly, between 0200h and 0400h on June 20, on the roadside, 7 km (4 miles) beyond Châtillon-sur-Indre (Indre), arriving later that day, at 1930h, at Rolmier near LeBlanc (Indre).

June 21, 1700h: leave Rolmier, arrive June 22, 0600h, at the Massé Farm, St. Ouën, 10 km (6.5 miles) before Bellac (Haute-Vienne).

Although walking was the primary activity, my father mentioned that several farmers along the way had been helpful, providing some bread, sometimes an egg or some chicken, and a glass of wine, as he walked his way south. This Massé farm is the first one cited by name in his diary, and apparently he had heard about the impending armistice by then, because he rested there for over 22 hours. Of course, he may also have been so exhausted that he had no choice but to stop and rest.

On June 23, he left at 0430h, arriving at 1600h at another farm, Ferme de la Chauvie, Le Clôtre, Commune of Javerdot, before St. Junien (Haute-Vienne). The next day, June 24, he left at 0500h, arriving at 1700h at La Chassagne, Videix (Haute-Vienne). This was his last temporary stop before being mustered out in Rochechouart (Haute-Vienne) on July 26.

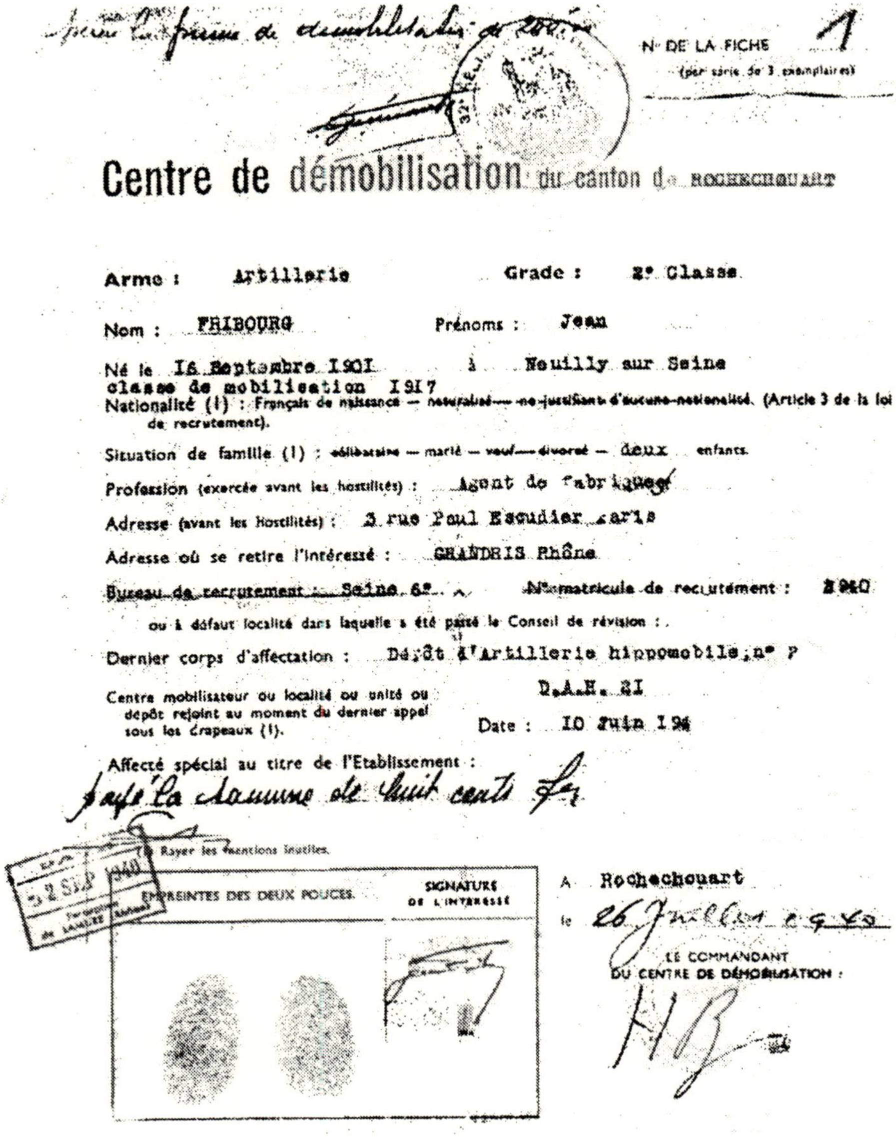

N° DE LA FICHE 1
(par série de 3 exemplaires)

Centre de démobilisation du canton de ROCHECHOUART

Arme : Artillerie Grade : 2e Classe

Nom : FRIBOURG Prénoms : Jean

Né le 16 Septembre 1901 à Neuilly sur Seine
classe de mobilisation 1917
Nationalité (1) : Français de naissance — ~~naturalisé — ne justifiant d'aucune nationalité~~. (Article 3 de la loi de recrutement).

Situation de famille (1) : ~~célibataire~~ — marié — ~~veuf — divorcé~~ — deux enfants.

Profession (exercée avant les hostilités) : Agent de fabrique

Adresse (avant les Hostilités) : 3 rue Paul Escudier Paris

Adresse où se retire l'intéressé : CHANDRIS Rhône

Bureau de recrutement : Seine 6e N° matricule de recrutement : 2940

ou à défaut localité dans laquelle a été passé le Conseil de révision :

Dernier corps d'affectation : Dépôt d'Artillerie hippomobile, n° ?

Centre mobilisateur ou localité ou unité ou dépôt rejoint au moment du dernier appel sous les drapeaux (1). D.A.H. 21

Date : 10 Juin 194

Affecté spécial au titre de l'Etablissement :

(1) Rayer les mentions inutiles.

EMPREINTES DES DEUX POUCES. SIGNATURE DE L'INTÉRESSÉ

A Rochechouart
le 26 Juillet 1940

LE COMMANDANT DU CENTRE DE DÉMOBILISATION :

My father's mustering out paper

My father's military equipment release

Another interesting document has survived to this day: the inventory of my father's military possessions at his discharge. This document, signed by the captain of the 101st Artillery Battery, certifies that Second Class soldier Jean Fribourg, upon discharge, has been given two days' rations and been paid for nine days, through August 4. It also states that he may keep his fatigue uniform, one handkerchief, one canteen, and that he has turned in all other military equipment issued to him, including his weapons.

When he started walking south, my father had a number of buddies with him. How many finished the entire trek with him, I do not know, but it was probably no more than the two friends pictured on a couple of photographs taken at the Videix farm. I recall his mentioning that some of the men he had started with had become so tired and sleepy that they laid down by the side of the road "for just a few minutes." They woke up as prisoners of war!

LIVING UNDER THE FRENCH QUISLINGS—1940 TO 1942

After being reunited in Nîmes, we looked for new lodgings. The impending birth of the baby would really crowd us in the small rooms at Rue Littré. In September, we moved to 5, Place d'Assas, not far from where we had been before. I have no recollection of what these lodgings were like. They were still in the downtown area, just two blocks from the Maison Carrée, because I remember walking from there to school later that fall. On October 16, my brother Sylvain was born. My mother had gone to a private birthing clinic (Clinique Rochet, 80, Chemin d'Uzès) some distance away from downtown, and the clinic building was on the right-hand side of a hill. I do not remember how my father took me there the next day. I remember being shown my brother through the closed window, while I was crouching through the bushes surrounding the building, because children were not allowed to visit.

In October, I started back in school, at the Lycée de Garçons on the Boulevard Victor Hugo, not far from the Arènes, entering in *Cinquième B*. There were two or three interior bare courtyards, bordered by monastery-like porticos all the way around, and students were forbidden to walk across the courtyards. Instead, it was mandated to walk only under the porticos, going around the courtyards. In 1986, when I briefly visited the building, asking for permission to look in, I observed that, with age, the courtyards had shrunk considerably, but had a profusion of plants hiding smelly latrines. The only teacher I recall is *Barbe-à-Poux* (Beard-full-of-Lice was his nickname), the mid-30s mathematics teacher who had a jet black beard reaching almost to his waist.

Leaving school in the afternoon to return home was an ordeal for me. When I had been going to school in Paris, there had been an occasional antisemitic attack on me, but usually there was only one or at most two aggressors, and the incidents were essentially verbal rather than physical. The fact that my friend Gert Rothschild was bigger than most of us also helped, although the son of the wine store owner on Rue Blanche, whose last name was Ripoteau and who had a mass of curly reddish-blond hair, was not easily deterred from insulting us. In Nîmes, on the other hand, at least once a week, sometimes more often, several antisemitic boys would wait for me and other Jewish boys, on the wide sidewalk fronting the school. If there were several of us Jews, we would form a tight phalanx and walk through the taunting bullies, usually being able to escape until the sport became boring and they dispersed.

Occasionally, however, because of the last-minute demands of a teacher, or some other reason, I ended up on the sidewalk alone or with just one other Jewish comrade. In that case, I sometimes had to fight my way through, using fists but no Marquess of Queensberry's rules. It was tough fighting my way through, but I always managed to keep my books and not break my eyeglasses, safely tucked away in the school-satchel on my back. My assailants retained some sense of misguided chivalry, so that if it got down to fisticuffs, there would only be one at a time attacking me. However, there seemed to be a limitless supply of assailants. Such fighting was strictly forbidden in school, and the teachers strictly enforced this "no fighting" rule inside the school. However, they washed their hands of whatever happened just one meter outside of the front door. Not one ever provided me with any protection on the sidewalk, although they could not have helped knowing what was happening. I learned early on that, since I was a *sale juif* (dirty Jew) I might as well fight dirty, which I did whenever necessary to make my escape.

As I recall, there was little that my parents felt they could do to help my situation. The "authorities" were not inclined to go out of their way to protect Jews, and the teachers appeared indifferent. My mother tried to soothe me with praise of my fortitude and urged me to find ways to get out of the attacks before they occurred. My father also talked to me, indicating that these bullies were misguided and to be pitied for their lack of intelligence, but that it would be best if I would not place myself in a situation where fisticuffs were inevitable.

After my father had rejoined us after discharge from the military, his parents also came to Nîmes from Toulouse, lodging at 23, rue de l'Horloge. Although the Maison Carrée was, and still is, an impressive Roman building, it could not be visited. I had always admired the beautiful architecture that dates from the Roman emperor Augustus. In 1986 Claude and I were able to visit the interior, a great bare disappointment. The Pont-du-Gard is not too far from town. I went to see it with the Boy Scout troop that I had joined, and again in 2001. This aqueduct is truly a marvelous relic of Roman civil engineering. I still have my membership registration, no. 115186, dated 1940, in the Eclaireurs de France, the secular Boy Scouts, which I joined after we had moved to Place d'Assas. I would go to the scout meetings on Thursday afternoons. There was no overt antisemitism in the EDF since, as a secular organization, there was never any mention of religion. That separation of church and state pervades French society, dating back to 1789, when the Church, associated with the monarchy, was irrevocably separated from the government by the revolutionary authorities, and has survived several attempts to abrogate it since then.

On Sundays the family would often go to the Jardin de la Fontaine, a beautiful park dating from Roman days, with the Temple de Diane in the back. Another outing destination was the Tour Magne, a huge but squat 2000-year old stone watchtower on top of the highest hill in the city, Mt. Cavalier. A real treat came one evening when I accompanied my father and sister to my first-ever opera, Carmen. The heroine of Gounod's masterpiece captivated my romantic heart! Since then, I have truly enjoyed romantic operas in French and Italian.

Everyday living was not easy that fall of 1940, and gradually became worse, week by week. Food could be obtained only with ration cards, and having coupons did not ensure finding the food. Queues were ubiquitous for everything. My mother could not use the pregnancy excuse any more to jump to the front of the line, and was loath to expose the very small baby to everybody's germs while standing in line. Rosette and I would go to wait in lines after school, queuing up for anything available, soap, toilet paper, meat, etc…We used to wrap small pieces of soap in foil, leaving only a small area, less than 1 cm^2 (0.16 in^2) exposed, in order to be able to use all small scraps. Later on, we boiled walnuts or chestnuts to extract a substance that substituted for soap. That fall, the only vegetables that could be purchased were turnips and rutabagas, and I have carried a lifelong dislike for these vegetables when cooked, although I recognized recently that raw turnips are pretty good.

Gradually, the Germans increased their stranglehold on the country, aided by willing and eager French collaborators watched over by Pétain's hand-picked goons in the *Milice*, which enforced the cult of his personality. His picture was plastered all over the place, and it was to be accorded as much respect as the singing of the *Marseillaise* (national anthem) or the deployment of the Tricolor flag. A mandatory census was initiated, and I recall my father having to fill in questionnaires demanding the names, addresses, nationality and religion of his grandparents and their parents. This was done to determine the Jewishness of every citizen according to the Nuremberg laws promulgated by the Third Reich, so that those who did not meet German racial criteria could be identified by the Vichy collaborators. My parents decided that this excessive pressure could be alleviated if they removed our family to the other side of the Mediterranean.

Algeria had been conquered by force of arms between 1830 and 1847. By 1940 it had been an integral part of France for some time and, under the provisions of the Franco-German armistice of June 1940, it was considered part of unoccupied (Vichy) France. Consequently, no special permits or papers were needed for French citizens to go there from metropolitan France and, at that time, there was no mention of religion or ethnicity on official documents. This lack of specificity was remedied by the Germans in November 1942 when they occupied Vichy France after the Allied landings in North Africa; at that time, not only documents were stamped with the Jewish or other necessary designation, but the wearing of the yellow star on outer garments became mandatory for Jews.

In February 1941 we left Nîmes by train for Marseille (Bouches-du-Rhône). There we embarked on my very first air trip on the seaplane that would carry us to Alger (Algiers). Upon arrival, we rented a very large room in the Hôtel de la Régence on the Place du Gouvernement, now known as the Place des Martyrs. This hotel was on the north side of the square, and the Great Mosque on the eastern side. A pedestrian entrance to the Casbah was on the western side, facing the harbor. This was my first exposure to a different culture. It was quite a shock to see the men in their white woolen *djellabahs* stuffing their faces with delicious sweets after they came out of the mosque in early evening during Ramadan, and to try to avert my eyes from the veiled women gliding out of the Casbah. Although I was under strict orders from my parents not to go into the Casbah, I did sneak in there several times, during the days only, to see the hordes of human streams passing among the odoriferous alleys. I also went up and down the Bab-el-Oued, a main business thoroughfare with covered sidewalks.

After a couple of weeks, my parents rented a house, Villa Zaïda, at 1, rue Calmette in El-Biar, a suburb high up above the city where the French Governor had his palace. The house was just a block or so from the electric trolley bus that we used to go downtown to shop or to attend school. The house was painted all white and had no internal doors, only beaded curtains to facilitate ventilation. The house had two levels, and so did the terraced garden, for they had been built on a very steep hill, just like all the neighboring structures. My parents purchased a security system for the house, and she became my pride and joy, a 3- or 4-year old German shepherd named Diane. She had not been trained very well, but obeyed me most of the time. When on a leash, though, she could drag me to any destination that she had chosen.

Shortly after moving in, I started school at the Lycée de Garçons, located about one or two blocks left from Boulevard Michelet as it starts rising up the hill toward the suburbs. It was not far from there that I also rejoined the Eclaireurs de France, Troop number 2, named the "*Youccas piquants*" (Spiny Yuccas). Going to school was both a pleasure and a calvary. I had always enjoyed learning and, as I progressed into higher grades, I found it not only pleasurable, but a refuge from the antisemitic distractions of the day. I was continuing to take the B sections, that is, natural sciences, mathematics, French, English, German, history, geography, chemistry (no lab), no Latin and no Greek, and doing well. Each day, I would take the trolley bus down the steep hill, walk a couple of blocks to the lycée, and time my arrival (about 0830h) so that I would spend the least possible time in the large interior courtyard before classes started. Similarly, after classes ended (about 1600h) I would not delay to leave to catch the trolley back up to El-Biar. This was done so as to minimize the time when I could be harassed or taunted verbally and sometimes physically by the antisemitic clique in the school.

There were four of us Jews in my section of 5 B, two Algerian Jews and one other who, like me, was a refugee from the metropolitan France. The Algerian Jews were accustomed to being called *sales Juifs* and doing the bidding of the bullies. They also recognized that not all Arabs or Berbers were antisemitic at that time, only a few, while most were indifferent to that issue. The two of us refugees from metropolitan France, and hence guessed (correctly) to be Jews, would not cede our place in line, pick up stuff they dropped on purpose, nor generally act subservient. Consequently, hazing was an almost daily occurrence. In my case, it was accentuated because in most of my classes, I was the top academic student. I shone in answering questions and in getting top grades on written quizzes. It is in Alger that I learned that, if I could not surmount adversaries physically, the best road to survival was to use my head. They could never take away what was inside my head, even when they were successful in stealing my pencils, or my ruler, or a book, or a jacket.

The group of bullies was not large, six or eight out of a class of some 40, but they had just two of us to intimidate. The worst time was in physical education class, which occurred two days a week. There, it was acceptable to push and shove, kick or punch, and I was not good on the gymnastic equipment, horses, rings, parallel bars. I could climb the ropes and do the gymnastics, but I was relatively slow in running. There were two ringleaders in the bully group, one was a tall, physically developed Arab (last name of Carrabia) who was not very smart and had been held back once or twice from promotion to the next grade. This gave him a well-deserved feeling of inferiority, and he boosted his ego at my expense. In particular, the minutes in the locker room after exercise, when we had to strip and take a shower, were occasions when he and others enjoyed abusing me physically. I have had a lifelong aversion to the smell and feel of locker rooms, and I believe I can trace that to the experience of these months in Alger.

The other ring-leader was a Frenchman, last name of Barré, about my size but more slender, with blond hair in a crew-cut. He had taken boxing lessons and was the son of a general. Once, when he had been particularly abusive to me, I "lost my cool" and issued the challenge "I'll meet you after school," which meant there would be a fist fight inside a circle of spectators on the sidewalk just beyond the school front door. I was really scared, because he had a reputation as a boxer, and I did not know what to do. However, the *sale juif* was lucky, I landed a solid blow on his left eye when he was pummeling my stomach, and then I hit his jaw so hard he fell down. There was a cheer from the spectators, classmates who hardly ever helped me when I was being abused and who were scared of the bullies. Barré was so surprised when he landed on his butt that, after he got up, he smiled at me, extended his hand, and said "no hard feelings." He never again bothered me as long as I was attending the school.

I was so proud of myself as I rode the trolley back up the hill to our house, I could not wait to tell my parents about the wonderful ending to the altercation. Little did I expect my mother's reaction, which was one of fury that I had endangered the survival of the entire family. She thought that the general's son would complain to his father about the *sale Juif,* and that the only doubt remaining was whether we would all be arrested later that evening or the next day! That night was one of the worst I ever spent, awake and wondering whether my proud and precipitous actions would result in peril for the family. In fact, the days went by, and nothing happened, except that the two of us boys proudly sported shiners in school.

Another lesson I have carried with me from these days is that one has to be self-sufficient in life. Of the 40 pupils in that 5 B class, four were Jews, six or eight were bullies, and the remainder were scared or indifferent bystanders. I learned early on that the two metropolitan Jews would not get any help from the great majority in standing up to the bullies, unless we were strong enough, physically and/or mentally, in getting them to give up or run. Physical action most of the time was unwise and a losing proposition, so using my head was essential; sometimes they could beat me, but in the long run they could not take away from me what I carried in my brain. At least, at that time, these people had not been won over to the German Final Solution.

My main release from the tensions at school and the self-driven push to learn as much as possible so as to excel in class performance was with the Boy Scouts. I was eager to progress in the scouts, becoming a tenderfoot on May 28, 1941, Second Class on August 11 at the end of a 3-week summer camp, and First Class later that fall. I became an Assistant Patrol Leader on June 12 and a Patrol leader (of the Eagle Patrol) on August 15, 1941. The summer camp tents were pitched in the pine woods just inland from a beach about 20 or 30 km (13 to 19 miles) outside of town. I remember getting my Messenger merit badge: in one day, having swum 500 m (1,600 ft), walked 5 km (3 miles) in less than one hour, ridden a bicycle on an asphalt road for 20 km (13 miles) in less than an hour, and transmitted and received messages in Morse code and in semaphore. I do not remember any antisemitic event in the Boy Scouts. I suspect that the adult leaders had indicated to the other members of the troop that ethnic or religious slurs were contrary to the Scout Oath and would not be tolerated. As a matter of fact, on November 27, 1941, shortly before my family left Alger, Norbert Aprosio, the really nice young man who was my Scoutmaster, wrote me an official attestation to the fact that I was a Patrol Leader and a glowing recommendation for being an excellent Boy Scout. This document stood me in good stead later in Cuba to obtain rapid promotion to Senior Patrol Leader, once I could speak Spanish.

Another memory deals with being awakened in the middle of the night by a noise, which turned out to have been made by an Arab trying to steal our hiking boots. I raised a hue and cry, and grappled with him. He had a knife with which he slashed the front of my right leg. The wound got infected and would not heal for a long time, because the only medication available was sulfa powder. To this day, the skin on that area is thin and much more susceptible to injury than the remainder of the leg. I also picked up a lifelong habit during these weeks on the beach. Before slipping shoes or boots on, I always turned them upside down. If you did not do that in such a setting, there might be a scorpion in there, which would be bad news. This habit has stood me in good stead when, in the army or in my early days at Tennessee, pranksters placed mice or other nasties in my boots. In the morning, I would turn my boots upside down, see the critter run off, and not say a word. Disappointed pranksters!

A major happening occurred in the middle of the last week of camp when, at a campfire, I was initiated into the fraternity of Boy Scouts who have a *totem*. I would forever more be known in scouting circles by this *totem*, rather than by my secular name. This event was a feared honor. It is very nice indeed to get a *totem*, but the ceremony is accompanied by considerable hazing carried out by those who already have been *totemized*, and witnessed by the entire troop. The *totem* has its origin with the presumed Native American habit of assigning names of animals to human beings. Presumably the chosen animal, with its qualifying adjective, describes salient characteristics of the individual. The *totemized* elders decide upon the name in advance. The candidate is asked whether the proposed *totem* is acceptable. It had better be, because the alternative may be less flattering. The second alternative is normally not acceptable, since it means delaying obtaining a *totem* for six months or a year, until the next big campfire at the earliest.

The *totem* that was chosen for me was "*Phoque se trotte*" (trotting or jogging seal, alternatively in slang, seal running away from work) possibly references to my somewhat chunky physique, my slow running gait, and my ability to use my head to escape the more dreary chores. In any case, this name had the additional benefit of lending itself to a pun, an activity in which even then I delighted. This pun comes about by pronouncing the three words rapidly, and thus coming out with "*Fox-trot*." Hence, the signature I designed for myself was the profile of a seal juggling a 78 rpm record on edge (the only kind in use at that time) on its nose.

Fox-trot (Phoque-se-trotte)

In 1941, an "Aryanization" office was set up in Algeria, and a 2 percent *numerus clausus* (quota) was imposed on Jews in the professions, such as physicians, lawyers, pharmacists, and nurses. The number of Jewish students in universities was drastically reduced to 3 percent. On November 18, 1941, came the time for the application of the law in secondary schools. In early afternoon, the school authorities posted on the bulletin board by the main entrance gate to the inner courtyard, the alphabetic list of those Jewish pupils who would be allowed to continue in school from that day on. My name was not on the list.

Henry Fribourg

This was in effect the French version of *Arisierung*, the German Nuremberg laws.

At 1400h, I was called to the principal's office, handed the curt and impolite (according to accepted letter-writing practice of the day) mimeographed notice reproduced here. (Sir, I regret to advise you that the commission charged with the duty to establish the list of Jewish pupils to be retained in the lycée did not include the name of your son. Therefore, he will not be admitted any more in our school) to hand to my father, and told to leave the school immediately. When I arrived home, earlier than usual, my parents were incensed. After all, my father had served in the French army, my grandfather Albert had, my grandfather Lucien's uncle had, one of my ancestors had received the *Médaille de Sainte Hélène*.

Monsieur,

J'ai le regret de vous faire connaître que la commission chargée de dresser la liste des élèves israélites à maintenir au Lycée, n'a pu retenir le nom de votre fils.

En conséquence, il ne sera plus admis dans notre établissement.

Je suis à votre disposition pour vous donner tous renseignements utiles.

Veuillez agréer, Monsieur, l'assurance de mes sentiments distingués.

Fait à Alger, le 18 Nov. 1941

Notice of my expulsion from school in Alger

Our families had been loyal and patriotic French citizens for at least one century before the Révolution Française in 1789 and had opted for French citizenship after the forcible annexation of Alsace-Lorraine by the Germans from 1871 to 1919, when that expansion of the Reich was nullified by the Treaty of Versailles.

These territorial ambiguities go back to the days of Charlemagne, otherwise known in Latin as Carlus Magnus or in German as Karl der Grosse. He wanted to treat his three sons equally, giving in 806 most of France to one, most of Germany to the second, and leaving the richer but smaller intervening lands to the third, Louis (Lothaire). Most of Louis' kingdom was made up of Alsace, Lorraine, and Burgundy, but it could not maintain itself as an independent kingdom. Burgundy for some time was able to maintain its independence, but had become an integral part of France by the 17th century. Some of the other lands have bounced back and forth through historical times between strong owners of the West (France) and of the East (Germany). Lorraine and Alsace lie to the west of the Rhine River, adjacent to France. Demographically, moreover, since the middle of the 18th century, residents of Lorraine and most of those of Alsace have preferred to be part of France rather than of Germany.

The next day, my mother and I went to the office of the principal, where she peremptorily and in no uncertain loud terms demanded to be admitted to his office, even though we had no appointment. This was a clear and outrageous violation of acceptable behavior in French society. She demanded from him that a report card be issued that day to me, rather than at the end of the trimester, that this report indicate that my conduct had been good and my school performance satisfactory, and that I had been expelled solely because I was Jewish. This document is proof of the betrayal of French citizens by the Vichy government in its eager kowtowing to the Germans.

I GAVE YOU LIFE TWICE

UNIVERSITÉ **Lycée de Garçons d'Alger** **ACADÉMIE**
DE FRANCE   D'ALGER
N° 61

SUR PAPIER LIBRE USAGE SCOLAIRE SEULEMENT

Le soussigné, Proviseur du Lycée de Garçons d'Alger, certifie que M. Fribourg Henri

né à Paris

le 10 ~~Février~~ Mars 19 29

a suivi, audit lycée, en qualité d'élève externe

la classe d' AB

depuis le 17 ~~Mai~~ Février 19 41
jusqu'au 17 Novembre 19 41

Certifie en outre que sa conduite a été bonne et son travail satisfaisant (atteint par le "numerus clausus")

Le Directeur

et que les sommes à sa charge ont été complètement payées.

Alger, le 19 Novembre 1941
Le Proviseur,

Good conduct and satisfactory schoolwork certificate in Alger

Henry Fribourg

Ministère de la Jeunesse, de l'Éducation nationale et de la Recherche

Le Ministre Paris, le 17 Juillet 200?

Cher Monsieur,

Vous avez bien voulu me faire part de la profonde injustice dont vous avez été victime en novembre 1941 de la part des autorités françaises, alors que vous étiez élève au lycée de garçons d'Alger.

Je conçois combien la blessure que vous a causée cette exclusion en effet totalement injustifiée peut être encore douloureuse aujourd'hui.

La mesure prise à votre encontre est au nombre de celles profondément regrettable, qui ont été adoptées durant cette période si sombre de notre histoire.

Je vous prie de croire, Cher Monsieur, en l'assurance de mes sentiments très cordiaux.

Luc Ferry

Monsieur Henry A. FRIBOURG
The University of Tennessee
Institute of Agriculture
Department of Plant and Soil Science
P.O. Box 1071
KNOXVILLE, TN 37901-1071
USA

BDC/AR/LF/ln° 124

110, rue de Grenelle – 75357 Paris 07 SP
Letter of regrets from Minister of Education Luc Ferry

For many years, ever since the late 1970s, I had written to each successive French Minister of National Education and each Prime Minister to ask whether they had any comments they would care to make or apology to tender in view of the way that I had been treated in November 1941, including copies of the two documents I have shown above. I had never received any reply. Nonetheless, I persevered, and eventually received the letter reproduced here, from Minister Luc Ferry, the grandson of the Jules Ferry for whom was named the lycée that housed my kindergarten class. The letter, states in part: "You informed me of the profoundly unjust treatment that you received at the hand of the French government when you were a student at the lycée in Alger. I understand the depth to which this exclusion wounded you and how this unjustified treatment can still be painful today. The treatment to which you were subjected is among those regrettable measures adopted during this dark period of our history. Cordially yours," This apology, 61 years after the event, was most gratifying to me, and reinforced my occasional optimism that France may, in the future, rightfully claim again to be moral and civilized.

THE ESCAPE—WINTER 1942

Although my parents must have been taking steps to figure out how to escape to the New World for some time, my expulsion from the lycée must have been the last straw that convinced my father that my mother was correct in wanting to leave Europe and German or French influence. I recall my father mentioning even before then, perhaps when the Aryanization laws were promulgated, that he had been able to correspond with a European Jewish man living in La Habana, whose last name was Dreyfuss, and that this man had indicated that he would be able to purchase five visas for us as soon as funds could be transferred to him. A figure of $1,000 or $2,000 per visa is a hazy, perhaps incorrect memory. I have no idea how this was done, but we did receive these visas on December 1, 1941. Unfortunately, I have no documentary evidence on these visas among the many documents I inherited from my parents.

I also have a vague recollection that an entity called *Agence Havas* was involved in some way in getting our visas, or perhaps in helping to book passage on a neutral Portuguese ship. A few days later we left Algeria. Having the visas was only the first step in a tortuous and difficult road, for exit visas for Frenchmen wanting to leave French territory were issued only in metropolitan France, not in Algeria. We were scheduled to embark on the S/S Nyassa in Lisbon, Portugal in December, so time was of the essence. The five of us crossed the Mediterranean again, by ship this time, to Marseille (Bouches-du-Rhône).

Rosette, Sylvain and Henri in Alger, October 1941

Upon arrival in Marseille, we took two adjoining rooms in the Hotel Splendide on Rue Grignan, just a few blocks from the Canebière, a very wide downtown street that goes down the hill toward the Old Harbor. The Hotel Splendide was one of the better ones in Marseille, and centrally located. Unfortunately, its attractiveness also meant that it was used by many German officers. We had to give them a wide berth, since we did not want to attract their attention. Sometimes, that was difficult, especially when they entered an elevator where we were already. It was indeed terrifying to be so close to these uniformed, boisterously loud, intimidating, mortal enemies. This became particularly chilling when my 8-year old sister, returning up to the room with me, said to me, in French naturally, "*Donnez-moi de l'espace vital*" (Give me breathing space, a mocking reference to Der Führer's frequent reference to Germany's need for *Lebensraum*). The German officers laughed, not understanding the mocking reference to their Leader!

    A major event for me was that my parents decided to purchase for me a suit with knickers, so that I could be warmer wearing them than with the short pants to which I was accustomed. Most boys wore short pants until the age of 12 or 13. I was much too young to wear the trousers that men wore. Knickers were "the" thing to wear for male teenagers, and I was thrilled to have my first pair. These kinds of pants originated as golfing attire and were tied below the knee, somewhat in the manner of bloused fatigues that I wore many years later in the US Army. The *mistral*, a cold wind from the north that blows down the Rhône valley, was fierce and made walking the streets a miserable experience at this time of the year. Notwithstanding the weather, we did do some window shopping, admiring the *santons*, Christmas ornaments peculiar to Provence, which we had never seen before.

    I remember accompanying my father to stand in line for innumerable hours, outside in the cold wind, to obtain the visas we needed from the Portuguese and Spanish consulates. All procedures had to be completed in a pre-determined sequence, and any deviation was unacceptable. Furthermore, the attack on Pearl Harbor just a few days earlier had made everybody jittery, because no one knew what the German reaction to the entry of the US into the war would be in Vichy France. First, my father obtained the exit visas that allowed the five of us, all French citizens, to leave French territory. As I recall, there was some kind of relatively short time limit, maybe six or eight weeks, after which the visas would become invalid. At the same time, he confirmed the booking of the cabin on the S/S Nyassa, one of the few Portuguese ships that were still plying the Atlantic. How much the bribes had to be for the travel agents, I do not know, but the cabin cost several thousand dollars, in advance. The cabin fares were not refundable, regardless of the reason for not reaching the ship before its departure from Lisbon. Having valid tickets, we then could apply for Portuguese transit visas, which were required before we could apply for Spanish transit visas. It took about a week or so to wait outside the Portuguese consulate in the cold and rain to apply for, and then receive, the Portuguese transit visas. I remember going with my father to pick them up, and then walking as fast as possible to go stand in line at the Spanish consulate. We did not get to the head of the line that day, and returned the following day.

It was on that day that Generalissimo Francisco Franco agreed with "his buddy" Hitler's request to close the Spanish borders to all "undesirables." My sister and I both recall overhearing conversations between our parents, when they were considering crossing the Pyrénées mountains on foot to be smuggled through Spain to Portugal. However, they decided against this alternative, reasoning that my sister would not be able to walk that far, and that there was too much danger from possible noises by our baby brother. Fortunately for us, there were many people in Marseille desirous of also getting to Lisbon to embark on the S/S Nyassa. The company modified the planned itinerary so that the ship would call at Casablanca, Morocco (also a French dependency at that time) before crossing the Atlantic, rather than heading straight out as originally intended. In a way, this made the trip easier for us, since we would not leave French territory until we boarded the ship. On the other hand, it would delay our departure from German control. In any case, we had no choice, and shipped across the Mediterranean, leaving Marseille for Oran, Algeria on January 13, 1942.

My grandparents Albert (*Bon-papa*) and Lucie (*Grand-maman*) had rejoined us from Nîmes, where they had been living since we had been there a year earlier, and where they had stayed while we were in Alger. It is in our hotel room there that I saw them for the last time, as we bid each other adieu the day before our sailing to Oran. They were not happy to see us leave, because my grandfather was convinced that, as a former officer in the French Army, he and his family would be immune to depredations from the Vichy government. Little did we know! It was an emotional scene when my mother insisted that our decision was right, that my parents wanted to save their children, and that the separation took place because my father's parents had refused to accompany us. Indeed, they could have come with us, but refused to leave their *patrie* (fatherland), France. My other grandparents Lucien (*Grand-père*) and Renée (*Grand-mère*) did not come to say goodbye from Pau. As a matter-of-fact, Grand-père was so upset with my mother's "abandonment" that he refused to correspond or talk with her until she went to visit her parents in Paris after the war had ended. It was then that he did apologize to my mother and admitted she had been right to leave with her family. To this day, I do not know why my mother was so certain of her intuition that leaving was necessary to survival, in spite of the objections of her parents.

On January 14, 1942 we arrived in Oran in late morning, transferred from the harbor to the railroad station, and boarded a train in late afternoon. This train was rather slow, and took us through the Moroccan cities of Fès, Meknès and Rabat on its way to Casablanca. The railroad cars were old, and had no lengthwise corridor; there were two doors to the outside per compartment, one on each side. Consequently, bathrooms were reachable only when the train stopped. At these stops, passengers also could purchase food from hawkers in the stations. The compartments were crammed full, with people on the floor as well as on the wooden seats.

On January 17, about mid-day, we were about 10 to 20 km (7 to 13 miles) northeast of Casablanca when the train came to a full stop in the middle of what appeared to be nowhere. There was a sign Sidi-something, perhaps Sidi-el-Ayashi, which is located about half-way between Fedhala and Casablanca. All persons who were to embark on a ship in Casablanca were ordered by armed French police to get off the train with their luggage. Many of the passengers were non-French refugees, and they accepted such mistreatment without complaint. My father protested vehemently, showing with his papers that he was French and a veteran, and was entitled to travel freely anywhere in French territory, such as Morocco was at that time. His entreaties were to no avail and were repulsed rudely.

Males were separated from females, and all were herded to large sheds with metal sides and roofs and concrete floors. I accompanied my father, whereas my sister and my 15-month old brother remained with my mother. There was no furniture of any kind in the structures: we kept our clothes in our suitcases, and slept on the concrete floor, the harsh surface of which was alleviated slightly with a few sprigs of straw furnished by the authorities. We were close by the beach, and the entire area was surrounded by barbed wire and armed guards.

I have no recollection of what we were given to eat, if anything, but I recall that there were several perpetual queues hundreds of people long. These queues terminated at one of the two water faucets, or at one of the four or five latrines available for the couple of thousand persons in the camp. My sister remembers seeing a corpse on the beach; I do not. I do recall the rage that we felt, so close to embarking on our ship, to be prevented from reaching the port of embarkation. As it turned out later, though we had not been told, the S/S Nyassa had delayed its departure from Lisbon, reasons unknown.

After a few days, my father was able to make contact with someone in authority who decided that French citizens should not have been interned and treated in this way. Our family was released to go into Casablanca, where we found lodgings in a downtown hotel. The daily news were distressing, because the projected arrival of the S/S Nyassa was delayed from day to day. We did not know whether the delays were due to shipping problems, Portuguese bureaucracy or inefficiency, or political complications. We spent our days walking around downtown Casablanca, finding it warmer, whiter, and cleaner than Alger. The name of the eager French police chief who ordered the removal of Jewish passengers from the train was made known, somehow, to the Free French forces in England. The individual was executed summarily by one of the first Free French officers who landed in Casablanca in November later that year. I remember well the satisfaction with which my father received the news in Cuba some time after the event.

Finally, on January 30, 1942, the Nyassa arrived in the harbor but, for some reason, was not able or allowed to dock. So we had to go in launches to the ship in late afternoon. The people from the camp were taken to dockside by train, and boarded the ship that evening. Our family had a second class cabin all to ourselves. My father had a bunk, my mother had the lowest one that she hardly ever left while the ship was in motion, and my sister and I shared the uppermost one, sleeping head to toe. My brother, who was then 15 months old, had a wardrobe drawer all to himself. I distinctly remember the great feeling of relief when we woke up the next morning and realized that the ship had moved out of territorial waters during the night. We were now out of direct German/Vichy French control. We had had no supper the previous evening, and the breakfast was served buffet-style. I well recall the astonishment with which we all viewed the enormous amount of food available. We had not seen that much food at one time for many months. I recall also the eagerness with which we ate bread, butter, eggs, fish, etc…and the terrible feeling when we found out that our stomachs, unused to so much food, rejected the load forcibly. There was a more than 95% incidence of seasickness among the passengers that morning.

In the middle of the Atlantic, January 1942

We were free! We could breathe again, although we still had many concerns for our safety. These were emphasized every time we looked over the guardrail and saw the huge Portuguese flag painted on each side of the ship, a notice to prowling submarines that this was a neutral ship. At night, many spotlights were directed over the gunwales to illuminate these flags. The ship was grossly overloaded with passengers, bunks five high in the holds for third class, and small cabins like ours in second class with more people than the occupancy for which they were designed.

Even the millionaires in first class complained about cramped quarters. There were French, German, Polish, Czech, Belgian, Dutch, stateless, and other refugees, most of them Jewish, but not all. There were a few *Hasidim* dressed in black caftans who felt compelled to flaunt their piousness in public, and many others who gave thanks privately and quietly.

I shared the baby-sitting duties for my brother with my father and my sister, for father was quite busy taking care of my seasick mother, who hardly ever left her bunk. When I could get away, I would play and talk with my friend Jean Wacziarg, a year older than I, who would become John Varney the day he landed in the US. As I recall, his family was originally from Czechoslovakia and had emigrated from their home to France in the late 1930s, long enough ago that he spoke French without any noticeable accent. The two of us explored the ship at length. Our favorite spot was at the bow, where we could feel the wind and watch the keel dip up and down through the waves. No seasickness there! It was there also that Jean told me all about the birds and the bees, my first and really only class in sex education.

After four or five days at sea, we were halted in the middle of the ocean by a German U-boat that surfaced not far from us, training its deck cannon on our ship. A boarding party searched the vessel for several hours, perhaps looking for forbidden merchandise, while we were all holding our breath. After the fruitless search was over, though, they left, leaving us feeling a lot better. Four or five days later, a British cutter came alongside to escort us into Hamilton harbor in Bermuda, for a British inspection of all of us dangerous refugees. I do not know if we had the benefit of an incompetent pilot, or whether the captain had out-of-date charts or could not read good ones, but the ship ended up on top of a sandbar in the middle of the harbor.

Considerable coal was burned in repeated efforts to get the ship off the sandbar, to no avail. Finally, several days later, a high enough tide came along to float the ship off the sandbar. Of course, by that time, we had all been declared harmless enough by the British to be allowed to proceed to our destinations. We were not harmless enough, however, to be allowed to go ashore for just a few hours at a time, in case we would happen to have in our midst dangerous saboteurs.

Although we had been scheduled originally to go directly from Bermuda to Cuba, the captain sought and received approval to go to Newport News, Virginia in order to replenish his coal supply, depleted by the efforts to get off the sandbar. In the meantime, it seems that the entrance to the coal chute had been inadvertently left open, and a young refugee boy, whose name I do not recall, fell to his death in that steep ramp. A couple of days later found us tied up at a coal-loading dock, my first-ever view of the United States. The morning after docking, those few passengers who had valid visas for the US were allowed to disembark, envied by many of the hundreds of us lining the guardrail. Just so that none of us would get any ideas, the American authorities posted Sea Patrol sentries, armed with rifles, on the deck, which they patrolled ceaselessly day and night. This was a visible demonstration of the American government's policy to not admit too many Jewish refugees. We stayed at this loading dock for three more days, and it was impossible to get or stay clean. Finally, the coal hatches were battened down, the armed guards disembarked, and the ship got under way, destination La Habana.

CUBA—1942 TO 1945

We arrived in La Habana harbor on the morning of February 25, 1942, seeing the old city on the right, with the cathedral where Columbus' ashes had rested until they were moved to Hispaniola in

El Morro

1898. On the left, El Morro castle guarded the harbor entrance. Some of the cells in the castle had special exits, openings sloping down to the walls overlooking the sea. Cell dwellers who had overextended their welcome were forced to slide down to the sharks waiting below. The ingenious Spaniards built these features, but subsequent rulers availed themselves of the facilities when they deemed it necessary.

Our papers were in order! We had escaped the Germans! We were free of persecution! Later that afternoon, after the ship had tied up to the quay, we walked down the gangplank, touched ground, walked one hundred meters (110 yards), and were told to get into small motorboats that took us to the island of Tiscornia, in the middle of the harbor. There, we were separated by gender, pushed into huge dormitories, and told this was a temporary quarantine for medical and document processing. This processing was completed in a couple of days, but we were not released. We found out that release required money!

In other words, the Cubans, who had sold us visas for thousands of dollars, were not satisfied. It would take more money to get out of their quarantine camp! At first, they exacted thousands of dollars per person for each release. The next week, the rate decreased to hundreds of dollars per person, and gradually kept on decreasing. As I recall, we got out after about three or four weeks, and my father had to pay two thousand dollars for the four of us (the baby was thrown in for free by the humanitarian bribe-taking guards).

Unfortunately for these venal members of the Fulgencio Batista government, the source of their extracurricular income was going to dry up soon. The S/S Nyassa was the next-to-last ship to get to Cuba with refugees. About a month after we arrived, the S/S Serpapinto came in, the last refugee ship to make it during World War II. So, by the end of the year, the Cubans finally figured out the only people left in Tiscornia were the ones who indeed had no money with which to bribe the authorities. They closed the camp and threw out the destitute refugees, so as not to have to house and feed them any longer.

We got rooms at the Hotel Inglaterra, a major hotel just across the street from the statue of José Martí (1853-1895), the poet who agitated for the liberation of his native island from Spain. Martí is held as the national hero of Cuba for he precipitated the 1895 Revolución and is considered the father of his country. The revolt started in the city of Bayamo, and so the national hymn of Cuba, commemorating this event, is the Himno Bayamés, words of heroic aggressiveness set to what my mother considered "Central European comic opera" music. It was after the US intervention, after the presumed attack on the Maine, that Cuba established its Constitution in 1902. However, while we lived in Cuba, the country was ruled by Fulgencio Batista, a former sergeant of artillery who had led a mutiny in 1933. He thereupon became a colonel. He had won presidential elections in 1940, after having been head of the armed forces for several years. His political nemesis was Dr. Grau San Martín, with whom he alternated in the office of President. Such a change occurred while we lived in Cuba, about 1944. [Later, Batista took over again in a coup in 1952. In December 1959, he was ousted by Fidel Castro. I heard the news during an intermission at a greyhound race track in Miami, when Claude and I took a Christmas camping vacation in Florida.]

On the other side of the plaza from the hotel was the National Theater, and the large, impressive, white-stone Capitol next door. We stayed in the hotel just a few days. It was an opportunity for me to walk the narrow streets of the Old City, the wide, tree-shaded Prado where adolescent girls and unmarried young women walked in the company of their *dueñas* (chaperones) while allowing young males to ogle them. However, it was bad form to whistle admiringly at women on the Prado, though it was done regularly throughout the rest of the city. Fidel put a stop to that! Near the Prado, at right angles to it, was the Calle O'Reilly, a very busy commercial street named after the Dublin-born Spanish nobleman who was governor of Cuba in the 1760s. After a kilometer or so, it crossed another very busy commercial street, the Calle Obispo, with arcades and many shops where such essentials as machetes of all sizes could be bought by *guajiros* (peasants) in from the country. On the sidewalk could be purchased slices of *lechón* (suckling pig roasted on a spit) which I was under strict instructions, for sanitary and health reasons, to leave alone (I never did indulge). All kinds of government-sponsored lottery tickets were also hawked in that area.

    We must have received help from the people who bought the visas for us in the first place, but I have no memory of them. I do recall walking down the street proudly wearing my wool knickers, the only dress clothes I had. They were extremely hot to wear in the tropical sun, even in winter. Worse, they attracted the taunts of teenage Cuban boys, unaccustomed to seeing such strange garb. So, only a few months after being so pleased to get knickers, I had to ask my parents to buy me long trousers, since short pants were not acceptable either in the Cuban environment. After a week or two, we moved to a ground-level apartment at 114 Calle 20 in the El Vedado suburb west of downtown La Habana. We lived there until May 31, 1944, when we moved to 1252 Calle 13, just around the corner, into a breezier and cooler second floor apartment (no air-conditioning in those days). That is where we lived until our departure for the US on April 10, 1945.

I GAVE YOU LIFE TWICE

Very soon after we moved to Vedado, my parents applied for my admission to Columbus School, a private secular American middle and high school located at 907 Calle 19, about six or seven blocks from where we lived. I suppose that the apartment location and the school selection were related. I was admitted to the school, where most classes were taught in English by expatriate American women. However, there were several courses taught in Cuban Spanish, and practically all students were native Cubans. I specify Cuban Spanish, because the accent and speed of delivery are specifically Cuban. To this day, if I meet a Latin American and speak a few words of greeting in Spanish, invariably I am asked "When did you leave Cuba?," for I have retained the distinctive accent of the island.

Rosette, Henri and Sylvain in Vedado, spring 1942

Since I knew no Spanish in 1942, and my two years of school English in France had emphasized written composition and grammar rather than the spoken word, communication was difficult. To make things easier for me, since no teacher spoke any French, I was assigned to a 6^{tth} grade home room, whose teacher in charge was Miss Patricia Doyle, the Latin teacher. Miss Doyle, originally from St. Louis, was a tall and bosomy blonde, in her thirties, with big blue eyes. If my halting English was not understood, I would talk to her in French. She would understand part of my statement and answer me in Latin, which I barely understood. However, she really wanted to help me, and she did, making my first three months in school bearable, even though those first three months were very difficult. I could not do the school work in English, even though I was learning English as fast as I could, but not progressing as rapidly as I wanted. During recess, I could not communicate with any of my classmates, who spoke Spanish the minute we got out of class.

At the same time, I was studying for my *Bar-Mitzvah* with the rabbi of a (the?) Reform congregation in Vedado. He was a German-accented English-speaking white-haired refugee with considerable body odor. The congregation used the 1940 edition of the Union Prayer Book. It was quite a revelation to us that it was possible to go to a Jewish house of worship and, with only relatively little effort, understand what was going on. On High Holyday services, there must have been several hundred worshipers in the large rented hall at Avenue H (I think) in Vedado. This wide street is one of the few avenues running perpendicular to the sea which was divided by landscaped lawns and islands. I had had my thirteenth birthday in March, while we were on Tiscornia Island. I guess that the rabbi and my parents came to the understanding that it was more urgent for me to have the *Bar-Mitzvah* as soon as possible than to take the time for me to learn all I should know for a traditional participation in a service.

So, building on the Hebrew lessons I had had from M. Hollander three years earlier, I learned to read the שמע (*Shema*), the first two paragraphs of the תפלה (*Tefila*), the עלינו (*Aleynu*), the Torah blessings, the *Kiddush*, and a few other prayers. I also learned about the various holy days, their meanings, duration, some historical background, and the elements of the events related in Genesis and Exodus. When the time came for the *Bar-Mitzvah* in mid-June, however, instead of reading my Torah portion, I underwent an unrehearsed public oral examination on the *bimah* (pulpit) in English. My gift from my parents for the occasion was a new Cuban-style brown short-sleeve dress shirt that would hang over matching long trousers. Apparently. I answered all the questions satisfactorily, and I was declared a Bar-Mitzvah. This unusual ceremony was the reason that in 1979, on my fiftieth birthday, I had another *Bar-Mitzvah*, a more traditional one this time, at Temple Beth El in Knoxville, Tennessee.

The teacher of English and algebra at Columbus School was Mrs. Sybil Kendall, a true daughter of the British Empire. Born in England, she was married to an Australian. She had four sons, each one born in a different part of the then British Empire, such as India and Canada. Her youngest son, whom I met late in 1942, had just enlisted into the Canadian Special Forces and was getting ready to leave Cuba. My parents asked Mrs. Kendall if she would give me some private tutoring during the summer vacation, so that I could follow normal classes with students of my own age group when school started again in the fall. Mrs. Kendall was a hard taskmaster, but she really taught me English grammar, composition, and literature, in a way that has served me well all my life. She gave me too much homework and too much reading to do. She gave me tongue twisters that I was to repeat aloud, and did, as I walked the 15 minutes each way to and from school. I did not like these, but she insisted, and it is thanks to her that I speak English without a French accent.

In addition to the homework Mrs. Kendall assigned me that summer of 1942, I decided to read the novel "The Swiss Family Robinson" in English. I already knew the story from having read it in French. Reading it in English was not as easy as I had anticipated. It took me all summer to read that book, using the dictionary for every single word I did not know, writing each in a notebook with its meaning. I recall working a whole day on each of the first few pages. After a while, I was able to speed it up. By the end of the summer, I could read and understand English. During the three years that Mrs. Kendall taught me English, I read parts of the writings of every significant author of the English (*i.e.*, British) language, from the days of Beowulf through Chaucer to the early parts of the 20th century. We stopped at that point, because Mrs. Kendall believed strongly that, before an author's writings were worthy of study, they should have withstood the test of time. It was therefore highly unlikely that unworthy authors had been winnowed out before their death. A few American writers were admitted to the worthy circle, such as Twain and Longfellow, but not too many. In addition to the Bard from Stratford-on-Avon, she particularly loved Keats, Yeats, and Lord Byron, and I did get to like them too.

Mrs. Kendall also taught the second and third years of algebra. I was ready to go into the second year in fall 1942, because school in France had already exposed me to a full year of this material, as well as geometry and trigonometry. I was not too good in math, certainly not as good as my father, and not up to his expectations. He tried to help me and teach me, but his approach was different from that in the American books we had, and help sessions usually terminated with some acrimony. Nevertheless, after a year or so, I determined that my progress into third-year algebra had advanced close to the limits of Mrs. Kendall's knowledge. The great delight then was to find a problem, a theorem, or a situation, that my father could explain to me and that I could master, but that Mrs. Kendall was unable to resolve on the spot, forcing her to do homework before the morrow. Great fun, and a way to equalize her unbending and demanding ways in English class.

In September 1942, in recognition of the progress I had made in English that summer, studying and working five or six days a week, I was promoted from sixth grade with Miss Doyle to eighth grade, which was led by Mrs. Frances Folsom. Mrs. Folsom was originally from Seattle, and was extremely pleased to be in La Habana, where it was warm and sunny every day, rather than in Seattle where, according to her, it was damp, cloudy, and rainy practically all the time. She wore rimless glasses, and originally appeared rather intimidating. She was the history teacher, and very good at it. I enjoyed history, and took several courses from her. She also doubled as the chemistry teacher, following the book rather closely. There was no laboratory, so I sometimes gathered up various pinches of materials to conduct experiments in our kitchen, to the dismay of my mother. I am pleased to report that I never did blow the kitchen up. After a few months, I became almost as knowledgeable as Mrs. Folsom, and delighted in reading a chapter ahead in the book, so as to be able to ask her legitimate questions about which she had not yet had time to read the answers! Nasty, nasty, but quite enjoyable!

Lest I leave the reader with the wrong impression, school and learning were the most important activities in my life. During our entire time in Cuba, we never considered that phase other than a temporary episode prior to our reaching the land of opportunity, just 150 km (90 miles) away over the northern horizon. Thus, all my being was devoted to preparing myself for the imagined competition of free-wheeling capitalism in the land of Wall Street, cowboys, Indians, skyscrapers, and the Great Plains. I therefore studied and learned as much as I could in order to be ready when the great day would come. I was also careful to let the fact that Columbus School had students of both genders, a new experience for me after the single gender schools I had attended all my life up to now in Europe and Algeria, not interfere with my education. It must have been very pleasing to my teachers to have such an eager student as I was. I truly wanted to learn, even though sometimes I could not resist the impulse to try to overtake them in their weaker areas. In fact, just before we left Cuba, Miss Eva M. Anderson, the principal, wrote in my transcript "He is the best student of the class of 1944-45 a superior student in every way, highly capable and conscientious, with a keen interest in learning and a serious purpose in mind."

In eighth grade, I took a year of geometry, and thoroughly enjoyed it. I was much better at it than algebra. Partly as a recognition of Pat Doyle's help to me the previous year, I enrolled in her Latin class, and took a year of it, learning all these terrible declensions and becoming able to translate Julius Caesar and Virgil. This small amount of Latin knowledge eventually turned out to be extremely useful to me later on in learning modern languages and scientific terminology.

In addition to the daily classes of English in the morning, I also had daily afternoon classes in Spanish at Columbus School. I particularly remember the semester in 1943 when I had Chemistry in English in the morning, and Physics in the afternoon in Spanish. After about six months, I was doing well in Spanish; the grammar being so similar to that of French, it was a snap. My greatest difficulty was mastering the Spanish "R" at the same time as I was trying to learn the English "R", since they are not only different from each other but also from the only "R" I knew, the French "R". I ended up taking three years of Spanish language and literature, reading Cervantes, Calderón de la Barca, and numerous other Spanish and Latin American authors, and mastering the rules that determine which syllables are accented with or without diacritical marks.

Being driven to be fully prepared when we entered the US, and not having other things to do, except for the scouting activities which I shall describe later, I decided to study several courses during the summer of 1943, after I had finished eighth grade. This was not as difficult as it might appear at first glance, because I found the American school system so much less demanding than the French curriculum in the lycées in Fontainebleau, Nîmes and Alger. It certainly was no big deal for me to do two, three or four hours of homework five days a week. So, in the spring of 1943, a strategy session was held in Miss Anderson's office with me and my parents. An agreement was reached that I would be allowed to enter the second year of high school the following autumn, provided I completed certain courses that summer and passed comprehensive examinations on them in the fall. Mrs Kendall was to oversee my studies during the summer, including English literature and algebra. When September came, I passed the examinations, including one that earned me two high school credits of French as well. The second year of high school was a snap. I had more time to study then than I had had during the summer, and so I was able to take five subjects rather than the usual four.

There was a half-hour recess each morning and afternoon when we walked in a column of twos to the baseball diamond half a block away. There was an attempt to make us walk in step by the non-English speaking female athletics teacher. I consciously refused to bend to her goal, especially since she tried to enforce her mandate by continuously clicking on a pair of irritating castanets.

Cuban boys are weaned on baseball. I knew nothing about the game. When the captains chose their players, I was invariably the last one chosen. The best athlete in my class, Jorge Sánchez, tried to be nice to me and sometimes would choose me on the penultimate selection turn rather than the last. He tried to teach me softball, but I could hardly ever hit the ball, let alone get on base. I was usually put in right field. Even there it was a 50/50 chance that I would not catch an easy fly, even though I was the proud owner of my personal fielding glove properly softened with neat's-foot oil. On the other hand, it was nice to not have to worry about bullies or antisemitism, and I got along pretty well. My strongest scholastic competitor was also a European, but by common agreement we ignored each other completely. He knew I was Jewish. His name was Koch, and he was the son of a diplomat (or a spy?) in the German consulate. I imagine he was under instructions from his father not to make conspicuously undiplomatic remarks about Jews while a guest of Cuba.

During the summer of 1944, I studied as much as I had the previous summer, in order to be a senior that fall. I was successful in this attempt, doing English with Mrs. Kendall, and Ancient History and American History with Mrs. Folsom. It was not too difficult to do this, since it entailed mostly reading. I was eager to be a senior, so that by the time we got to the US, I could go to college. It was not inappropriate to make such plans at that time, for by then the progress of the war clearly showed that it would be over soon. We would then probably be allowed into the US.

In the late fall, I went on several successive Saturdays to the big private and expensive secondary school, Colegio de Belén, to take the College Board Examinations, administered out of Princeton, New Jersey, precursors to the SAT exams of today. There was little known about these exams then, as only fragments of previous tests were available for review. It was an anxious time for me, because there was no way to study for these examinations, I was told, and there were no study books available, as there are nowadays. Nevertheless, I did reasonably well in these tests, especially because of the skills in literary analysis I had learned from Mrs. Kendall.

In joint conversations with my parents and Miss Anderson, I had decided to apply for admission to Cornell University, Duke University, and the University of Wisconsin at Madison. My field of study was to be pre-forestry, and that accounts for Duke, in addition to the fact that Miss Anderson was very strong on that university. I believe she was from North Carolina. Cornell was in contention because my physics teacher, from whom I had learned some of that science in Spanish every afternoon, was a Cornell graduate and spoke eloquently of his alma mater. The selection of UW was perhaps more circuitous, although every one agreed it was a very good school. An added consideration was that a new English teacher, from whom I was taking a course in American literature that year, was a recent graduate from Madison, and she was a real "looker"—so I reasoned there might be more like her at Madison if I went there. I was accepted by all three schools, and each offered me some kind of scholarship. I decided on Wisconsin because of the lower fees and the lure of beauties on the shores of Lake Mendota.

The two major obstacles to our receiving immigration visas related to my mother and my grandparents. In the case of my mother, it was the fact that she had been born in Austria. The facts that her father had been working in Vienna and that both her parents were French citizens when she was born were not relevant as a mitigating circumstance to the US Immigration Service, even though she could prove that she had possessed French citizenship ever since her father had registered her at the French consulate in Vienna shortly after her birth, and again when she was automatically reinstated in her French citizenship according to the terms of Treaty of Versailles on June 28, 1919 (see page 44).

The fact that my grandparents were still in Europe also was held against us. It was thought the Germans might blackmail us to spy for them in exchange for beneficial treatment of our relatives. What nonsense from the reactionary, right-wing, antisemitic officials of the Roosevelt administration and the Cordell Hull- and Edward Stettinius-led State Department that were enforcing strictly the provisions of the quota characteristics of immigration laws promulgated by Congress! Little did we know then about the attitudes of the US government toward Jewish refugees. It was only years later that the conscious ignoring of pleas for help to Roosevelt and Churchill were revealed. But in 1944, for us, Franklin Roosevelt was still a hero, the fearless leader of the Free World (Freedom from Fear, Freedom from Want, etc…) who was going to vanquish the nasty Germans and save everybody.

In May 1942, just four months after our arrival in Cuba, we had applied for immigration visas to the US. They were denied. A second set of applications was filed, but they too were turned down, in November 1943. My parents learned many years later that another reason for the refusal was that one of our sponsors, an Oury distant cousin from New Orleans whom we had never met or spoken to, was considered an Axis sympathizer by the US Government. The third applications were filed on April 12, 1944, before the Honorable R.F. Washington, Vice Consul of the United States of America in La Habana. I remember my parents mentioning the name of this official with considerable fear and dislike, for he was an arrogant, overbearing individual, who gave the impression of being quite unsympathetic to Jewish refugees. I recognized later that he probably felt that Jews had suffered a lot less than his people, for he was an ethnic African-American. The fact remained that he held our fate in his hands. My father, proud as he was, had to swallow his pride and behave not just politely but subserviently to this perhaps overworked, but certainly powerful, apparently able-bodied (to have been serving in the Army) civilian bureaucrat.

I still have a carbon copy of the affidavit typewritten in April 1944 in La Habana, Cuba, by my father to support the visa applications to enter the United States. After attesting to his and his parents' life history, his schooling and his military service, my father recounted his marriage, the births of his children, his walk through

France, and the escape of his family during the Retreat. He recounted our flight to Alger and the fact that "Our son Henri, although the best pupil of his class, was, as a Jew, expelled from his school. So, seeing the Nazi measures put into application by the collaborators of the enemy, we had only one thought: to leave all French territories and to settle definitely in the United States. As we were very anxious to set out the soonest possible, and to avoid a loss of time, we asked for a Cuban visa which was delivered to us on December 1, 1941." He wrote further: "But came Pearl Harbor. The frontier between France and Spain was closed. After many days of anxiety, during which we feared to be unable to depart, we took advantage in January 1942 of the steps taken by the "Hicem," a branch of the American "Joint Committee," which obtained, the transit via Casablanca, where the S/S Nyassa would put in we went on board at Casablanca on January 30, 1942. Meanwhile, our homes, furniture, in Paris and in Fontainebleau were being stolen. After arriving in Cuba, on February 25, 1942, our immigration application was filed at the end of May 1942. We began then to cherish a great hope in our hearts: at last we would soon enter the United States, we would have once more a life of work, and we would prepare the future of our children in the way of American Democracy. But this long hoped-for visa was denied us. This was for us a painful disappointment waited with hope the answer to our second application; but a second denial, in November 1943, was a deep disappointment for us. Here in Cuba we cannot work in any productive manner. We dare hope that this time the Visa Division will give us a favorable answer. After so many torments, so many anguishes, so many losses we have only one wish, that of living and settling in the United States. We dare hope that our call will be heard and that the above explications will convince the American Administration of our real and sincere adherence to the Principles of American Democracy. This is an affidavit signed by JEAN FRIBOURG in Havana, on April 12, 1944."

I have reproduced portions of this 2-page single-spaced document to bring to the reader the reality of the conditions in those days, when applicants for immigration to the US need not only abase themselves in front of arrogant bureaucrats, but had to furnish the names of sponsors willing to swear that they would see to the financial needs of the applicants for the first five years of their residence in the country, should the immigrants not be able to provide for themselves! Quite a contrast to the more recent environment, when excuses are made by politicians to provide amnesties to undocumented immigrants residing illegally in the country, as long as they have been able to evade the authorities for a few years while sometimes living on the public dole.

My primary source of recreation while we were in Cuba was Troop 2 of the Boy Scouts de Cuba in Marianao, a suburb adjacent to the Vedado suburb where we lived. I joined in 1943. I suspect the delay was due to my inability to speak much Spanish before that time. My identification booklet indicates that I became an Assistant Patrol Leader on August 28 and a Patrol Leader of the *Águila* (Eagle) patrol on December 4, 1943. It was not until February 7, 1944, that I completed the requirements for both Second Class and First Class. On October 1, 1944, I was promoted to Assistant Scoutmaster. By then, I also had earned merit badges in swimming, interpreting, first aid, reading, hiking, safety, and both personal and public health.

Girl Scout Rosette and Boy Scout Henri

Most of my free time, one or two days a week, was devoted to these activities, and I carefully planned my study times so that they would not interfere with Boy Scout outings. On infrequent hikes into the countryside, I learned to enjoy chewing on a peeled section of sugar cane stem, and to avoid walking through a stand of *picapica*, a plant much fiercer in its effects on human skin than European nettles, with which I had become accustomed in the palace gardens at Fontainebleau, not far from the apartments of Madame de Pompadour. My mother had been embarrassed to tell me about her. I had not understood the reasons until I looked for Madame de Pompadour in the encyclopedia. It was there that I determined that my mother disapproved of the manner in which this courtesan had found favor with King Louis XV.

The Cuban Boy Scout uniform, khaki short-sleeved shirt and short pants, was comfortable in the warm tropical climate, but often subjected us to ridicule, since neighborhood toughs, unacquainted with short pants, yelled at us to stop running around in our *calzoncillos* (underwear). These insults were complements to the others to which I had become accustomed, that of being yelled at as a "*polaco*." Street Cubans were familiar only with Cubans or North American foreigners, called by the despicable word "*gringo*." There was in their eyes, however, an even lower form of humanity: the "*polacos*," referring to Jewish refuges from Poland who had arrived in Cuba in the 1920s and 1930s. By extension, this term was applied to all European refugees. This label infuriated my parents, and me as well. I never did know if the term was pejorative toward all non-North American or hispanic foreigners, or whether it contained also tinges of antisemitism.

It was not until I started writing this memoir that I realized fully the magnitude of the stresses under which my parents must have been living. My father was an intellectual, an avid reader, a student of mathematics and of economics as they influenced the stock market. In France, he had been a successful sales representative, because he could explain and communicate clearly. He could not do this in Cuba, speaking Spanish poorly and with a marked French accent. My father was not good at any kind of manual activity. The Cubans, in their effort to distribute refugee wealth in what they considered a more suitable manner, had decreed that European refugees (or possibly all foreigners) were allowed to contribute 100% of the capital for selected approved commercial enterprises. In return, refugees would be permitted to retain 49% of the business control in partnership with a Cuban national.

My Parents as I remember them (photo of 1960's)

The latter would have 51% of the voting power, the obligation to do nothing, and a license to steal it all with complete impunity. This must have been extremely galling and depressing for my father, who was not gainfully employed.

My father spent his Cuban days reading books in French and studying English, which he learned to understand and write very well, building on the several years of earlier school study of English. He never did shed his marked French accent, although he spoke English more grammatically correctly than most of his interlocutors once we reached the US. Remember that in those days there were no such things as language tapes, records or DVDs. He also had much time to counsel me, to interact with my sister as she grew from age 10 to age 13, and to babysit my brother, developing from age 2 to age 5. My mother probably had the least change in occupation, since she kept our home, studied English like my father, cooked good meals with meager resources while learning all about Cuban fruits and vegetables. She made sure we went to services on the Sabbath, and enforced mild discipline so that father's harsher requirements would not need to be invoked.

The refusals of the US to let us in the country, where my father could earn his living and contribute to the war effort, were severe blows to all of us. He was also noting the gradual disappearance of the assets that had been salvaged in that bedroll over which I had watched in 1940. In fact, the options for gainful employment were extremely limited, while the opportunities to be robbed were limitless. Future generations will understand perhaps why it has been very difficult for me to feel much sympathy for many of the Cubans "suffering" in Florida because of Fidel Castro. I cannot empathize much with the well-to-do Cubans who escaped to Miami. They prospered in the US without any restrictions placed on their activities, in a manner similar to that in which the US has welcomed legal immigrants for decades, and even illegal immigrants more recently. It is only because of my father's economic success and prescient investing in pre-war France, and the ability to salvage foreign stock certificates and jewelry during the Retreat, that the family was able to survive in moderately comfortable conditions from 1940 until my father was able and allowed to again earn a living in 1946, and that my siblings and I could obtain the education that made our future successes possible.

 Both our parents were deeply concerned about their parents. For a while, we received heavily censored letters, and later some postcards. The censorship consisted of words, phrases or entire sentences blacked out or cut from the letters. In 1942, one of these communications arrived sometimes as frequently as once a month but, as the war dragged on, after the occupation of Vichy France by the Germans, they became more infrequent, and eventually stopped altogether in early 1944.

 After the German occupiers were chased out of France later that year, it was a long time before we heard from my maternal grandparents. It was a great relief to learn they had survived. We also learned from them and René Morquer that my grandfather Albert had died in Bugeat (Corrèze) on November 27, 1943 of pneumonia. In fact, he might have lived had it not been for lack of medical attention enforced by the German occupiers.

Henry Fribourg

MINISTÈRE
DES
PRISONNIERS, DÉPORTÉS
ET RÉFUGIÉS.

DIRECTION DE LA CAPTIVITÉ.

SOUS-DIRECTION
DES FICHIERS ET STATISTIQUES.

MODÈLE A

RÉPUBLIQUE FRANÇAISE.

CERTIFICAT.

N° 028084

Le Chef du bureau des Fichiers des (1) DEPORTES POLITIQUES (R) certifie, d'après des documents que possède son service que M (2) Madame Veuve FRIBOURG née ACH Lucie, né le 17.7.73 à BOULAY - MOSELLE, a été (3) INTERNEE à DRANCY du 6.4.44 au 29.4.44 date de sa déportation

Le présent certificat a été délivré pour valoir ce que de droit.

23.7.45

NOM ET ADRESSE
de l'intéressé :
Madame OURY
2 rue Thimo...
PARIS

Pour le Sous-Directeur des Fichiers et Statistiques :
Le Chef du 2e bureau,
P.O.

(1) Déportés ou Internés politiques ou Prisonniers de guerre ou Travailleurs déportés.
(2) Monsieur ou Madame ou Mademoiselle.
(3) Déporté ou Prisonnier de guerre ou Interné

J 507717.

My grandmother's deportation certificate

My father had nightmares for many years after learning that his mother had been transported from Bugeat to the internment camp of Drancy, near Paris, on April 6, 1944. On April 29, 1944, she was shipped in a cattle car to the Auschwitz extermination camp in Convoy 72. This information is documented in the book by Serge Klarsfeld, "Memorial to the Jews Deported from France 1942-1944," published by the Beate Klarsfeld Foundation in New York, in French in 1978 and in English in 1983.

The reader may wonder at the extent of known details about these gruesome events. The Germans kept meticulous records of the deportations they conducted, generating manifests for each train shipment which listed the name of every deportee, along with birth date and place. Up to six or seven carbon copies were made, so that every appropriate entity could be notified. After the war, Serge Klarsfeld, aided by his wife, was able to obtain the fifth, sixth or seventh carbon copies of these manifests and painstakingly hand-copied the records, prior to publishing the tens of thousands of names in the book cited above. We never did learn whether or not my grandmother survived the cattle car trip or whether she was gassed in Auschwitz.

We had a short-wave radio from which we could glean more news than from the Cuban stations. As I recall, we received more news from the BBC (British Broadcasting Company) than from American stations. This was because the BBC transmitted news from the Free French Government in Exile. Early in our stay in Cuba, we obtained Général Charles de Gaulle's symbol, *Croix de Lorraine* lapel buttons, which we wore proudly. We also read the newspaper, *El Diario de la Mañana* (The Morning Daily), and the weekly *Bohemia*, patterned after but considerably cheaper than Life magazine. This reminds me that we often stated, within the confines of our apartment only, that Cuba had to be a country with a great future, since we thought the present could be improved, and it was clear that all improvements would occur *mañana* (tomorrow). I did have a map of Europe in my bedroom on which I marked and followed the movement of armies in Africa and Russia, and later in western Europe. The course of the war in the Pacific held little interest for me, except in the general sense that it was unthinkable the US should lose to Germany's allies.

Henry Fribourg

Across the street from our apartment, on the northeast corner, was a grocery and general store (*bodega*) run by a *chino* (Chinaman), one of many Chinese shopkeepers in Cuba. It was most often my lot to go across the street to purchase some of our food, since I could argue and bargain in Spanish much better than my mother, who often felt she was being taken advantage of. I also learned there the value of keeping one's mouth shut, for the block police informers, well known to everybody, were often there. It was most unhealthy to talk politics, which as a foreigner I never did, nor even to complain about living conditions within their hearing. My mother, though, often took the streetcar into the downtown areas where vegetables, fruits, and meats were sold at sidewalk open stalls. In the fall of 1944, a hurricane swept over Cuba, and the eye passed over Vedado. It was an eerie experience, and our beds and furniture got soaked, because we had been advised to open all windows so that the changes in atmospheric pressure would not shatter the window panes, even though we had taped them. The windows did not break, but we sure got wet. After a day or so, my mother asked me to go across the street to fetch some grocery items. I recall crawling on the ground both ways, because I could not stand in the hurricane winds.

I can still smell Cuban *bodegas*, permeated with the odor of salted cod emanating from an open keg. Dried cod was then a staple of meals, accompanied by rice or sometimes cassava. I never did acquire a taste for cassava, even after repeated trips to the tropics. Green vegetables were not regularly available, a normal feature of tropical climates, particularly before the advent of frozen food. On the other hand, many delicious fruits could be had, some of which I have pined for during all these years, such as *añón* (sweetsop), *mamey* (mammee), mangoes and avocados picked from the tree rather than ripened in ethylene and shipped in refrigerated containers, truly fresh pineapple, and many different kinds of sweet bananas. We also often had plantains, fried in olive oil. A staple blue collar worker sandwich, which I learned to appreciate during Boy Scout hikes, consisted of 15 to 20 cm (6 to 8 in) of a Cuban bread baguette, liberally soaked with olive oil and laden with numerous pungent fresh onion slices.

Occasionally, maybe once a month or so in spring and summer, I would get an invitation to join a wealthy school friend at his family's oceanside swimming club in the posh suburb of

Marianao, to the west of Vedado. This would be quite a treat, for the only safe place to go swimming in the area was at private clubs. I would reach the one where I was invited periodically after a long ride in a *"guagua"* (pronounced wahwah). My mother preferred to ride streetcars, which were relatively clean and not so crowded. A *guagua* was a dilapidated, old, noisy, smelly, uncomfortably hot and extremely crowded speeding city bus weaving in and out of traffic. Added features were the acquisition of fleas and the loss of wallets to pickpockets. The swimming clubs had a narrow beach and a clubhouse, and often a diving platform some distance from shore. The primary feature, though, was a shark-proof net which protected the whole swimming area and presumably was inspected daily for tears. In fact, sharks were feared greatly, perhaps disproportionately to their danger. On the other hand, it was not infrequent to learn of a swimmer being attacked by sharks offshore from the Malecón, the great oceanside boulevard stretching from downtown to the Hotel Internacional, an opulent watering hole of American millionaires and Mafia executives. At the club, we would also play some games of *"frontón,"* a game similar to jai-alai, but using tennis rackets rather than *cestas* in a 3-sided walled court. A fast game or two would get us warm enough to enjoy the cool sea afterward.

After a year in La Habana, my parents bought me a bicycle. It was my birthday gift in 1943. This was my ticket to independence, for now I could go almost anywhere in the city. As I think back on it, another reason for not joining the Boy Scouts until that year was my inability to go to meetings, which took place in a park at the back of the University of La Habana, at the boundary between La Habana and Vedado, three or four km (1.5 to 2.5 miles) from where we lived. In the long run it was much cheaper for me to ride my bicycle than to have to pay the fare for public transportation. There were many streetcars crisscrossing the city, and I had learned their routes well before getting my bicycle. So, shortly after getting my wheels, I was able to join the ranks of other bicycle riders who would grab with their left hand one of the three metal bars at the bottom of the windows which prevented passengers from sticking their arms out. Steering the bicycle with the right hand, this method, today known as skitching, ensured rapid free motive power. This was especially appreciated during the hot part of the day. One had to take care to be sure of the destination of the grabbed car, knowing in advance where the streetcar was due to change direction, and steer the bicycle wheels free of the tracks. Adventurous boys would pull the same trick with the *guaguas*, but I stopped that after my first try. It was just too difficult and dangerous to anticipate the weavings of the bus through traffic. I only had one minor bicycle accident in all that time. I slid too fast around a corner on wet pavement, tore a hole in my pants, and skinned my right knee. The pants were mended by my mother, but entreaties for trouser replacement fell on deaf ears.

Occasionally I would be able to save enough money out of my small allowance to go to the movies. Usually I went alone, considering the outing a learning experience to be had in the comfort of one of the very few air-conditioned buildings in the city. It was educational, especially during the early days in Cuba, because the movies were English-spoken with Spanish sub-titles, and I needed practice in both languages. In early 1945, I went downtown to see my first color movie ever, "Gone With the Wind." It was a wonderful outing. A few months later, I was delighted to see the Disney film "Fantasia" with Stravinsky's Rite of Spring music.

In 1944, I first purchased a box of Partagás cigarettes, fairly strong, but which I learned to like on an occasional basis. I think it was all right for me to smoke a cigarette at home after the evening meal, especially when my father indulged himself with one of the best Cuban cigars, Hauptmann, that came in individual sealed tubes. The two of us might play a game of chess, while through the open windows would drift the sound of Cuban music accompanying the tinkle of dominoes from the adjoining patios and terraces. It was at about that time also that somehow I ended up in a party at La Tropicana, a famous nightclub, with public dancing in an open courtyard. I was scared by the approaches of a man who was high on marijuana, and who tried to get me to smoke. Having been warned about the dangers of this drug, I refused; his behavior was frightening. Never again did I have any desire to be in the company of drug users.

On February 20, 1945, we received our visas to enter the US. Mine was number QIU 583, as recorded in my French passport number 18493/138, issued by the *Délégation du Gouvernement Provisoire de la République Française à Cuba,* in other words, the Free French. We were then still enamored of our French patriotism, and flaunted our association with the de Gaulle movement by wearing on our lapels the tricolor pin with a Cross of Lorraine in the white field. It took several years for me to realize that the French government, with or without de Gaulle, had no intention of properly correcting the wrongs inflicted upon our family and many others by the French collaborators of the Germans. I shall explore this later on. It took a bit of arranging for us to make all our plans for departure from Cuba. I recall vaguely the name of an organization, HIAS, that may have helped us some in this regard. It was not until April 10, 1945, that we embarked on plane NC 30011 (company unknown, but probably Pan American) at Rancho Boyeros Airport, destination Miami.

During the interim period, I was issued my Boy Scout International Passport on March 15, signed by the Cuban National Scout Chief, Angel Loustalot, and his international minister, Luis R. Ríos. On March 6, I received a very laudatory final transcript from Miss Anderson at Columbus School. It must have been an exciting and busy time, but I have no special recollection of any other momentous event. We were elated to be leaving Cuba to go to the land of opportunity where my father could work, where I could go to college, and where there were seasons rather than the continuous warm tropical temperature. Yes, the years we had spent in warm climates had been very tiring toward the end, as the sameness of the year-around temperatures seemed to lower our energy levels. In later life, I have always enjoyed getting back to tropical areas for visits, but I would never want to settle permanently where it never gets cold.

BECOMING A NORTH AMERICAN
- 1945 to 1951

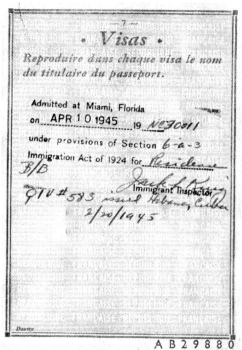

My legal US immigration visa

On April 10, 1945, in late morning, the five of us disembarked jubilantly in Miami, were admitted by Immigration as legal immigrants to reside in the US, recovered our hand luggage (the remainder had been sent in a crate by ship to New York City), and took a taxicab to a boarding house. That afternoon, my parents determined that one important piece of hand luggage had been left behind at the airport. Since I spoke English best in the family, I was given a few dollars to take the bus and retrieve the lost bag. I underwent several rude awakenings that afternoon.

First of all, I had never boarded a bus that had only one employee. All previous experiences had led me to believe that a ticket-taker who was not the driver was essential, and was a person from whom one could obtain information. An unsympathetic driver who expected money to be dropped into a counting machine and who would not talk when the bus was in motion was a new experience. For years, in France, Algeria, and Cuba, I had been accustomed to buses operated jointly by a driver and one, sometimes two, ticket collectors. After reaching the end of the bus line at "the airport," I realized there had to be more than one airport in Miami, because this airport was not the one at which we had landed. In fact, it took me about five or six hours to locate and reach the correct airport, retrieve the lost luggage, and return to my parents, who were very concerned about my welfare.

Before I returned, however, I discovered the American drugstore of the 1940s. I treated myself to an ice cream soda, for I was hot and thirsty from my several bus rides. On the recommendation of the clerk, I also bought a tin of Prince Albert pipe tobacco. Finally, I found out that afternoon that the English I knew from my studies in La Habana was not the English spoken in Miami. Not only that, but because all my teachers of English had been women, whose voices are pitched higher than men's, I was unable to comprehend men. It took me over a month to get used to the pitch of men, although I could understand women just fine.

On April 12, early in the morning, we boarded a Seaboard Line train for New York City, about 24 to 30 hours away. It was during this ride that I first tried out the gift that I had received from my parents one month earlier for my sixteenth birthday, a French *"bruyère"* (briar) pipe. I found the Prince Albert tobacco pretty harsh and not to my liking, but I did persevere and got sick to my stomach in the antechamber to the lavatory. I must admit, though, that I persisted in learning how to smoke, and persisted in this habit until the eve of my heart bypass surgery on November 17, 1988. On April 13, we arrived at Pennsylvania Station in New York City. All flags were at half-mast. We did not know why. It did not take long, though, to learn that President Roosevelt had died in Georgia while we were on the train.

We were welcomed in New York City by Eliane and Denis Brach. My mother and sister had met Eliane in the internment camp near Casablanca, and we all were passengers on the Nyassa to Cuba. The Brachs had been able to leave Cuba for the US in late 1943 or early 1944. My sister reminded me that Eliane also enjoyed riding the ship across the Atlantic at the forward part of the prow, earning from the younger generation the nickname of *La Gueule de Proue* (The Great Talker of the Prow). Her 17-year old only son Rolland had enlisted in the Free French forces. He was taken prisoner of war in the North African desert campaign in Libya and died when the German ship taking him north across the Mediterranean was torpedoed.

The Brachs had an antiques store on the second floor of a building on the east side of Madison Avenue in Manhattan, somewhere between 60th and 70th streets. We visited the store the next day. They had acted as our official sponsors for our third immigration applications. At that time, being a sponsor to an immigrant was not a mere formality, but rather a solemn promise to provide for the immigrants if they could not sustain themselves. Quite a contrast with the situation nowadays, when some people consider it inappropriate to deny welfare payments to non-citizen illegal immigrants. In the meantime, we got rooms in a hotel on the east side of Herald Square, across the street from Macy's.

There was a Horn and Hardart automat around the corner. Such an "automatic" restaurant was a revelation. An entire sidewall, 20 or more m (60 or more ft) long, was lined with little doors, from waist height to shoulder height, which had 15 x 30 cm (6 x 12 in) windows. Customers could see the dish, sandwich, or other food item displayed in the cubbyhole behind the glass. Upon insertion of the correct change in an adjoining coin slot, the door lock would release and the customer could extract the food. When the door closed back, an employee would replenish the supply from the other side of the wall. I eventually recovered from liking these restaurants, but my father remained infatuated with them for many years for lunching when he worked in downtown Manhattan. Quite a contrast with his deep appreciation for gourmet dining, fine wines, imported cheeses, and other epicurean delights in different circumstances.

After a few days, we moved to a very small apartment in the Flatbush section of Brooklyn, at 39 East 17th Street, on the second floor. Just a few blocks away was Erasmus High School, and I attended there for about a week or two. However, the administrators of that school, which then had academic pretensions, decided I would not be allowed to graduate from their high school that coming June, because they thought they should determine themselves whether I was as good a student as my record in Cuba suggested. We found out that Haaren High School, three long blocks west of Columbus Circle in Manhattan, and a half-hour express subway ride away, would indeed accept my record from Columbus School.

So, I commuted from Flatbush by subway every day, acquiring a lifelong distaste for rush-hour New York subways, and graduated from Haaren High School in June 1945. This was just a few days after I saw the triumphal parade of General Eisenhower riding on the back ledge of a convertible limousine circling the column in Columbus Circle upon his return from victory in Europe. The experience of attending a large urban school was a shock. I was not accustomed to chaotic classes of fifty unruly African-American, Hispanic and Caucasian students who had no intention of learning anything, who were disrespectful to their teachers, and who acted like hoodlums, as some indeed were. The few of us who wanted to learn had to do it surreptitiously. I was fortunate to speak Spanish fluently. A tall well-muscled Puerto Rican boy, with whom I commuted daily, accepted that I help him with his math homework. In return, he was my bodyguard and let it be known that I should be treated like a "brother."

The day we moved into the apartment in Flatbush, my mother sent me to the nearest food store, just a block or two away. It was there I first became acquainted with a check-out line and counter. After the young girl totaled my bill, she asked whether I wanted a "beg." I had to ask her to repeat herself, and did not understand what she meant until she took out a paper shopping bag from under the counter and showed it to me. That was my initiation to the Brooklyn accent.

On May 10, my parents had to submit to another unforeseen indignity. This time it was not from French lackeys of the Germans or from greedy Cubans, but from American bureaucrats. In order to be able to receive funds from Europe, or to send some to my maternal grandparents, they had to apply to the Treasury Department for a "license to engage in a foreign exchange transaction." In particular, my mother had to explain again at length, in a document of which a carbon copy has survived, that she was a French national, and not an enemy alien, by virtue of her having been born in Vienna. In fact, this was done so that my mother, a French Allied citizen with a legal immigrant status, could write checks out of the checking account opened after arrival in the US, and so that she could have access to the safety box rented at Bankers Trust after reaching New York. The licenses were granted to each of my parents on July 10, 1945 (numbers 696849-T and 696850-T). Another indignity which I learned about while filing some of my parents' papers was that my father obtained, on September 25, 1951, a Certificate of Literacy issued by the University of the State of New York. What a ridiculous affront and farce to have required such a certificate from my father, a French university graduate, who could probably write English better than his examiners, despite his marked French accent!

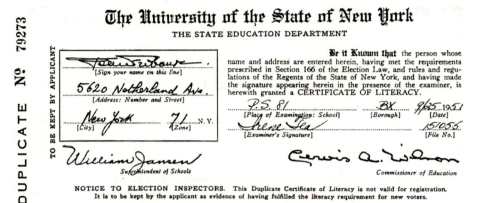

My father's certificate of Literacy

Soon after graduation, I left for Camp Achvah, in the Catskills, known in New York City as the "Jewish Alps," where I was supposed to be an assistant counselor for the summer. This was a conservative to orthodox Jewish camp. I forget how I was hired, but it must have been through the intercession of some of my parents' friends. I planned to have a restful summer before going off to college in September and also to be out of the city during the poliomyelitis season. As an assistant counselor, I would not be remunerated, but neither would I have to pay for my room and board. I was utterly unsuited to being a big brother to four 7- and 8-yr old undisciplined American brats unaccustomed to obeying older people.

I was also cured forever of traditional rites with prayers no one understood, after having used the Union Prayer Book in English for over three years. I also lost any doubts I might ever have had about the presumed essentiality of ritually clean food served cold on the Sabbath, when I had to work twice as hard as during the week to ensure the little monsters would put on white shirts and ties for the 4-hour service in the morning, the 2-hour service in the afternoon, and then the evening Havdalah service.

I GAVE YOU LIFE TWICE

Eventually, over the following two decades, after considerable study after joining the Reform Temple in Knoxville, I developed a view toward religion that made sense to me. The uniqueness and indivisibility of God, as stated in the שמע (*Shema*), is fundamental to my acceptance of Judaism. I have continued to observe the major holy days of the faith, although I observe the Sabbath by delighting in the natural world and reading more than by religious utterances. On the other hand, on occasion, I find some comfort in repeating prayers that have been uttered for hundreds of years by my ancestors. In spite of that, it has been a very difficult struggle for me to reconcile the genocides and major epidemics that have occurred on Earth, such as but not limited to, the Holocaust, the Crusades, the Black Death, the several African and Asian tribal wars of recent decades, etc…with the idea of a God that watches over every minute detail of human existence. If God were so powerful, all-knowing and merciful, why would such wholesale butcheries and sufferings be permitted to occur? I do see God when I look at a color photograph of a distant nebula, or at an electron photograph of a microorganism or molecule—but not when I think back at the agony that my grandmother had to suffer. An overall deity—yes, a personal God—no way!

Once a week at Camp Achvah, though, I had a day off, and I used it to walk in the mountains, as far away as I could get from the noise and tensions of the camp. Things really looked up when I made the acquaintance of another junior counselor, Helen, who felt like I did and accompanied me on the hikes. However, all we ever did in the woods was hike!

Sabbath dinner at 201 West 54th Street, New York City, 1947

When September arrived, my parents had moved to an apartment at 201 West 54th Street in Manhattan, at the corner of Seventh Avenue, not far from Broadway and three blocks from Carnegie Hall, the then, and soon-to-be again this year, home of the New York Philharmonic. A few days after my return from Camp Achvah, I took the NY Central train from Grand Central Station to Chicago Union Station, from where I had to transfer to La Salle Street Station to connect with the Northwestern train to Madison, Wisconsin. I had one small suitcase and a steamer trunk so heavy I could barely lift it. I got a room at a seedy hotel near the station, only to find out that the university campus was about five km (3 miles) away. That evening, I was quite homesick. So I went across the street to the cinema to see the "Song of Bernadette" and caught a cold in the overly-air-conditioned movie house.

Within a few days, however, I had found both lodgings and the job I had to have. Indeed, my parents had explained to me that it was essential that I earn essentially all of my room and board, since I insisted on going away to college, rather than staying at home to go to school, but they would help pay for my clothes and books. It would also be very important for me to earn good enough grades so that I could continue to be eligible for tuition scholarships. However, I felt it was essential that I go away to college, because my convictions on appropriate behavior and activities sometimes did not agree with my father's European-type discipline and ideas. Clashes would have been inevitable if I had stayed at home. As a matter of fact, one of the reasons I chose Wisconsin over Cornell, although I never did state that reason to my parents, was that Madison, Wisconsin was much farther from New York City than Ithaca, New York.

I moved to the home of Dr. and Mrs. Neff, in a mansion high on Maple Bluff, eight km (5 miles) in a straight line across Lake Mendota from the university, but 14 km (8 miles) away by road. I did cross the lake on foot a few times during the winter, when the lake surface was frozen, after having strapped on my wooden cross-country skis. The noise of the water bumping against the floating ice was somewhat disconcerting until one got used to it. Dr. Neff was a prominent ophthalmologist, and his wife aspired to be the "hostess with the mostest" in Madison. In exchange for my room and meals, I was to serve the evening meal six days a week, dressed in a white shirt, dark trousers, black bow tie, and white coat. The coat and tie were furnished. Mrs. Neff taught me how to set the table properly, how to serve from the diner's left and clear away from the right (or was it the other way around?). I was also expected to wash all the dishes and pots and pans after the cook was through dirtying every item in the kitchen. When there had been a dozen dinner guests, the cleanup could last until very late in the evening. Remember there were no electric dishwashers in those days.

After a few months, though, recognizing that I was being taken advantage of, I looked for other lodgings, especially because the bus did not run after midnight back to where I parked my bicycle five km (3 miles) from the Neff house. This made dates to concerts, movies, and plays almost impossible. Riding those five km (3 miles) on my bicycle after it started snowing in late November was challenging. The difficulty was compounded at all times by the numerous unrestrained dogs along the route. Dr. Neff was not happy that I had to forego the opportunity to work in the garden with him on Saturdays for an extra 50 cents an hour (10% over the minimum wage!) because I felt I needed the time to study.

In the meantime, my studies were going well. I still spoke English with a slight but noticeable French/British accent. I wrote well enough that, on the strength of my performance in the first three essays assigned in Freshman English composition, I was exempted from the entire one-year course of Freshman English. Instead, I was required to register in a sophomore literature course taught by Professor Cassidy. This scholar had studied extensively English vocalization by Wisconsinites, and later wrote several books on the subject. He had a radio program each Saturday morning during which he challenged anyone to talk to him for a few minutes, and he would tell them, over the air, where their Wisconsin home was located, within ten miles. My friends Ernesto and Roberto Freund from San Salvador, and Phi Dodell from Brooklyn, challenged me to go to the radio station to test Dr. Cassidy's expertise before the latter had really become acquainted with me in class. After two sentences, he stated that I was neither from Wisconsin nor from the Midwest, and with two more sentences he had determined I was not American-born, probably from Western Europe!

At that time, the University of Wisconsin had major growing pains, with 12,000 students enrolled (more than double the pre-war enrollment), of whom many were veterans on the G.I. Bill. It was not easy for me to compete with these motivated older students, paid by the government to attend school. They had plenty of time to study, since they did not need to earn their living, like I did. Nevertheless, I worked at many part-time occupations, as bus-boy, dishwasher, waiter, painter's helper, apprentice carpenter—20 to 30 hours a week during the school year, and full-time during vacations, especially before and after summer school, in order to pay for room, meals, in-state tuition, and an occasional play or concert at student prices. I was able to maintain my grade point average high enough so that the university would pay my out-of-state fees every year I was at Madison. My parents did send me the money for a round-trip train ticket to New York, though, so I could visit each New Year's vacation, and helped me by buying me some clothes at each visit and providing money for some of my books.

As a male freshman, I had been automatically enrolled in R.O.T.C. (Reserve Officers Training Corps). I considered this class an absolute waste of time, not caring to dress up in uniform and march in cadence through the slush of a Wisconsin winter. At the end of the first semester, I visited the office of the Dean of Students and asked to be informed as to why, as a French citizen, I had to take R.O.T.C. The dean exempted me on the spot, and I had retrieved several hours each week for conducting activities more important to me.

I learned early on that it was essential that I be completely organized, down to the most minute detail, in order not only to maintain my grades and earn my keep, but also to leave a little bit of time for dates and other entertainment. One of the most pleasurable events was the free dance class on Sunday evenings in the ballroom of the Student Union. These events were well attended, and it was there that I learned some ballroom dancing of the day, Latin American dances, European folk dances of many kinds, and square dancing. Of course, it was also a choice spot to meet girls. Another memorable event occurred during my junior year, when I had volunteered to serve on a student committee that hosted notable speakers that had come to speak on the campus: I was assigned to sit on the left of Carl

Sandburg at the 2-hour dinner and discussion with the committee that preceded his address. It was a thrill to converse with him. He became in interested in me when I told him I had read a biography of Abraham Lincoln when I was a high school student in Cuba.

It was during the year-end vacation periods that I became well acquainted with New York City, its streets, subway system, on- and off-Broadway theaters, Greenwich Village, museums and monuments. My father had found employment in the New York office in downtown Manhattan for the Point 4 program created by President Truman as a stopgap help to the just-liberated European countries. This program eventually metamorphosed into the much more comprehensive Marshall Plan, for which my father also worked in Manhattan for a number of years. My father's command of French and written English, as well as his knowledge of the business world, stood him in good stead as he helped negotiate and write bilingual contracts. In 1945, when he started with Point 4, my father was 44. It was not until much later, when I was in my fifties, that I fully appreciated the magnitude of his achievement. He created a new life for himself and his family, at that mature age, in an environment which was still alien to him. I do not know if I could have done such a major about-face when I was in my forties. Eventually, he became a small businessman with an antiques shop on Madison Avenue. Although this business was not very successful, it provided an excuse for yearly trips to France to locate and purchase antique furniture, paintings and objets d'art likely to be of interest to American shoppers. Eventually, in his 60s, he proudly rose to be Comptroller and Vice President for Renault, Inc., the US subsidiary of the French company.

My mother was a homemaker and an accomplished cook. A listing of the dishes I remember is bound to be long and incomplete, but would have to include roast leg of lamb, Vichyssoise soup, egg custards, tossed salads, cold salmon and lamb chops. She excelled in these activities, never aspiring to any other profession, although she worked for many years in offices in downtown Manhattan, primarily a Franco-American cable company, because it was necessary to supplement my father's income. I suspect that this need for income was primarily due to needing to help finance her children's education. She was proudest of the fact that, by her obstinacy, she had saved her family from the Final Solution and the German ovens. She often delighted in stating she "had given life to her children twice" ("*Je vous ai donné la vie deux fois*"), once at birth and again in 1942, when she insisted the family had to leave Europe.

During those years, my father was trying to come to terms with the manner of his parents' deaths. The French Government did not make it any easier. All real estate belonging to Jews had been stolen by the Germans or their French minions during the occupation. In some cases, the properties had then been sold at bargain prices to Frenchmen who could not help knowing that these were confiscated Jewish assets. After the Libération, one would think that all such transactions would have been automatically declared invalid and the properties returned immediately to their rightful owners or their heirs. In fact, it took many years of protracted negotiations, numerous letters, and many proceedings before my parents decided to stop trying to obtain the full value of what had been stolen. One instance in which there may have been no loss was the sale of the apartment building at 3, rue Paul Escudier. Documents were saved which show that each apartment was sold separately by my father to various individuals in 1957 and 1958.

My grandparents Oury returned after the war to their apartment on Rue Thimonnier in Paris. Some of their neighbors had cached many of their furnishings. I do know that it took over ten years for the illegal occupants to leave my parents' house at 97, rue St. Honoré in Fontainebleau. They claimed they were entitled to shelter, even though they knew that they occupied a house bought at bargain prices as a Jewish asset. I wish I had questioned my father in greater detail about these matters. It is my impression that he recovered on the order of ten cents on the dollar values of the dwelling because of the bad will of the authorities and the fact that currency inflation and devaluation were ignored. He did file for some war indemnity from the Germans, and received some token payments from them.

It also took many years before the French Government authorized the awarding of the mention "Mort pour la France" to my grandmother Lucie Fribourg. The memorial stone erected to her memory next to the tomb of my grandfather Albert, in the Cimetière Nouveau at Neuilly-sur-Seine, not far from La Défense, should forever be maintained with the inscription selected by my father "Mort pour la France—Assassinée par les Allemands." This monument is erected on a burial plot (Plot 15823, Division 1C, Series 5bis) bought "in perpetuity" by my grandfather on August 30, 1910. Hence, annual maintenance fees ensure that the stone remains clean and the inscriptions visible.

Seven of my father's ancestors, including my great-grandfather Henri Caïn Fribourg and his wife Anna Ségnitz, are buried in 30 Div CD/2 Sud, 10 in the Jewish section of the Montparnasse Cemetery in Paris. In this municipal cemetery, when a direct descendant of the deceased fails to renew the 33-year lease and to pay for yearly maintenance, the coffins are exhumed and the exhumed remains are transferred to a common grave. This practice is followed to make room for more recently-deceased persons.

I have observed a similar practice in the Jewish community cemetery in Epernay (Marne), where my grandparents Renée and Lucien Oury, and their son Robert, are buried. In her Last Will and Testament, my mother enjoined her three children to maintain an affiliation with the Epernay Jewish community, in order to ensure continued maintenance of her parents' graves. My father also included a similar provision in his Last Will and Testament regarding the tombs of his ancestors. It is my fervent hope that my children, my nieces and nephews, and their descendants, will continue the practice of contributing the necessary annual maintenance fees to these three cemeteries in France. No such provision need to be taken for the graves of Claude's parents, or mine, because they are all buried in or near New York City, where perpetual care could be, and has been, purchased.

My paternal grandparents had an apartment in Paris at 116, rue de la Folie Méricourt, and a house on Rue Royale in Fontainebleau, which were both stolen and auctioned off. My father tried, but could not get any compensation from the French government before his death in 1975. However, on July 16, 1995, Président Jacques Chirac of the French Republic solemnly recognized France's unremitting debt to the 76,000 Jews deported from France during the Holocaust, including my grandmother. After a thorough study, the French Government on September 10, 1999, created the *Commission pour l'indemnisation des victimes de spoliations intervenues du fait des*

Henry Fribourg

législations antisémites en vigueur pendant l'Occupation (Commission for the Compensation of Victims of Spoliations Resulting from Anti-Semitic Legislation in Force during the Occupation).

On October 23, 2000, on behalf of my sister, my brother and myself, I filed a petition accompanied by seventeen documents in which I proposed that the French government indemnify us for the losses incurred by my grandparents. The supporting documents included copies of our birth certificates and of those of our father and our grandparents; marriage certificates of my parents and grandparents; reinstatements of my grandmother into French citizenship after World War I; my grandmother's deportation card certificate and her death certificate with the notation "*Mort pour la France*"; and my father's and my grandfather's military records. The total claim for the Paris apartment and the Fontainebleau house, with their antique furniture and paintings, was realistic, according to appraisals which I was able to obtain from real estate firms in France. The number 411 was assigned to the file.

At its meeting of November 15, 2002, the Commission recognized the legitimate rights of my grandparents' living descendants and awarded us, to be divided equally among us three, a compensation amounting to less than 2 % of the appraised value. The payments were received on June 17, 2003, seven months after the decision had been made and 32 months after the filing of the petition. In addition, in accordance with the December 2001 agreement between the French and US governments, small payments were received by us to compensate for bank account balances stolen from our four grandparents during the war. Nonetheless, we deem that the French government's public acknowledgment, however belated, of its complicity in the robbery and murder of its Jewish French citizens 60 years ago, is a victory for re-awakened morality. The amount of money by itself was not a major consideration for us, and we plan to donate much of it to worthy organizations dedicated to remembering and educating the public about the Holocaust. As an original donation, the three of us have committed to establish a Holocaust Library Collection at Brandeis University in Waltham, Massachusetts, in memory of our grandparents believing, with Benjamin Franklin at the founding of his library, that "To pour forth benefits for the common good is divine."

As I reach this point in my tale, I hope that some of what I have recounted explains the use of the word "betrayals" in the subtitle of this account. I refer to betrayals by the French Government of its Jewish citizens after centuries of faithful citizenship. Admittedly, many individuals helped us, some at considerable risk to themselves. Neighbors helped my grandparents, either by hiding them or their possessions, and by hiding the fact that they were Jewish. Some neighbors of my parents in Paris hid some of our possessions, particularly the Pasdeloup family. Other refugees in Cuba and New York helped us, as well as friends we all made later in the US. The conclusion I have drawn from my own family's experiences is that you can have many friends and most can be trusted, but governments cannot and must not be trusted. Where Jews are concerned, governments are not trustworthy and some major religious and political groupings are antagonistic.

Eternal vigilance is the price of freedom. For Jews, eternal vigilance is also the price of survival. Remember that we survived from May 1940 to late 1945 on the savings of my parents, and because these assets were sufficient and portable. As each of you inherits, earns and accumulates assets, remember that diversification is not only desirable for insuring varied sources of income, but having eggs in many different baskets is likely to spread risk and perhaps reduce it. It was only after considerable soul-searching that, during my lifetime, I bought more real estate than that needed for a primary dwelling.

While I was away at college, my sister Rosette attended Washington Irving High School in New York City from 1946 to 1949. Her recollections of earlier schooling are not clear. I know she went to the Girls' Primary School on Rue Chaptal when we were in Paris and, in Alger, she went to a girls' school situated not far from my lycée. She started learning English in Cuba at the English School. Rosette attended Brooklyn College for her B.A. obtained in 1953, with a joint major in Spanish and Comparative Literature, and a minor in French. Three years after I had left the University of Wisconsin in Madison, she went there, to some extent for the same reason as I, for her M.A. in Spanish in 1954. After obtaining this degree, she was a member of the foreign language faculty of Lake Erie College, a private girls' liberal arts institution near Cleveland, Ohio, until she got married in 1955. Since then, from time to time as she lived in New York City and London (UK), she has tutored private students.

My brother Sylvain had his entire education in the US, since he was four a half years old when he arrived in New York. He attended the Rudolf Steiner School before entering the Bronx High School of Science in 1954. Upon graduating from there in 1958, he attended Columbia University, first as a mathematics major. After a couple of years, he switched to a pre-medical program, while taking a number of elective courses in Far Eastern civilizations. He then attended the New York University School of Medicine from which he received his M.D. in 1966. He was an intern at Bellevue Hospital in 1966-1967 and served in the US Public Health Service at the Center for Disease Control, Epidemiology Program in 1967-1969. Following this service, he became a resident in obstetrics and gynecology at Mount Sinai Hospital in New York from 1969 to 1973, after which he moved to the Los Angeles area where he practiced his profession for many years.

On July 21, 1948, Rosette and I traveled as passengers on a Danish freighter, the Vibeke Maersk, from New York to Antwerp, Belgium. During the two-week trip, I read and completed the written assignments for the first half of a University of Wisconsin correspondence course in physical geography, using the great textbook by Trewartha. I mailed the material upon arrival by train in Paris. We lived with our grandparents Oury, getting re-acquainted with them and our native city. Unfortunately, this was the summer of the Berlin airlift, when Cold War tensions got pretty high after the Russians forbade traffic in and out of Berlin and all supplies had to come in by airplane. Our father judged that we should return to the US as soon as possible. Consequently, we had to cut our planned visit short by several weeks.

When we left my grandparents on August 9, I entreated them to come see us in the US, but they never did. My grandmother knew she would get seasick on a ship, and she was afraid of flying. So, I never did see them again. Rosette and I arrived in New York on August 22 via the Gudrun Maersk. I had completed the other half of the geography course on the return trip. These two voyages were undertaken on freighters to save money but in fact they were very pleasant. There were only six passengers on each trip. We ate at the captain's table: Danish smorgasbord every day, three times a day. We soon learned to select just two or three dishes at each meal. We drank what the captain provided, aquavit and beer on the way east, beer and aquavit when returning west. We had trouble finding drinking water for 16-year old Rosette. I enjoyed the freedom on the ships, the low population density, and the leisurely pace.

Since we were still French citizens and traveled on French passports, I had to register for the French universal military conscription at the French Consulate in New York City. I was classified as *"Bon pour le Service"* ("Good for military service") in 1948. The evidence for this lies in my military record book, numbered 4671 in the First Region, issued in Paris on March 20, 1949 and delivered to me in New York City. It shows that I was adjudged good for army service on July 22, 1949, but was given a deferment because of my foreign residence.

It was with considerable relief and joy that I became an American citizen on June 18, 1951, upon my petition Number 596758, receiving Citizenship Certificate Number 6950438 in the Southern District of New York. To obviate the troubles I had continuously encountered about the spelling of my first and middle names, I had them changed officially at that time from "Henri Auguste" to "Henry August." I recall the Judge, in his magisterial black robes, asking me in front of my mother why I wanted to become a citizen, who was the Father of the Country, and what were the Four Freedoms enunciated by President Roosevelt. Fortunately, I knew all the answers, gleaned both from history books I had read and the small booklet provided earlier by the Naturalization and Immigration Service. My parents had preceded me in obtaining their citizenship, because they were in residence in New York City where the petitions had been filed. My father became a US citizen on December 18, 1950 (No. 6915237) and my mother on January 8, 1951 (No. 6915783). My sister became a citizen when she turned 18, while my brother, who was not adult at the time, acquired American citizenship at the same time as our mother.

After I had been an American citizen for over twenty years, and had served two years in the US Army, I found out that, should I ever return to France and remain there for more than 90 days at a time, the French government could demand that I serve as many years in the French Army as the men in my age group had served. The French government would not agree to forego this right, even though I had served in the army of an allied country, maintaining that no male French citizen can lose his citizenship prior to age 50. The poor unfortunates of my age group had the 'great' opportunity, for the glory of France and in a vicious struggle, to spend three or four years fighting Algerians who wanted to throw off the colonial yoke. To avoid the possibility of having to spend three or four years of involuntary servitude in the French military, I petitioned the Ministère du Travail, de l'Emploi et de la Population of the République Française to free me from allegiance to France. According to the French government, my spouse and my two children had acquired French citizenship from me. I therefore had to petition for each of them also. After almost a year and the payment of five hundred dollars per person, the République Française graciously freed us all of allegiance on July 31, 1972, publishing these news for all to see in the Journal Officiel of August 13, 1972, number 189.

BECOMING A PROFESSIONAL AGRONOMIST

Toward the end of my first semester at Madison, I had to obtain the approval of my course of study for the spring semester from the advisor to whom I had been assigned, a faculty member in Dairy and Food Technology. He insisted that I had to take a required course, "Survey of Animal Husbandry" during the second semester. I maintained I would take it later, because I wanted to continue with the second semester of the first year of calculus, as well as complete the first year in chemistry and botany. The advisor insisted that I would not need integral calculus for a pre-forestry curriculum. After leaving his office without an agreement satisfactory to me, I made a beeline for the office of the Dean of Instruction in Agriculture, Dean Kivlin, a tall well-muscled elderly gentleman with a flowing shock of white hair and a dark blue suit. He listened to my tale, authorized me to take calculus, and suggested I give him the name of the faculty member whom I wished to have as advisor. That is when I learned a lesson that has stood me well for many years: when you are convinced you are right, do not argue with underlings, but make your case to the "top dog." You will usually obtain satisfaction.

When I became a sophomore, I switched from pre-forestry to a joint major in Agronomy (crops only at the University of Wisconsin - a situation that pertains to this day) and Soils (different department, different building), not only because of the attractiveness of the subject matters to me, but primarily because of two faculty members who became my joint advisors, Dr. Robert Muckenhirn and Dr. Henry Ahlgren. I shall always remember Dr. Muckenhirn for his unfailing smile, reserved humor, and his understanding support. Dr. Ahlgren was an outstanding teacher and forage crops investigator who later became a top administrator at Wisconsin. He retired some 15 years ago but still lived in Madison five years ago. He was pleased when I wrote him at that time, and sent me an anthology of poems he had collected over the years.

During my sophomore year, I had tried out and been selected for a part in a play put on by the Department of French and Italian. I suppose I was picked more because I spoke French without an American accent than because of my negligible Thespian qualities. Nevertheless, I enjoyed the experience greatly. The comradeship with the student actresses, the glory of being a small star, and the thunderous applause at the end of the performances, all were exhilarating. It was then that I was approached by Professor Lévesque, co-author with Dr. Harris, the department head, of a French conversational beginning textbook, and was asked whether I would be willing to be one of the voices in the conversations that were to be recorded from the book. As I recall, I was paid several hundred dollars, more money than I had ever had, for reading French in a recording studio for a few hours a week for several weeks. What a windfall!

I realized then that Dr. Harris needed native speakers to lead the conversational laboratories in beginning French that were going to use his book the following year. It was somewhat irregular that a rising junior in Agriculture be hired at the rank of Instructor in another college, but he hurdled the bureaucratic obstacles satisfactorily. During my last two academic years in Madison I earned two-and-a-half times as much by teaching French eight hours a week as I could by waiting on tables or washing dishes for 30 hours, and I had much more free time. I became a regular at the French House where, as a member of the instructional staff, I could get good, almost free meals and meet many female students enamored of the idea of Frenchness.

In January 1949, I had successfully completed my undergraduate studies at the University of Wisconsin and received my degree at the end of the fall semester. One of the courses I took that fall was the senior course in wildlife management taught by Aldo Leopold. Leopold is renowned as the founder of wildlife science, and that fall was the last time he taught the course before his death. Then I moved to Ithaca, New York, where I had been offered a Grange Fellowship to study for my M.S. degree under Dr. Roy Blaser, one of the foremost forage scientists in the world.

I did go back to Madison in June to receive the actual diploma and attend the graduation ceremony with my friend and 1946 roommate Philip Dodell. I remember well being impressed by the fact that the commencement speaker was the Secretary General of the United Nations, Trygve Lie. Phil was from Brooklyn and both he and his mother wanted him to become a physician. His grades were not high enough to surmount the Jewish quota limits for admission to medical schools, so he became a science teacher in New York City high schools. After about ten years, he was admitted to the University of Louisville Medical School and later established a general practice on Long Island. He and his wife Myra attended my wedding, but we later lost track of each other. The four of us accidentally met again on a sightseeing boat in a fjord outside of Bergen, Norway, in 1994, after he had retired from a 20-year career as an allergist in Phoenix, Arizona.

B. S. cum laude, University of Wisconsin, Madison June 1949

I found the going tough at Cornell, where I started the spring semester in February 1949. Nobody had prepared me for the rigors and expectations of graduate school. As an undergraduate, I had become highly efficient in my use of time for disciplined study, and had found that intense concentration in class ensured a B grade. Home study and extra effort built on top of that for an A. But in graduate school, the aim was not to learn the textbook, but to learn the subject matter in depth. The intensity of study expected of me became clear after a month or so. I had a date on Saturday night, and another date, with a different girl, on Sunday evening. On Monday morning, Dr. Blaser asked me how come I had so much free time that I felt I could be absent from my desk on two consecutive evenings, or was I studying at home on weekends rather than at the office, as I did during the week? Then, a few months later, Dr. Blaser confided to one of his other students, a doctoral candidate, Roy Sigafus, who later was on the faculty at the University of Kentucky, that I would never amount to anything because I did not appear to be devoted enough to professional development. This offhand remark, presumably not meant to be repeated to me, was indeed told me in confidence by Roy Sigafus. I shall always be grateful for his indiscretion, which turned out to energize me for many years, perhaps to this day, for I became determined to prove Dr. Blaser wrong. In the late 1970s, when the two of us were attending a professional meeting in Beltsville, Maryland, and he came up to me and said "Henry, I have been watching you in your work at Tennessee, and you have done well, congratulations," I was finally able to shuck this load from my shoulders.

When I was his student, Dr. Blaser was a hard taskmaster. His socratic style, used impartially throughout his life with all interlocutors, be they colleagues, farmers, or students, consisted of continuous rapid-fire challenges to facts, theories, hypotheses, and all other statements. It was not easy for a new 20-year old graduate student to handle such a challenge. It took me a couple of decades to become able to deal with such a conversation. And then I realized how excellent it was for stimulating graduate students to become thoughtful professionals able to stand on their own two feet, so I used the method with my own students, but doing it gradually as each grew in knowledge and competence.

The campus of Cornell University is 350 meters (1,000 ft) above the city of Ithaca on the shores of Lake Cayuga, one of the glacial finger lakes of western New York State. My transportation, a heavy second-hand bicycle, was not suited to coming back from downtown. Indeed, it was not suited to going downtown, for I once received a speeding ticket for exceeding the 50 km/hour (30 mph) speed limit on the hill descending to town. My parents gave me $250 to purchase my first car, a 1937 Plymouth sedan. It served me well for a year and a half. I used it to go to New York City several times. On the last trip, though, it threw a rod near Morristown at three in the morning, and I kept driving. I recovered $20 for the wreck from a used car dealer on Queens Boulevard. From then on, I stuck to my bicycle, for it required few repairs and I could afford them. Occasional long distance trips to New York City were made with a friend who was the proud owner of a Model A Ford sedan, which I learned to drive.

In the fall, Dr. Blaser left Cornell to take a position at Virginia Polytechnic Institute and University, where he remained for the rest of his career and developed a very successful forage program. My new major professor was Dr. W. Keith Kennedy, a highly energetic, tall, long-legged, ambitious, demanding, former infantry captain. Under his direction, I finished my Master of Science degree. However, his research interests were somewhat different from mine, so I applied to other schools for continuing my studies. I also did not care for the arrogant Cornell spirit that seemed to pervade the campus. By then, I had decided to earn my doctorate and become a professional investigator and teacher in the field of forage crops.

I applied to several of the best graduate schools with the most renowned agronomic and forage programs, including Iowa State, Purdue, and North Carolina State. I sealed my non-acceptance by NC State when I answered the question on race in the Graduate School Admission form by writing "human." Both Purdue and Iowa State offered me assistantships. I could have studied under Dr. George O. Mott at Purdue, a former classmate of Roy Blaser at the University of Nebraska, also a highly renowned forage scientist, and a gentleman, with whom I later became well acquainted when I visited the Campinas agricultural research station in the state of São Paulo, Brasil, when he was there for several years. However, he insisted that my admission be contingent on getting a recommendation from an Indiana farmer for whom I was to work for six months. This requirement was to compensate for the fact that I had not been raised on a farm. I told him I would be willing to work for the farmer, but only after I had been admitted unconditionally. After meeting with Dr. Iver J. Johnson at the Agronomy Meetings in Cincinnati in November 1950, and being influenced by his kind and magnetic personality, I decided to accept his offer to go to Ames, Iowa.

My assistantship in the Agronomy Department at Ames, where I started in February 1951, paid me $100 a month. I had a 1-room basement apartment in town for $30 a month, with a shower/bathroom down the hall. The remaining $70 were sufficient for bread, cheese and salami for lunch, a cafeteria supper, a restaurant meal once a week, use of a washing machine in a washeteria, an occasional movie, a subscription to Time magazine, and sometimes I had up to $10 left over at the end of the month. I could stockpile these savings and indulge myself in a 2-day weekend in Des Moines once a quarter for attendance at a Friday evening service at the

Reform temple, a good meal, and a cultural event. In late afternoon during warm weather, I would play some tennis three or four times a week when the weather allowed and, every evening without fail, I would read for at least 30 minutes before falling asleep. The reading matter would usually consist of university library books that had absolutely no relationship whatever to my study program. I thoroughly enjoyed my three-and-a-half years of study and professional apprenticeship at Iowa State, although recreational opportunities were limited. Many of my student colleagues were married and some had children. The few of us who were bachelors relaxed with one or two lines of bowling in the Student Union after supper before returning to the office in the evening. Since there were not too many distractions, it was easy to study and learn in Ames.

The VIth International Grassland Congress (IGC) was scheduled to take place on the campus of Pennsylvania State University in early July 1952. I wanted to attend, but had no funds for that purpose. Unlike the University of Tennessee until recently, Iowa State did not provide substantive support for either faculty members or graduate students to attend professional meetings. In winter 1952, I wrote W.R. Chapline, a USDA scientist in Washington, D.C. and Executive Secretary for the upcoming Congress, of my predicament. I explained that I was poor and a graduate student in forages, but that I did speak, read and write French and Spanish, and would be willing to work for my travel and meeting expenses. Several weeks later, I received a letter from the Department of State, offering me a 6- or 7-week job. I was to spend a month in Washington to be trained as an interpreter while I compiled a French-English-Spanish lexicon of agricultural and forage terminology. Then, I was to function as an interpreter at the Congress. The remuneration was to be $55 a day plus expenses, at a time when my assistantship paid me less than twice that each month! Dr. Johnson was surprised at my good fortune and gracious enough to acquiesce to my request for a leave of absence without pay, provided I got some of my student colleagues to carry on the essential research work for me during my absence.

At the end of the spring quarter, I went in June to Washington for what turned out to be an almost uninterrupted series of 12-hour or longer work days, 7-days weekly, for the next two-and-a-half months.

For six to eight hours a day, I received instruction in both simultaneous and consecutive interpreting, with supplementary lessons in elocution, voice projection, note-taking, and other tricks of the trade. Many of these came from Mr. Edmund Glenn, Chief Interpreter, a 190-cm (6-ft 4-in) Hungarian native with a booming bass voice whose stentorian antics I shall always remember. He instructed me on using my diaphragm in speaking so that I could be heard in the last row of a 1,000-seat auditorium without the benefit of any amplification. Such training stood me in good stead later on in Latin America and Africa, as well as at field days in Tennessee. Before and after these training sessions, I worked with several French/English and Spanish/English professional interpreters. These highly educated people knew literature, history, economics, political science, but their knowledge of agriculture and its terminology was rudimentary, and their scientific knowledge was very limited. Thus, I became their teacher while we compiled the lexicon on index cards that later were alphabetized prior to being typed on stencils for mimeographing. A job that would be simple nowadays required considerable effort in those days.

When the IGC convened at State College, PA, I already had been there several days as a member of the advance party. I worked like a dog for two weeks, enjoying every minute of it, helping the professional interpreters understand the texts of upcoming plenary talks that had technical contents, and standing by in the booths to scribble translations of words not yet in the lexicon. My salary had been increased to $65 a day when the Congress started. I inferred from this raise that Mr. Glenn, a hard person to satisfy, must have been pleased with my performance. He spoke Hungarian, Russian, German, French, English, plus two other languages, and had served as President Truman's interpreter at the Potsdam meetings with Stalin.

About half-way through the Congress, Mr. Glenn asked me if I would be willing to tackle an additional job, being the interpreter for the Western Tour that was to follow the closure of the Congress. There were to be four tours into various parts of the US and Canada. The Western Tour was to travel by Pullman train, with occasional bus rides, from Chicago through Nebraska to Utah, Idaho and Montana, then New Mexico and Arizona, followed by Texas, Colorado and Missouri, returning to Chicago after three weeks. To save money, they were looking for one interpreter to handle the three official languages: English, French and Spanish. I would be paid $100 a day plus all expenses, but unlike the multiple interpreters on the shorter tours to the Northeast, Midwest, and South, I would be alone to handle all language problems. Dr. Iver Johnson was at the meeting, and he acceded to my request for an additional three weeks of leave.

So, my next big adventure started as about 75 congress participants and I boarded the train for the first leg to Chicago, where we were met by the leader/guide/organizer, Colonel Wentworth, normally employed by Armour and Co. The tour had been organized very well, and a meticulously-drawn schedule had to be followed. Although the Colonel was 50 kg (110 lb) overweight, he could move fast. I never did learn whether he was an infantry colonel or a Kentucky colonel, but he did love a good shot of bourbon, and was not stingy with his liquor. He worked for in public relations, I believe, in the Chicago stockyards and knew every cowboy worthy of the name living west of the Mississippi River. We had French speakers from Europe and Africa, and Spanish speakers from Latin America and Spain. There were Portuguese speakers from Portugal and Brazil, Italians, Germans and several Scandinavians. I tried to make them all feel wanted in my country, which I was discovering along with them.

We were welcomed into each state or agricultural university by one or more "big shot," usually a dean, director or vice-president. Most evenings there was a banquet with an after-dinner speaker. Sometimes luncheons or even formal breakfasts took place. Invariably, seated at the head table, I would gulp my food down while interpreting for those chosen from our group to sit next to the local dignitaries. Then, after each after-dinner speaker had declaimed, I delivered a translation in Spanish, and one in French, of the entire speech. Each interpretation had to be half as long and strove to be twice as good as the original. There were also speeches in the other direction, as members of the group alternated in thanking our hosts for their hospitality. During the day, of course, there were numerous explanatory speeches on all the professional aspects, experiments, equipment, livestock, landscapes, etc…that we were shown. I learned right from the beginning to use Latin names only to describe plants and animals, common names being just too confusing as I shifted from one language to another.

Most American greeters felt it necessary to insert at least one joke, sometimes more, in their speeches, not recognizing that what is funny in English to an American audience might fail to amuse, or might be offensive, to a Frenchman or a Latin American, or even to a Britisher. So, early in the tour, I got into the habit of inserting my own jokes, proven effective for a particular language, at the appropriate place in the interpreted speech. The original speaker was most gratified that an appreciative laughter greeted the translation at the proper place in the speech, most often not realizing the laughter greeted a completely different joke. After a while, though, the laughter was even more pronounced than the original English version had elicited, because some of the multilinguists in the group were taking bets about which joke out of my limited inventory I was going to use with which speech!

Needless to say, I enjoyed myself immensely on the trip, earning much money, and learning more about agriculture and the West than I ever had. I also made many friends from among the group. One of those was a Brazilian animal scientist who, a few months later, was to become the organizing secretary of an Inter-American Meeting in Livestock Production meeting sponsored by the Food and Agriculture Organization (FAO) of the UN. He requested them to hire me as one of the five interpreters for the conference. When FAO called to offer me the job ($125 a day plus all expenses), I declined at first, explaining that I spoke no Portuguese. They assured me I would have to deal only with French, English and Spanish, persons charged with local arrangements would take care of Portuguese. Just so that I could order meals, find a room, and understand directions, though, I picked up a grammar, a dictionary, and a phrase book, and studied Portuguese for a couple of months before departure.

My plane landed at five in the afternoon in São Paulo, where I was met by the American working for FAO who was in charge of the Congress and would be my boss. He took me to the hotel to clean up, and then at 7:30, we went to dinner with two Brazilians connected with the Congress, neither of whom spoke either English or Spanish, and so I had to interpret from and to Portuguese! We went by train to

Henry Fribourg

Baurú a few days later, where the Congress was to take place at a technical agricultural school. After the meeting, we traveled for a week throughout the state of São Paulo, visiting *fazendas* (ranches), eating *churrasco* (grilled barbeque), and learning about tropical livestock production and problems. I have to admit that, for someone who had not been expected to, and thought he could not, interpret Portuguese, I became good enough to understand and be understood. I also earned every penny I was paid. The work days started for me before breakfast and did not end until everybody was in bed and we had translated the reports and summaries of the day into the four official languages.

The next year, 1953, was when I was taking the most difficult and advanced course work at Ames, in biochemistry, plant physiology, statistics, soil science, plant breeding, and crop ecology, preparing to undergo the written and oral comprehensive examinations required of doctoral candidates. I was successful in these and was admitted to candidacy. All that remained was the writing of a dissertation on the use of plowed-under leguminous plants (*Leguminosae* spp.) as nitrogen sources for corn (*Zea mays*), which I completed in summer 1954. For a couple of years prior to that time, I had been receiving deferments from my draft board, in New York City, at a time when military service was expected of every able-bodied male. I had been able to convince this urban draft board that agricultural studies were vital to the efforts sustaining the so-called police action in Korea.

In early summer 1954, I accepted another part-time job with FAO, this time as Chief Interpreter for an Inter-Caribbean Conference to be held in Jamaica in June and July. I got to visit most parts of the island, not only in the touristic areas, but also in the interior. I was told by the spouse of the Minister of Agriculture that I had learned well the local dancing styles, to the extent that she thought I probably had "some drops of Negro blood in my ancestry"! One of the hosts for the conference, whom I had met earlier in the tour for the IGC, was Dr. Thomas Lecky, a native Jamaican, who at that time was in his fifties. He had obtained his doctorate in animal genetics and breeding at the University of Edinburgh, internationally renowned for its prominence in that field. Dr. Lecky showed us the results of his work, which had the objective of developing a productive meat/dairy cattle breed adapted to the harsh climatic and poor forage conditions of Jamaica. The breed was to be called the Jamaica Red, for obvious reasons. In February 2003, while on a vacation in Jamaica, I was very pleased to observe many herds of Jamaica Red cattle that were obviously thriving, some forty years after the breed was released to the public.

Upon returning to Ames, I finished writing my dissertation, passed the final oral examination, and was granted the Ph.D. in August, walking across the stage with Dr. Iver Johnson, my major professor, who placed the doctoral hood over my head. Dr. Johnson had been an outstanding mentor to me, as he was to many other students. I considered him, and still do, as my academic and professional father, and mourned him when he died a few years ago. In early September, I left Ames for a few days of vacation in New York City with the family, prior to reporting for military service on September 15.

The new Ph.D. in Ames, Iowa, August 1954

FROM Ph.D. TO Pfc.

I was sworn into the Army of the United States in downtown Manhattan on September 15, 1954 and assigned the Service Number US 51 325 633. Prior to reporting for duty, I had shaven off the moustache I had worn ever since living in Cuba, having deemed it prudent not to attract the attention of sergeants with what was then a rare and unusual facial adornment. A busload of us proceded to Fort Dix, in New Jersey, to be processed, vaccinated, issued uniforms, and assigned to a basic training outfit in the 69th Division. My platoon sergeant's name was Fredericks, a wiry muscular very dark-skinned African-American with infantry combat experience in Korea. He was a demanding but extremely fair supervisor, and he gained the respect and liking of just about every recruit in the platoon. Many of these were educated persons who had benefited from deferments to finish college programs. One of them was Gilbert Grosvenor who later on succeeded his father and grandfather at the helm of the National Geographic Society. Many of my recruit colleagues had hoped that the Korean police action would be over before they would be drafted. Only a few were vocally bitter that they had not escaped their duty.

During the sixteen weeks of basic training, I found out several things that I did not know about my physical and mental strengths. It was a surprise to learn that I could do hard, repetitive, numbing physical activities day after day, six and a half days a week, with only four or five hours of sleep each night. It was also a revelation to learn that I could do some physical exercises of which I did not know I was capable. For instance, I did not know I could walk and run in the soft dry sands of the pine woods of New Jersey while carrying a 25-kg (55-lb) pack and a 5-kg (11-lb) weapon (M-1, or Garand rifle) for 11 km (5 miles) in an hour.

It was interesting to observe how well the basic training program had been planned and organized to challenge and develop the physical and mental attributes of recruits while building their muscles and esprit-de-corps. It was also unfortunate that much of it was vociferously mishandled by foul-mouthed, barely-literate non-commissioned officers, mostly of African-American and Puerto Rican heritage. On the other hand, some of the more sadistic training officers were white males, such as a Captain Reynolds who was in charge of our company for a short while. He was relieved of command after a recruit, whom he thought was malingering and that he had forced to run in front of his jeep, died of shock and exhaustion. Another recruit from my barracks died when a rifle which had not been cleared (visually ascertaining that the firing chamber was empty after use on the firing range) discharged in the barracks. The recruit had placed his uncleared weapon in the gunrack on the ground floor, and gone to lie down on his bunk on the second floor. When someone else climbed the stairs, thus shaking the building, the weapon discharged. The bullet went up through the first floor ceiling, passed through his bunk on the second floor, and killed the sleeping careless recruit instantly. There were a few officers' and noncoms' heads that rolled as a consequence. After that incident, firing range personnel were insistently careful that all weapons be cleared prior to troops departing from the firing range.

I got to be in pretty good physical shape. By the time I received a one-week pass to go home in December after graduation from basic training, I was so inured to sleeping in the cold and on a hard bunk that I chose to sleep on the floor of my parents' living room at 5620 Netherland Avenue in Riverdale, with the window open. It was disconcerting to my mother that I preferred this arrangement to the living room sofa because I found the temperature of the apartment so stifling and the couch so soft. One evening, I missed the last bus to Riverdale from the subway terminus. Rather than take a taxi and spend a lot of money I did not have, I just walked the 8 km (5 miles) in just an hour and a quarter. Of course, in those days, it was not dangerous to walk alone at night in this area.

When I went back to Fort Dix, the buses were very full. I had to stand the whole way, about an hour and a half. That is when I found out that I was now able to sleep standing up, for the last thing I remembered before arriving at Dix was the bus entering the Lincoln Tunnel. Upon return to camp I had to endure the blandishments of several "recruiters" who, on the basis of the mandatory examinations taken during basic training, wanted me to sign up for Officers' Candidate School (OCS). I would have been willing to go, as long as my commitment was to be only for two years, the time for which I had been drafted. The least time they would offer was four years. I decided to remain an enlisted man and not become an officer and a gentleman at that time. Even so, affluence was within reach. After getting twenty dollars a month as a recruit, I was going to get almost eighty dollars a month, plus free clothes, lodging, medical care, and food! What a life! All I had to do as an E-2 was obey stupid orders, not be noticeable, and stay out of trouble.

On the basis of my education, I was assigned to the US Army Chemical Corps as an SPP (Special & Professional Personnel) at Camp Detrick, in Frederick, Maryland. The fact that I had worked at Ames on a Detrick contract that Dr. Johnson had received may have helped. In that research, which I conducted for Dr. Johnson, we determined the minimum rates of the herbicides 2,4-D and 2,4,5-T that would adversely affect the survival of hundreds of soybean genotypes. The mission of Camp Detrick was to do research and development in biological warfare. The small group to which I was attached had five civilians, two or three with M.S. degrees and the others with B.S. degrees. They were the bosses. The boss of the bosses was Roy, a consummate politician and an incompetent scientist. In the latter regard, he was not unique in the group. Then there were about five to seven of us enlisted men (the number varied from time to time, as draft obligations expired) who all held Ph.D. degrees in various branches of biology. We generated most of the ideas; we did all the literature research, and practically all of the lab and field work. We were aided by a couple of R.O.T.C. cadets, otherwise known as 90-day wonders, who had received commissions as second lieutenants with their B.S. degrees. Usually, they recognized early on that their knowledge of biological research was extremely limited, and they would be well advised to take counsel from us enlisted personnel, however much this might be a blow to their officers' ego. Once in a while, one would come along that we had to educate the hard way. After the first major error he would usually tend to follow our advice. Occasionally, we would have to host an Army master sergeant or a Navy chief petty officer sent to our group for a month or two of "familiarization" with biological warfare. These were more resistant to education than the second "louies" but eventually we would bring them to our way of thinking.

The mission of our small group was to determine the efficacy of various means of distributing from airplanes agents that would damage or destroy crop plants. In those days, physiological weed control was in its infancy, and we were pushing its frontiers, testing with crop plants rather than weeds. Transport planes flying at different altitudes and speeds would discharge aerosols of colorless liquids, simulating herbicides, to which had been added known concentrations of dyes. Our job was to determine the quantity and geographic distribution of the dye at ground level. Alternatively, we would distribute spores of fungal diseases that affect crop plants, for instance, wheat or oat rusts. Our field trials were held in areas less populated than Maryland.

I shall admit here that I had no qualms about doing this kind of work at that time. In those days, atomic and hydrogen bombs were the deterrent *par excellence*. To us, killing plants seemed a much more humane way to conduct warfare than killing people. Little did we know how, later on, the results of our work would be misused in Vietnam with Agent Orange and its contaminant dioxin. We had not foreseen that Lyndon Johnson, Richard Nixon, and their aides would spray indiscriminately and devastate entire ecosystems and their inhabitants to defoliate the rain forest. It was then that I realized again that generals are not to be trusted. Sometimes, their civilian overseers, such as Robert McNamara and some of his successors, are not any better. McNamara egged Lyndon Johnson on and required 30 years before eventually recognizing and confessing his mistakes publicly. A little late for the tens of thousands of victims for whose deaths he was responsible! In addition, the ordering of unprotected enlisted personnel, not told to wear rubber gloves and breathing masks, to handle Agent Orange, is another example of the abominations that can be visited upon unsuspecting drafted citizens and volunteers by their leaders.

To do our field trials, we would go to an Air Force base at Avon Park, Florida, and to a Strategic Air Command (SAC) base at Rapid City, South Dakota. We spent time on private farms or agricultural experiment stations in the rice-growing swamps of coastal East Texas, where the size of native mosquitoes is legendary, and in the wheat-growing areas of the Red River Valley, near Grand Forks, South Dakota, where the small lively mosquitoes were just as bad as the large Texas variety. To determine the scatter of the dyes, we would set out aluminum plates over a grid many kilometers wide and deep, and measure the dye deposited on the plates by colorimetric determination. When we studied the spread of disease-causing fungal spores, such as wheat rust, we captured the spores on sticky surfaces and spent hours counting spores observed in a set number of microscope fields. When we were on these trips, usually one-half to two-thirds of the year, we traveled in civilian clothes and had considerable freedom. Many times, the duty was boring, the so-called research unnecessary because it was already published or could be easily inferred from known information, the waste of materiel astounding, and the orders repetitive or ridiculous. Nevertheless, we SPPs carried on valiantly, fighting the battles of Campus Detrick with obedient determination, knowing that these assignments were considerably preferable to pulling infantry duty in Korea.

In the spring of 1955, my father decided to sell to me, at a very modest price, with payment deferred until I could afford to pay, his 1951 Power Glide Chevrolet sedan. My parents had used this car on a trip to Europe and brought it back to the US. I believe the Power Glide was one of the early cars with automatic transmissions. It was very difficult to travel from camp without a car, and I hoped that the availability of a vehicle would improve my non-existent social life. It did, since I then could go on pass to Baltimore, Washington, Newark, New York City, and other places. However, my pay as an E-2 was insufficient to pay for gas, oil and insurance. Most of us SPPs had fairly fixed schedules, and we knew well in advance about trips, KP (kitchen police) duty, etc…So, many of us had evening jobs to earn extra income.

I ended up joining the ranks of the traveling sales representatives for a company selling fine Rosenthal china and beautiful Gorham sterling silver place settings. I underwent a training course which provided me, in writing, with all the appropriate responses to make once I had wormed an appointment from an unsuspecting young woman, preferably one who had already set a wedding date. I tried to have one appointment each night from Monday through Thursday. If I made one sale a week, I broke even; two or more sales resulted in profit. I found the experience valuable and revolting. I needed the money, but I had to use all the ploys and lies suggested for making a sale, even if the prospective buyer appeared to me unable to afford the considerable monthly payments she undertook.

Many days in the office at Detrick were spent just waiting around for orders. My friend Warren Stoutamire and I established a considerable number of one- and two-gallon aquaria in which we studied the inheritance of color patterns in guppies. That kept us amused and challenged. It was also a challenge to our colleague Vladimir Walters, an ichthyologist who eventually went into oceanography. Once I had a car, I was able to volunteer to go to the map collection of the Library of Congress to investigate the geographical distribution of soybeans in China. This became a challenging and interesting task. I got to be out of camp and into Washington for many duty days during the week, dressed in civilian clothes most of the time. I had the opportunity to wander the stacks of the Library, as well as those of the US Department of Agriculture before it was moved from downtown to Beltsville, Maryland. I learned to recognize various key Chinese ideograms and wrote a 100-page report for which Roy thanked me. He then promptly filed it, never to see the light of day again, as far as I know. Perhaps he waited for my discharge from service and then put his name on it before sending it on to the Pentagon. On May 21, 1956, I was promoted from E-2 to E-3, otherwise known as a Private First Class (Pfc.). A couple of weeks before I went on terminal leave prior to my return to civilian status, I was promoted to the exalted rank of Specialist Fourth Class (E-4), a rank formerly known as corporal for those unlike me who were entitled to command other soldiers.

The drafted SPPs who made up the enlisted personnel working on research at Detrick were highly trained individuals, Ph.D. recipients or engineers with some experience. Military life did not sit well with most of us. We were supposed to use our knowledge and professional experience during working hours. During the other hours each day, we were under the control of infantry or career non-coms or officers, most of whom did not have the faintest idea of what we did at work. They expected spit-and-polish, creased trousers, snappy salutes, and presence at reveille and retreat (lowering the flag in the late afternoon). Most of us were quite willing to work during the day, but we did not look forward to the periodic 24-hour KP duty. Occasionally, we also had to undergo inspections, either standing at attention by our bunks in the barracks, or in ranks in the street. Bunks were supposed to be made so that a coin would bounce up from the top blanket after being dropped by an officer, and the white collar (top sheet turned back over the blanket end nearest the pillow) was supposed to be exactly 9.88 cm (4 in) wide. We did not have to pull guard duty, because security was provided by a special detachment of military police. From time to time, some eager officer would come along who decided that we needed to shape up! Collars that did not meet the prescribed width exactly would result in the bed being unmade forcefully by the inspector, and a suspension of the usual weekend pass. Similar disproportionate penalties were imposed for infractions that were minor in our eyes and had no influence on our jobs, but were violations of petty military discipline.

So, the SPPs retaliated imaginatively! When an inspection in ranks was called, all personnel were dressed appropriately, except that non-matching civilian socks of bright hues were showing below the trouser cuffs. A lieutenant-colonel almost fell victim to apoplexy when that happened! A gung-ho captain decided to have a barracks inspection on a Saturday, a day when we normally would not have to be on the post. To save him the trouble of tearing up any bunk that did not meet his exact criteria, not a single bed was made in the entire detachment of several hundred SPPs! Admittedly, these offenses could have been construed as mutiny, but how would it look on a colonel's record to have been party to a court-martial involving hundreds of soldiers whose only offense was wearing loud civilian socks at an open-ranks inspection, or not making their beds on a week-end morning?

An offending disciplinarian became the object of daily complaints to the Inspector General (IG) by successive groups of fifty or more enlisted men, many more than the IG could accommodate daily in the hours allotted to the task. After two to three weeks, the personnel situation was remedied by the IG, tired of having to listen to all the complaints. Many enlisted men joined an informal Greek-letter fraternity, MI!, advertising its logo on walls and sidewalks. These graffiti lasted many weeks, until some high-level officer figured out that those were the transliterated initials of the English phrase "f#*@ the Army," and demanded an immediate cleanup. The hall where movies were shown was stifling hot in summertime. An edict came down that ties were to be worn with shirts when attending the cinema because officers' wives had complained about the casual dress of the enlisted men. Tee-shirts were then substituted for the short-sleeved sports shirts we had been wearing, and garish ties were knotted around our necks. The colonel's wife soon decided that the earlier laissez-faire attitude resulted in better over-all sartorial appearances than the new edict demanded. These are the petty ways in which we battled frivolous or stupid orders.

    Another activity that I carried on was to collect the numerous genealogical notes that my grandmother Renée had written down over the years. I organized them and built genealogical trees on large sheets of paper. This was before the advent of portable computers and word processors. So, in order to be legible, I decided each person would have a box 2.5 cm high and 5 cm wide (1 x 2 in) in which I would record name, and dates and places of birth and death in India ink. Marriages would be recorded as links between the appropriate boxes. I also requested my father to write down or recall for me all he could about his side of the family. I ended with two large rolls of paper, about 60 cm (24 in) high and five or more meters (over 16 ft) wide. In the 1990s, I purchased a personal ancestor program, and eventually had entered almost 1,500 names into this record by the end of 1996. At that time, having acquired a color computer with larger memory and with graphics capability, I transferred all the data to a newer program. This software was not only compatible with my personal computer system and a color monitor, it also had much greater flexibility of use and in providing numerous options for report generation. Two years later, while visiting with a distant cousin in France who is an avid genealogical investigator, I learned of still another American software program. This software program was much superior in ease of data entry and availability of desired records. I shifted all my records to that format, a conversion that was relatively easy to conduct. I have continued to work with this program, expanding the data base laterally to include more living relatives, and also backward to record ancestors predating the French Révolution. It is my deepest felt hope that this will turn out to be a meaningful legacy to future generations, illuminating their past to buttress their way into the future, and I shall present some of the results of this endeavor in a subsequent chapter.

FINDING MY LOVE AND FOUNDING A FAMILY

In the fall of 1954, my sister Rosette had met Jean Pierre Besman, and they were married on May 29, 1955. It was a very nice, traditional wedding, at which there were many people, much food, and dancing to good (fox-trot, waltzes, occasional slow jitterbug) music. Since I had no light-weight suits, I decided to attend in my Class A summer uniform of a Private First Class (khaki shirt and trousers, brown tie, brown shoes shined to a mirror-like sheen, one stripe on each sleeve) in the Chemical Corps.

It was at this wedding that I met the wonderful girl who would later become my wife. It was only later that Claude Brunschwig—generally known as Claudia in the US—and I figured out that our meeting was not entirely accidental. In fact, Eliane Brach, who not only was a friend of my parents but also of

Sylvain, Rosette and Henry on her wedding day

the Max Brunschwig family, and a distant cousin of Jean Pierre Besman, had ensured that the Brunschwigs were invited and that I would meet Claude. After spending most of Rosette's wedding with Claude, I was pretty sure that, if she would accept me, she was the one with whom I wanted to spend the rest of my life.

Claude Brunschwig, 1956

There was a slight delay to my courtship, since Claude was due to go to France with her maternal grandmother Mathilde Wolff Lévi for the summer. However, there was a letter waiting for her when she returned at the end of the summer, asking her for a date. From September on, whenever I was not on a field trip for the Army, there were few weekends when I did not leave Fort Detrick (the facility had been promoted from Camp to Fort) in late afternoon on Friday, to arrive in New York City late Friday evening or Very early on Saturday morning.

I would stay the weekend, and leave New York at eight Sunday night, arriving back at the barracks at two in the morning, in time for reveille at 0600h. In the fall, I stayed at my parents' apartment at 2440 Sedgwick Avenue in the Bronx, and commuted from there to Kew Gardens, in the borough of Queens, where the Brunschwigs lived at 80-23 Grenfell Street. We became engaged in November, and there was a big luncheon and engagement party at the Brunschwigs'. After that, I often would be invited to sleep in a spare bedroom in Kew Gardens. That was a lot easier than traveling 60 km (40 miles) of highways between the two homes in the early hours of the morning, especially if it had snowed. During our courtship, we went to many plays on- and off-Broadway, and to as many restaurants and nightclubs as I could afford on a Pfc's pay. As a serviceman I was often able to get cut-rate tickets to the shows and concerts.

During winter and spring 1956, I mailed over 300 letters and résumés to locate employment for after my discharge. It may have been a mistake, I realized then, to have completed my doctoral degree before I was drafted. The people at Iowa State did send me the usual job announcements, but I received them three months after they had been issued, after everybody else in the country had had a crack at them! Nevertheless, I did locate about six vacancies, and had three job interviews. I interviewed at the University of Tennessee in July, and was offered a job as Assistant Professor of Agronomy at $6,000 per year, a respectable salary for those days. On that same trip, as I flew from St. Paul, Minnesota, where the army had me working in wheat fields near Crookston, I also interviewed with Monsanto in St. Louis. Monsanto offered me a job at $9,000 a year to be a country-wide technical representative. After considering it, I turned it down to accept the offer from Tennessee. I declined the Monsanto offer for several reasons: I did not want to be on airplanes six to eight months of the year, my boss would have been a chemist with no understanding of agriculture, and I did not care for the St. Louis climate. In fact, it was lucky I turned it down because two years later the company abolished its agricultural division, although they revived it several years later, eventually becoming prominent for the Roundup (glyphosate) herbicide and genetically-modified seed.

Claude and I scheduled our wedding so that it would occur at the beginning of the month of leave I had accrued from the Army, giving us time for a honeymoon before I reported for work in Knoxville. We were married on August 12, 1956 (Elul 5, 5716) at the Homestead Hotel in Kew Gardens by Rabbi Salamon Faber. Officially, the Borough of Queens, City of New York, recorded the marriage as No. 6883—56. There were about 150 people there, and there was much good food and much dancing. A temporary but large *chuppa* had been erected in the air-conditioned hall, I smashed a glass into smithereens, Claude was radiant.

August 12, 1956

I was very happy, although I did get rather emotional during the ceremony.

For our honeymoon, we took the Chevrolet Power Glide and drove to Québec, where we had reserved a room in a moderately-priced motel on the outskirts of town, sitting in the middle of a large meadow. We visited the city mostly on foot, some in a horse-drawn carriage, and had a wonderful time. We visited various places in New York State in the Adirondacks, in New Hampshire, and along the St. Lawrence River. I surprised Claude by driving to Connecticut and to Jewett City, where we visited the neighbors of the poultry farm where she had grown up during the war. Upon returning to New York City, we rented a small trailer and loaded it and the car with all our worldly possessions. We also had about $2,000 in wedding gift money, which we used to purchase essential furniture in Knoxville. It took us three days to drive to Knoxville. It was very hot. The engine was overloaded and overheating. We barely made it up some of the hills in southwest Virginia. At that time, there were no freeways south of Washington, D.C. After we had left the capital, we had to travel on 800 km (500 miles) of winding two-lane Appalachian roads, accompanied by local pickup trucks, long-distance trailer trucks, and much local traffic through every town.

When we arrived in Knoxville, about the tenth of September 1956, we found out there were only three apartment developments in the entire city. We rented a small one-bedroom apartment in Taliwa Court, off Chapman Highway. The buildings then belonged to the university, and the rent was affordable, $120 a month plus utilities. We stayed there one year, while I learned about Tennessee agriculture and Claude completed her third year of college at UT, since our wedding had interrupted her schooling at Queens College in New York.

We also diligently tried to overcome the culture shocks which assaulted us. Claude learned that, when she was asked from where she was, she should answer "Connecticut", where she had lived several years, she would be much more welcome than if she said "New York", where she had resided most recently. We were shocked to note that, in downtown Knoxville, rest rooms were labeled "Men", "Women", and "Colored", and one could drink cold water from either a "White" or a "Colored" fountain. We were most pleased when these signs disappeared in the early 1960s.

The next year, we moved to a larger apartment in Shelbourne Towers, nearer the campus. I started my research program in forage crops ecology in earnest, and Claude graduated from the College of Education. About the same time, I received an unexpected promotion to Associate Professor. After a year and a half in Shelbourne Towers, we moved again, this time to a small rental house at the end of Timbergrove Drive, in the Rocky Hill area. It was our intention to learn about house ownership and maintenance before taking the big step of buying our own house. Claude was then teaching first grade at Flenniken School, on the Old Maryville Pike, a position she had taken right after graduation. She was then one of the very few Jewish teachers in the Knoxville City Schools, and we were actually surprised that she was hired.

We were then also undergoing the process of qualifying for becoming adoptive parents. Indeed we had learned that, for medical reasons not previously evident, it would not be possible for us to have children the usual way. In those days, it was possible to adopt babies shortly after birth. However, to qualify, we had to undergo an inquisition that extended over many months. This examination process was conducted by female social workers who, while well-intentioned, were limited in their capacity to comprehend the thinking processes of people not of their own Appalachian culture and fundamental Christian religious upbringing. The fact that we had not then joined a religious house of worship became an impediment that we were told had to be remedied before we could be considered suitable potential parents. We were also the first Jewish couple that Knox County Child and Family Services had ever had as clients, and they really had a problem with that. In addition, we did not talk the language properly, being "damn Yankees." Eventually, after we had joined the Reform Temple Beth El and had successfully passed the gauntlet of numerous inane questions of the category "When did you stop beating your wife?," we became qualified to become adoptive parents. And so, in January 1961, we took our 3-month old son Daniel home to 1215 Timbergrove Drive.

5435 Yosemite Trail, Knoxville

During these many months that we were expecting our family to increase, we were also supervising the building of our home by Paul Shirley at 5435 Yosemite Trail in the Timbercrest subdivision. We had worked hard with many floor plan proposals, and eventually became satisfied that we had designed what we desired. Unfortunately, we had to delete a couple of features I had wanted, such as two more meters (6 ft) in the length of the living room and a wrap-around balcony in the back from the living room to the master bedroom. I have always been sorry we had to eliminate these features for cost reasons, but I had been advised that a home mortgage should not exceed three times one's annual income. Since I was making $6,800 a year, and Claude would have to stop working indefinitely when the baby came, we felt that the $19,600 we were going to have to mortgage was all we should handle, rather than the $25,000 the larger house with balcony would have entailed.

Since I had been in the military during the Korean War, I was entitled to obtain a G.I. loan for my mortgage. So, we qualified for a 30-year G.I. mortgage at 5.25%. Pretty good deal! During the spring and early summer of 1961, I learned to use a chain-saw, and cut the undesirable trees and brush from the lot we had selected in the Timbercrest subdivision. We tied old boards around the trunks of the trees we wanted to keep, primarily dogwoods, a maple, and other desirable trees. This procedure succeeded in protecting established trees from the equipment used to dig the trenches for the footings and the septic field. Claude and Daniel would watch, the latter on a blanket in the middle of what later became the backyard. The house was built in summer and fall, and we moved in shortly after

Thanksgiving 1961. We lived there until June 2000, when we moved to a 1,700 sq.ft. retirement home in the Buckingham portion of Shannondale Retirement Homes.

Daniel and Renée, 1964

Two years after Daniel entered the family, we were blessed with another child, our daughter Renée, almost exactly two years younger. We were all three delighted with the new addition. I must say also that this time, the Child and Family Services were not at all as demanding in their questions, and we were judged to be suitable parents in record time. So, by December 1962, our family had been completed, and we all were very happy. At the outset, Claude and I had decided to speak French to Daniel, so that he would have the advantage of being bilingual. This decision was one of the major problems we had with the social workers at Child and Family Services, for they found it difficult to accept such a novel idea in child-rearing. However, when they observed that Daniel was behaving normally for his age, and could also converse in Appalachian Anglo-Saxon, they were amazed and reluctantly set their objections aside. We continued the practice with Renée. Unfortunately, by the time she was two and a half or three, both children had gotten into the habit of speaking English together and with their neighbor friends. It became more and more difficult "to be different," and eventually we stopped insisting that French be the primary language of the household. I hope that neither of my children will regret this lack of self-discipline and autocracy on our part.

CLAUDE AND HER FAMILY'S ESCAPE

Claude was born in Ixelles, a section of metropolitan Bruxelles, on August 7, 1936. Consequently, she was less than five years old when the German armies invaded neutral Belgium on May 10, 1940, and her memories of the events that followed are sketchy. Recollections of later conversations with her parents and other relatives, and a few letters that have survived in the family since then, provide the foundation for the tale that follows.

Max Brunschwig, Claude's father, was born in Basel, Switzerland, in 1905 and therefore was a Swiss citizen. In fact, his family had been living in the Basel area since the middle of the 17th century. His grandmother, Marie Nordmann, was the sixth great-granddaughter of Nephtali Nordmann and the fifth great-granddaughter of Bernard Diedisheim, both of whom had settled in the Basel area at that time (See Appendix I).

Simone and Max Brunschwig, 1960s

Max's father had been born in Durmenach, a village in Alsace about 25 km (18 miles) west of and overlooking Basel. He left Durmenach during the 1890s to escape the *pogroms* that were then occurring in the region. Max's great-great-grandfather Moyse was the first member of the family born in Durmenach in 1780, but earlier generations had lived not far away in Blotzheim since at least 1675.

Simone Lévi, Claude's mother, was born in 1912 in Haguenau (Bas-Rhin) in an Alsace occupied by Kaiser Wilhelm II's armies. Her birth is recorded in German in the records still maintained at the city hall, where I saw them a couple of years ago. Of course, she regained French citizenship after the signing of the Versailles Treaty in 1919. Both her father's and mother's ancestors had roots in that region of Lower (northern) Alsace (See Appendix II). Claude's great-great-grandfather, Léopold Lévy (the family changed the spelling of the family name to Lévi two generations later) was born in 1790 in the area. On her grandmother's side, Claude's fourth great-grandfather, Abraham Wolff, was born in 1738 in Metting, but he moved to Sarre-Union where his children were born. Some of his direct descendants still reside in Sarre-Union.

Claude Brunschwig, 1939

Claude and her younger sister Monique were both born in Bruxelles, because their father was working there as a haberdashery fabrics sales representative with his older brother Bernard. Neither brother trusted the German assurances that they respected Belgium's neutrality, and both of their families escaped. Max maintained his car fully fueled, and kept his garage stocked with extra jerrycans of gasoline and food supplies. When they were awakened very early on the morning of May 10 by the sound of exploding bombs and artillery shells, they turned on the radio and learned of the German invasion. Max hurriedly loaded his family in the car and proceeded west toward Ostend and the North Sea. Unable to book passage to England, he drove into France, just a few steps ahead of the invaders, passing through Plombières (Vosges), and eventually arriving in Brive-la-Gaillarde (Corrèze) shortly before the time when the armistice was signed by Pétain.

Since Max was a Swiss citizen, his daughters also had obtained Swiss passports. Claude obtained her passport number 831078/183 on February 17, 1937 in Bruxelles. The passport was renewed on September 20, 1940 in Toulouse and again on August 11, 1941 in Casablanca. Max and his daughters were able to obtain visas for the United States, along with his French wife, under the little-used Swiss quota. He was fortunate that his older sister Berthe and her husband Max Bollag were residing at that time in New York City and could undertake to assume total financial responsibility for them, as required by immigration laws. In fact, the Bollags had been on a trip the previous year to attend the 1939 World's Fair in New York, and either had been unable to return to Switzerland or had determined to remain in the US during the war that exploded during the Fair. The Max Brunschwig family obtained immigration visas in short order.

Claude does not remember crossing the Mediterranean but her passport stamps show that she was allowed to leave Marseille on May 12, 1941, aboard the S/S Voyageur Wyoming. She received immigration visa number 7 (Swiss) from the US consul in Casablanca on August 28, 1941, under Swiss quota number 811. On September 4, 1941, she received a French exit visa for a one-way trip to the US. Claude has no memories of the trip to Morocco, but she does remember internment at Sidi-el-Ayashi, the same camp where I was to reside briefly several months later. In September 1941, the Max Brunschwig family boarded the Portuguese S/S Serpapinto, mentioned earlier as the last ship to reach Cuba in 1942, and landed in New York shortly thereafter. We have no record of the exact date, but on January 27, 1942, just four months later, Claude, while residing in Jamaica, New York City, was quarantined because she was afflicted with scarlet fever.

During World War II, in the US, food production was considered an important and essential occupation. Max Brunschwig became a poultry farmer, reading books to become familiar with his new occupation. He enlisted his wife's and daughters' help to feed, catch, slaughter, pluck, clean and market the chickens and eggs produced on their farm in Jewett City, in rural Connecticut. Both Claude and her sister still remember their awe when seeing a chicken bounce and hop around without a head for a minute or so after their father

Connecticut poultry farmers (left to right): Monique, Max, Claude and Simone Brunschwig, 1942

had decapitated it. Claude remembers the feathers sticking to her wet hands when plucking the chicken after it had first been dunked into a bucket of very hot water. She also remembers playing hide and seek in the tall corn field with her sister Monique. It was a magic forest!

The farmer's daughters: Monique (left) and Claude with their Rhode Island Reds, 1942

The family also had a Victory Garden, a cow named Lily, and Claude remembers her mother churning butter. The churn was a large glass container with wooden paddles that were cranked by hand. Claude attended Riverside School in Jewett City. As in many homes in those days, there was no refrigerator; rather the ice man delivered ice periodically to replenish the supply in the icebox.

Leaving the farm after it was sold a year after the end of the war was very difficult for 10-year old Claude. She cried a long time as the family drove toward Kew Gardens in Queens, New York, where other members of the family had settled. Shortly after the move to Kew Gardens, *Mémé* (Claude's maternal grandmother, Mathilde Wolff Lévi) came over by ship from France to stay with the family. Mémé had survived the war and the German occupation by using false identification papers. In order to prepare for their grandmother's arrival, the girls, Claude and Monique practiced, rehearsed and memorized two of the fables Jean de la Fontaine (1621 - 1695) in order to be able to recite them to Mémé's upon her arrival. Of course, this was their mother's idea; she prodded, pushed and helped the girls memorize these long poems. To this day, Claude still can recite "La Cigale et la Fourmi" and" Le Corbeau et le Renard" from memory.

Summers usually meant summer camp. Even though this may have been somewhat of a financial hardship for the Brunschwig family, the girls went off to summer camp every summer because of the health dangers during the polio season. Claude remembers going to a YWCA camp with other girls of different ethnic and religious backgrounds. Later, she went to a private farm camp where she took care of the owners' small grandson. There was another camp where she was a counselor to three or four little boys. She dearly loved playing mother or big sister to these youngsters, thinking that eventually she would like to be a kindergarten teacher. It was at those camps that she learned many American folk and camp songs.

The Brunschwigs had moved to Kew Gardens so that their daughters would grow up in a less rural environment than Jewett City. Max learned at New York University to be an optician, a profession he practiced in midtown Manhattan during the day, and at home in the evenings and weekends. Simone took a course to learn shorthand. She then traveled an hour and a half round trip each day by subway to work as a bilingual secretary on Broad Street in the Manhattan financial district. In the meantime, Claude attended Public School 99, not far from her home, and Forest Hills High School. Later, she attended Queens College, from which I tore her away at the end of her sophomore year.

A SATISFYING CAREER

It is not my intention to discuss in detail in this biography my activities as an agronomist and crop ecologist employed by the University of Tennessee from 1956 until my retirement in June 2001. Nonetheless, this autobiography would be less than complete if I did not include the more salient aspects of my 46 years on the faculty of the University of Tennessee (UT). My professional career was successful and personally satisfying. Most of the time, I was supposed to spend 80% of my time in research on forage crops, those plants consumed by livestock, and 20% in teaching. I was able to make contributions which have been helpful to the forage and livestock producers of Tennessee, have advanced humanity's knowledge of forage crops, and have been recognized by awards from my peers, professional societies, and academic institutions. Most of my teaching was in graduate courses, and I took pride in passing on my knowledge to students, while maintaining high standards of excellence. I am gratified that several of my former graduate students have excelled in their careers.

I shall now briefly describe what I consider my major research achievements. Summer annual grasses, such as forage sorghums (*Sorghum* spp.) and pearlmillet (*Pennisetum americanum*), are used extensively for supplemental pastures and feed for dairy cows to maintain high levels of milk production during the dry and hot summer months. I was one of the first investigators to study the management required for these plants to grow back vigorously after cutting or grazing, and to determine that high stubbles were necessary for some, but not for all, cultivars (varieties). My research on these plants is well documented in the scientific literature and in popular articles, and I am the author of the chapter on these plants in the last three editions of the most-used American textbook on forage crops.

Prior to my coming to Tennessee, bermudagrass (*Cynodon* spp.) was considered a weed. In fact, it covers an estimated 350,000 hectares (860,000 acres) or more in the state, mostly in West Tennessee. I determined ways of using this warm-season plant in a useful and economical way for beef production. The research showed how to produce up to 13.5 Mg per ha (12 tons per acre) of hay annually with the improved bermudagrass cultivar Midland when only 1/3 to 1/4 of that amount can be produced with common bermudagrass. I investigated ways to manage pastures of Midland and common bermudagrasses to produce over 450 kg per ha (400 lb per acre) per year liveweight beef gains, about twice what producers did in the 1960s. I found out how to manage bermudagrass pastures to introduce and maintain a cool-season grass, tall fescue, in the sod, thereby increasing the normal grazing season of five months to almost ten months. I have led in the successful effort to find means to maintain legumes in bermudagrass pastures. Although most of the initial research with this crop in Tennessee was done by me alone, much of the later research involving cattle was conducted in collaboration with animal scientists and agricultural economists. I have led such team research, where interpersonal and interdepartmental relations are sometimes delicate and require tact and diplomacy.

  I recognized early in my career that crop plants do not live in a vacuum, but rather that their life and performance for human use depend on many inter-relationships. I carried out much macro- and micro-climatic work, and have published in this area. I was the first to verify the validity of a mathematical precipitation model, derived in the Midwest, for both theoretical soundness and practical use in the upper Southeast. My publications in probability occurrences of climatic parameters for Tennessee have been useful not only to agriculturists of all kinds, but also to engineers, industrialists, architects and planners, and the real estate and tourism industries.

  Soil characteristics and properties greatly influence crop plant performance. I am one of the few crop scientists who has collaborated with soil scientists to help characterize the potential value of different soils on the landscape as these affect forage crops. With foresters and pedologists, I have compared the value of forage crops and trees for use on soils marginal for row crop and small grains production.

  There are over 1.4 million hectares (3.5 million acres) of tall fescue [*Lolium arundinaceum* (=*Festuca arundinacea*)] in Tennessee. That represents half of the land in pastures, one-fourth of the total farmland in the state, and one-tenth of the US area in that pasture grass. Research in improving the usefulness of this pasture species lagged for many years, because tools were not available for repeatedly identifying negative quality factors. I was instrumental in alerting the Tennessee Agricultural Experiment Station to the tall fescue fungal endophyte problem as soon as reports from other states in the late 1970s indicated that the fungus *Neotyphodium coenophialum* (formerly *Acremonium coenophialum*) was a probable causative agent. As a result, Tennessee was able to create new research programs in this area. For the last twenty-five years of my career, the University of Tennessee was in the forefront of the studies on this problem and related aspects of attempts to circumvent the low quality of infested tall fescue pastures. Research under way at the time of my retirement promised to lead to 50 to 100 percent greater cattle gains from tall fescue pastures, improved reproductive competence in cows, and to elucidate interactions among forage and grazing systems, environment, and beef cattle genotypes. In cooperation with colleagues in Animal Science, I helped quantify methane exhalations by freely-grazing ruminants, methane being one of the greenhouse gases instrumental in possible climatic changes.

Renovation with clovers (*Trifolium* spp.) is one of the best ways to improve an endophyte infested tall fescue pasture. In the 1950s, I determined that some widespread insects are detrimental to clover stands and that some herbicidal chemicals could help in the establishment of clover in tall fescue pastures. More recently, research on tall fescue renovation initiated in Tennessee was emulated in other states and is the basic underpinning of an extensive agricultural extension program in Tennessee and adjoining states. I established that a subtropical legume, hyacinth bean (*Dolichos lablab*), grows well in hot and dry weather in Tennessee. There is no other forage legume of that quality and yield potential in the state, since calves can double their normal summer growth rate while creep-grazing that species.

When I was in the US Army at Fort Detrick, I became acquainted with the computing capabilities of computers, using an IBM 650 to calculate some fairly involved statistics. The IBM 650, which occupied a very large room, had thousands of vacuum tubes, required several dozen human servants, and had to be programmed and provided data with punched cards coded with zeros and ones. One of the problems we solved took five of us two weeks to program, and then the computer required three and a half days to complete its calculations. I estimate that a similar problem in 2003 would require 15 minutes of my time to program, and the answer could be computed on my desktop personal computer in less than a minute!

When computers arrived on the UT campus, I led in their use and contributed my knowledge by publishing well-documented software programs for teaching and research. I pioneered the joint use of statistics and computers to help explain the effect of concomitant variates on crop and livestock characteristics of value to agriculturists and scientists. I was the first to publish on the use of factor analysis in agronomic research and to show its usefulness, in conjunction with multiple regression techniques, for developing quantitative models describing crop plant and beef cattle responses. If my father had still been alive at that time, he would undoubtedly have been gratified that I finally had appreciated the value of mathematics and its application to real-life problems!

My research on the influence of stage of development of plants at harvest for silage production is basic to the recommendations used throughout the state for both beef and dairy cattle. The contributions in this area were recognized when I was invited to participate in an American Society of Agronomy symposium on that subject.

As my academic mentors used to say, a research endeavor is not completed until the results have been analyzed, summarized, and reported in a publication, so that members of the scientific community and of the public can utilize them. During the course of my career, I published over four hundred titles. To illustrate the scope and extent of my interests and activities, I have selected the more significant titles and listed them in Appendix III.

Lastly, I have not been content to do research only. I have willingly shared my knowledge and experiences with students and the general public, at home and internationally. My teaching fields were forage crops and their management, crop ecology, statistics in agriculture and experimental design, and crop climatology. I designed and taught such courses at the graduate level on numerous occasions at the University of Tennessee. I also participated in practical courses for agricultural extension agents who wanted to refresh or advance their competence in forage crops and beef cattle management, and was a featured speaker to producers at numerous field days throughout the state. I was the major professor for 14 doctoral students and 23 master of science students, and also served on 46 other graduate advising and examining committees. I am very proud of my former students, who successfully completed the rigorous training to which I subjected them, and especially those who have achieved recognition as experiment station directors, research innovators, outstanding teachers, and some even as administrators.

During my academic career, I received numerous honors, and I shall cite some of them here. As a student, I was initiated in Phi Eta Sigma (honorary society for freshmen) in 1946, in Alpha Zeta and Gamma Sigma Delta in 1948 (honorary societies for agriculture), and in Phi Kappa Phi (honorary society in recognition of good academics) and The Society of the Sigma Xi (honorary society for research) in 1954.

The highest honor that a member of scientific societies can receive is to be elected a Fellow. This award was extended me in 1973 by the American Society of Agronomy and in 1996 by the Crop Science Society of America. In 1975, I received the Gamma Sigma Delta Award of Merit for Research, and in 1977, the National Merit Award from the American Forage and Grassland Council and a Special Service Award from the National Weather Service. In 1996 I was named to the Career Professional Award of the Southern Branch of the American Society of Agronomy. I was Associate Editor of two professional journals, Crop Science in 1986 -1989 and the Journal of Production Agriculture in 1986 -1991. In 1982 -1985, I was elected to serve on the Board of Directors of the Crop Science Society of America and of the American Society of Agronomy.

I GAVE YOU LIFE TWICE

The University of Tennessee honored me in 1974 by choosing me as Macebearer for that year. The Macebearer is the faculty member who carries the official symbol of the University at commencement exercises. In 1975 and again in 1986, I was invited to deliver the Annual Phi Kappa Phi lecture at the University. The UT Chancellor's Research Scholar Merit Award was awarded me in 1982, and the Chancellor's Citation for Extraordinary Service to the University in 1985. As the long-time chair of the Faculty Benefits Committee of the Faculty Senate, I served on the University of Tennessee Board of Trustees in 1982-1984 and 1986-1988. I participated in judging of the Southern Appalachian Science & Engineering Fair for many years, and was Chair of Judging, with over 700 participating judges, for the 1988 International Science & Engineering Fair in Knoxville.

My mother was very proud when I was selected to carry the University of Tennessee Mace at the head of the commencement ceremonial in 1975

One of the greatest innovative ideas that the US ever had was the land-grant concept. In 1861, Abraham Lincoln approved the original congressional acts, modified and improved several times since, whereby western lands (belonging to the American Indians—but that is another story) were granted to each state to be sold, with the proceeds to be used for the establishment of an institution of higher learning in the "mechanic arts and agriculture." The land-grant colleges of the US, through their agricultural experiment stations, colleges of agriculture, and agricultural extension services, were the foundation on which modern agricultural productivity and efficiency were able to rise and flourish. In the middle of the 19th century, one farmer could, with some difficulty, feed his family; 150 years later, the same person, supported by capital investments and a developed societal infrastructure, could feed another 150 persons. Thus, the US could provide food and feed for many other lands in the world. Other countries and cultures have tried to, and have had great difficulty in adopting this concept, although many have tried. I am convinced that, along with the Constitution of the United States and its guarantee of religious tolerance and of the rule of the majority while safeguarding the rights of the minorities, the land-grant concept was one of the main reasons why our country became such a great country and world power in the 20th century, by helping to foster a prosperous agriculture to undergird the entire economy.

The recounting of the professional recognitions which I received over the years was not only pride in my accomplishments, but also a means of establishing my credentials for the comments which follow. The unfortunate by-product of the efficient and prosperous US agriculture has been an estrangement of the increasingly urban population from the source of its daily bread, to the extent that many children nowadays believe, *e.g.*, that milk comes from a carton rather than from the udder of a cow or goat. Politicians often reflect, and sometimes amplify, the ignorance of their constituents. Consequently, over the last fifty years, there has been a steady and rapidly accelerating decrease in government support of agricultural research, teaching and extension, which have thus become victims of their success.

This decreasing support was accompanied by the consequences brought on by institutional administrations with limited ability to visualize the needs of investigators to modernize their capabilities. Thus, starting in the 1980s, many institutions began falling back in their capability to compete on the national and international scientific scenes. Now, new administrations are attempting a 180-degree turn, forcibly pushing faculty members to change their historical approaches. That is very difficult to accomplish. In the quest to change direction, existing programs, resources and personnel, even in successful programs, are being sacrificed. Individual teachers and investigators have had to beg for support from private sources or to sell their services to agencies with self-serving objectives.

As professionals have searched for the "almighty dollar," they have been forced to bend the mission of research, teaching and extension for the public good to compete successfully for grants. University groups that used to be aggregates of scholars toiling for the public good have become assemblages of technicians competing for scarce resources who try to ingratiate themselves to grantors. To succeed, individuals have had to pander to the short-term objectives of granting agencies and to the demands of administrators of limited vision. Administrators have often confused the adoption and use of seductive new tools as progress, rather than subjugating these powerful techniques to the needs of the overall mission for the public good and the long-term needs of agriculture and its participants. They have gone so far as to refuse to fill empty positions created by retirements in nationally and internationally recognized programs when these disciplines did not qualify in one of the hallowed bioengineering or molecular categories. Consequently, when a molecular breakthrough may occur in a few years, there will be very few, if any, scientists capable of adapting the new technique or material to the exigencies of the real world. What a shame!

IN SEARCH OF OUR BELIEFS AND ANCESTORS

When Claude and I were residing in Knoxville, and particularly while our children lived with us, we attended services on a fairly regular basis at Temple Beth El, starting in 1958. Since my religious education had been so abbreviated that it could not be characterized other than as kindergarten knowledge, I participated for many years in the adult education program. My interest in learning more about Judaism as a religion had been awakened during a conversation with Rabbi David Seligson of Central Synagogue in Manhattan. He and his wife had become friends with my parents. They ate in each others' home once or twice a year, when my father and the rabbi could engage in free-ranging conversations on many topics other than religious ones, as well as philosophy and theology. While I was a graduate student visiting my parents during a vacation, I happened to talk with Rabbi Seligson and point out that I had little use for infantile mouthings of repetitious incantations. He invited me to come to his office, when I felt like it, to discuss these ideas. Eventually, I took him up on the invitation during a New Year's vacation period in the early 1950s. When I visited him, what had been a half-hour appointment stretched into more than two hours. He gently pointed out to me what I should have realized, that my knowledge of Judaism was rudimentary, and that the questions I had always raised in my mind had been broached, explored, and written about by many people over the centuries. He urged me to become more knowledgeable by reading a number of books he suggested.

While I could not follow his suggestions as long as I was in graduate school, being otherwise too occupied, I gradually engaged myself in some study after joining Temple Beth El. I became involved in the Adult Education program, eventually acting as leader for several years. After some fifteen years of intermittent study, I developed other interests, but not before I had formed a philosophy which recognized the probable existence of the deity, admired the unique Jewish contribution to monotheism and prophetic religion, and rejected the idea of a personal God. The latter belief was sorely tested later, in the mid-1970s, but survived, when both my son and my mother were severely ill at the same time. Nonetheless, for many years I have been very active in synagogue affairs, being a member of the Board of Directors, chair of many committees, and eventually being elected to a number of positions of leadership, including two terms as President. To this day, I serve on the Board of Directors and remain chair of the Cemetery Committee, a self-imposed duty of love which I fulfill willingly. My attendance at weekly services has diminished, probably in proportion to the trend among Reform Judaism clergy and laity to resurrect traditional or medieval customs and practices which traditional and rational Reform (and I) abandoned many years ago.

As I reflect on the religious paths followed by my ancestors, it becomes clear that they adhered to their Jewish precepts throughout the emancipation that followed the 1789 Révolution, their evolution from rural cattle and horse traders to city dwellers, and their acquisition of the culture and thoughts of the milieu to which they evolved. Although my paternal grandparents kept only a small fraction of traditional Jewish religious observances, they never hid their adherence to Judaism. My grandfather Albert was convinced that his status as a French citizen and an officer in the Army reserve would protect him and his wife from persecution by the French government—a conviction that was destroyed in 1943. My maternal grandparents were observant of liberal Judaism and, as I recall, attended services on most Sabbaths. My mother liked to follow this practice, and my parents were members of Central Synagogue while they resided in New York City. Many Americans may not realize or appreciate the magnificent contribution of the Constitution of the United States and of the Bill of Rights to their life and freedom. My family and I do. After experiencing the covert and sometimes overt and official discrimination against Jews that I have recounted, it is wondrous to be living as an American and as a Jew in a society where official distinction based on religion does not exist and covert discrimination, wherever it may still occur, is practiced furtively because most persons do not espouse it.

As I mentioned earlier, I developed an interest in genealogy in the 1950s, as it applied to my family. In the 1990s, when computer software became available to make the recording, storing, and processing of numerous family records an easily achievable enterprise, I searched for and recorded much information. Much of this knowledge was gathered by consulting microfilmed records obtainable from the Library of the Church of Latter Day Saints. Correspondents in France, also consumed by the same desire for information, served also as sources for my research. Some of these co-investigators are distantly related either to me or to my wife, and others are persons who like to consult archival records in departmental or municipal libraries and communicate the results of their search to interested persons. I have now in excess of seven thousand persons in the electronic file, related either to me or to my wife, and dating back, in some branches of the family, to the mid 17th century.

Main street of the Fribourg ancestral home, Erstroff (Moselle) in 1999

My great-grandfather Henri Caïn Fribourg was the last of his family to be born in Erstroff (Moselle), where his family had been born and resided since the middle of the 17th century. It is now a village of about 200 inhabitants, although in 1792, it had 473 persons living in 89 dwellings. Nonetheless, there is a city hall, a primary school, a carpentry shop, and there used to be a synagogue, probably destroyed in World War II.

Salomon Rosenwald, my grandmother Lucie Ach's ancestor, was born in 1774 and settled his family in Sarre-Union (Bas-Rhin). It is possible that this family was acquainted with that of Claude's grandmother, Mathilde Wolff, whose grandfather Moïse Wolff, born there in 1809, founded a hardware store (see Appendix II) where a second cousin of Claude's, Jacques Wolff, a teacher, still resides.

My mother's ancestors, both on her mother's and her father's side, mostly came from the Moselle *département*, being traceable back to the late 17th and early 18th centuries. In those days, royal decrees, laws, and common practices, prohibited Jews from owning land or practicing most professions. Consequently, most of our ancestors were horse traders or cattle brokers, one of the activities not prohibited them before the French Révolution and its accompanying emancipation.

Bay windows are part of the front room of the Wolff (Claude's grandmother) ancestral home in Sarre-Union (Bas-Rhin) in 1999

Claude's family traces its antecedents to Berlé Diedisheim, who was a head of household in Allschwil (formerly Allschwyl) near Basel (Switzerland) in 1690. It is probable that he or his parents had come from Deidesheim in Rhenish Bavaria (see Appendix I). Members of this family later went to live in Héguenheim and neighboring Durmenach, in southern Alsace, where the Brunschwig family had its home until the end of the 19th century, when her great-grandfather moved to Basel, in order to escape some of the *pogroms* then prevalent in rural Alsace.

The few preceding comments illustrate the kind of information available to those willing to make the effort to search out genealogical sources of information, whether they be birth and death certificates, marriage contracts (*ketubah* in Hebrew), tombstone inscriptions, tax and legal records, or other material. It would be neither possible nor appropriate to show here all the genealogical trees and branches and information which I have accumulated. If I were to show only the names, dates and places of birth, death and marriage, and occupation of all the descendants of our earliest ancestors, each ancestor would require from four to over ten pages of fine text for listing all the persons. Instead, I shall show my wife's and my direct ancestors. Such listings will highlight the scope of our current knowledge, but the reader must realize that the siblings of the ancestors, in all generations, are not shown. Hence, the descendants of these siblings also are omitted. Should any relatives read this memoir and wish to obtain copies of the much more detailed records I have, or contribute to the assemblage, I hope that they will not hesitate to contact me or my survivors.

Caïn Fribourg (1752-1832) and his son Kauffman (1782-1866) were cattle traders in Erstroff, as depicted in the lithograph "Jewish cattle traders in Lorraine ca. 1899" by L. Benoit

[*NOTE*: The Ahnentafel (American) or Stradonitz (French) numbering systems provide a very useful standard numbering system for direct ancestors, and are represented in the following pages by numbers preceded by the # symbol. The first person is assigned the number 1, that person's father is 2, and that person's mother is 3. In general, if a person's number is n, the father's number is 2n and the mother's is 2n+1.]

HENRY'S ANCESTORS

1. Henry August Fribourg, b. 10 Mar 1929, Paris 2, Seine, France. He married Claudia Georgette Brunschwig, 12 Aug 1956, in Homestead Hotel, Kew Gardens, NYC, USA, b. 7 Aug 1936, Ixelles, Bruxelles, Belgium.

Parents:

2. Jean Fribourg, b. 16 Sep 1901, Neuilly-sur-Seine, Hauts-de-Seine, France, d. 3 Jan 1975, Claremont, Los Angeles, CA, USA, buried: Brooklyn, New York, NY, USA. He married Yvonne Juliette Oury, 24 Jun 1928, in Paris 9, Seine, France.
3. Yvonne Juliette Oury, b. 2 Jul 1904, Vienna, Austria, d. 20 Feb 1988, Knoxville, Tennessee, USA, buried: Brooklyn, New York, NY, USA.

Grand Parents:

4. Albert Fribourg, b. 24 Apr 1865, Paris, Seine, France, d. 27 Nov 1943, Bugeat, Corrèze, France, buried: 23 Sep 1946, Neuilly-sur-Seine, Hauts-de-Seine, France. He married Lucie Ach, 26 Jan 1897, in La-Ferté-ss-Jouarre, Seine-et-Marne, France.
5. Lucie Ach, b. 17 Jul 1873, Boulay, Moselle, France, d. 15 May 1944, Auschwitz, Poland, murdered, Third Reich.
6. Lucien Oury, b. 9 Oct 1872, Château-Salins, Moselle, France, d. 12 Apr 1952, Paris, Seine, France, buried: Epernay, Marne, France. He married Renée Samuel, 7 Jul 1903, in Epernay, Marne, France.
7. Renée Samuel, b. 21 Apr 1885, Epernay, Marne, France, d. 11 Sep 1958, Paris 9, Seine, France, buried: Epernay, Marne, France.

Henry Fribourg

Great Grand Parents:

8. Henri Caïn Fribourg, b. 18 May 1837, Erstroff, Moselle, France, d. 27 Feb 1904, Paris, Seine, France, buried: Montparnasse Cemet., Paris, Seine, France. He married Annie "Nanny" Ségnitz, 4 Jul 1864.
9. Annie "Nanny" Ségnitz, b. 4 Aug 1838, Gelnhausen, Hesse-Nassau, Germany, d. 15 Jun 1920, Paris, Seine, France, buried: Montparnasse Cemet., Paris, Seine, France.
10. Auguste Ach, b. 29 May 1838, Boulay, Moselle, France, d. 29 Jul 1910, Neuilly-sur-Seine, Hauts-de-Seine, France. He married Ernestine ("Nounoute") Rosenwald.
11. Ernestine ("Nounoute") Rosenwald, b. 23 (25) May 1848, Sarre-Union, Bas-Rhin, France, d. 10 Feb 1935, Paris, Seine, France.
12. Léon Oury, b. 1819, Château-Salins, Moselle, France, d. 19 Dec 1895. He married (1) Colette Lazard, d. 17 Jul 1855, Charmes, Vosges, France. He married (2) Juliette Daltroff, Aft 1855, b. 29 Jan 1836, d. 17 Oct 1902.
13. Juliette Daltroff, b. 29 Jan 1836, d. 17 Oct 1902.
14. Adolphe Samuel, b. 27 Jul 1856, Longeville-lès-Metz, Moselle, France, d. 16 Feb 1904, Epernay, Marne, France, buried: Epernay, Marne, France. He married Mathilde Roubach, 30 Aug 1892, in Epernay, Marne, France.
15. Mathilde Roubach, b. 23 Apr 1862, Sarrebourg, Moselle, France, d. 18 Jan 1939, Epernay, Marne, France, buried: Epernay, Marne, France.

Great Great Grand Parents:

16. Kauffman Fribourg, b. 15 Mar 1782, Erstroff, Moselle, France, d. 26 Apr 1866, Erstroff, Moselle, France. He married (1) Fleurette (Lamber) Lambert, 28 Oct 1815, in Montigny-lès-Metz, Moselle, France, b. 3 Jan 1795, Augny (Erstroff?), Moselle, France, d. 7 Mar 1835, Erstroff, Moselle, France, buried: 8 Mar 1835. He married (2) Sophie (Vogel) Kahn, 11 Jul 1835, in Erstroff, Moselle, France, b. 25 Oct 1805, Bouxwiller, Bas-Rhin, France, d. Bef 27 Apr 1866. He

	married (3) Fanie (Fany) (Cahem) Cahen, b. 1806, d. Aft 27 Apr 1866. He married (4) Babette Lévy, b. 1800.
17.	Sophie (Vogel) Kahn, b. 25 Oct 1805, Bouxwiller, Bas-Rhin, France, d. Bef 27 Apr 1866.
18.	Moïse Ségnitz, b. Abt 1790, d. Abt 1845. He married Clara (Rosa) Kohn.
19.	Clara (Rosa) Kohn, b. 1806, d. 21 Nov 1879, Paris, Seine, France, buried: Montparnasse Cemet., Paris, Seine, France.
20.	Bénédict (Solomon Benoit Isaac) Ach, b. 1 Jan 1808, Boulay, Moselle, France, d. 4 Oct 1854, Buenos Aires, Argentina. He married Bibi (Bibie) Worms, 15 Jul 1834, in Boulay, Moselle, France.
21.	Bibi (Bibie) Worms, b. 25 Jan 1817, Volmerange-lès-Boulay, Moselle, France, d. 1890, Boulay, Moselle, France. She married (1) Bénédict (Solomon Benoit Isaac) Ach, 15 Jul 1834, in Boulay, Moselle, France, b. 1 Jan 1808, Boulay, Moselle, France, d. 4 Oct 1854, Buenos Aires, Argentina. She married (2) Samuel Lévy, 29 Jul 1874, in Bolchen (Boulay), Moselle, France, b. Ethionville.
22.	Moïse Rosenwald, b. 8 Apr 1810, Sarre-Union, Bas-Rhin, France, d. 20 Nov 1865. He married Célestine Lévy.
23.	Célestine Lévy, d. 6 Mar 1866?.
24.	Salomon Oury, b. 7 May 1795, Vannecourt, Moselle, France, d. 22 Jun 1872, Château-Salins, Moselle, France. He married (1) Minette Joseph, b. 1805, Lixheim, Moselle, France, d. 2 Nov 1878, Château-Salins, Moselle, France. He married (2) Adelaïde (Lion) Joseph, b. 1792, Vannecourt, Moselle, France, d. 26 Jan 1828, Château-Salins, Moselle, France. He married (3) Brunette Daltroff, b. 1799, d. 12 Jan 1820, Château-Salins, Moselle, France.
25.	Adelaïde (Lion) Joseph, b. 1792, Vannecourt, Moselle, France, d. 26 Jan 1828, Château-Salins, Moselle, France.
26.	Jacob Daltroff, b. 16 Mar 1807, Château-Salins, Moselle, France, d. 2 Sep 1853, Château-Salins, Moselle, France. He married Minette Oppenheim.
27.	Minette Oppenheim, b. 1806, Metz, Moselle, France, d. 1 Oct 1880, Château-Salins, Moselle, France.

28. Salomon (Salmiche) Samuel, b. 1819, Vantoux, Moselle, France, d. 16 Sep 1896, Epernay, Marne, France. He married Henriette Hayem.
29. Henriette Hayem, b. 1826, Longeville-lès-Metz, Moselle, France, d. 26 Apr 1892, Epernay, Marne, France.
30. Lazare Roubach, b. 1829, Hellimer, Moselle, France, d. 10 Oct 1909, Sarrebourg, Moselle, France. He married Caroline Lévy.
31. Caroline Lévy, b. 1830, Nancy, Meurthe-et-Moselle, France, d. 17 Jan 1909, Sarrebourg, Moselle, France, buried: 18 Jan 1909.

3rd Great Grand Parents:

32. Caen (Caïn, Cayim) Fribourg, b. 1750 (1752?), Erstroff, Moselle, France, d. 1 Mar 1832, Erstroff, Moselle, France. He married (1) Katiche (Cathiche, Kelchen, Catherine) Lambert (Lamber), b. Abt 1751, d. 22 Dec 1820, Erstroff, Moselle, France. He married (2) Kailigen (Keilligen) Kayen, Aft 1820.
33. Katiche (Cathiche, Kelchen, Catherine) Lambert (Lamber), b. Abt 1751, d. 22 Dec 1820, Erstroff, Moselle, France.
34. Salomon Kahn, b. 1766, d. Aft 1832, Bouxwiller, Bas-Rhin, France. He married Régine Raphaël.
35. Régine Raphaël, b. 1770, d. Aft 1832, Bouxwiller, Bas-Rhin, France.
40. Isaac Ach, b. 1762, d. 1847. He married Berde (Berelle; Bizel) Samuel.
41. Berde (Berelle; Bizel) Samuel, b. 1772, d. Abt 1879.
42. Michel Worms, b. 1791, Denting, Moselle, France, d. Abt 1862, Boulay, Moselle, France. He married Rachel Samuel.
43. Rachel Samuel, b. 1792.
44. Salomon Rosenwald, b. 1774, d. Aft 1819. He married Sibille Wolff.
45. Sibille Wolff.
48. (Charles) Charlot Oury, b. 1767, Donnelay, Moselle, France, d. 19 Jun 1832, Château-Salins, Moselle, France. He married Rosette Brisac, Bef 1796.

I GAVE YOU LIFE TWICE

49. Rosette Brisac, b. 1764, d. 26 Oct 1821, Vantoux, Moselle, France.
52. Louis (Boris, Isaï) Daltroff, b. 1764, d. 2 Jun 1808, Château-Salins, Moselle, France. He married (1) _____ _____. He married (2) Guiton Vormus, b. 1775, Delme, Château-Salins, Moselle, France, d. 4 Nov 1838, Château-Salins, Moselle, France.
53. Guiton Vormus, b. 1775, Delme, Château-Salins, Moselle, France, d. 4 Nov 1838, Château-Salins, Moselle, France. She married (1) Louis (Boris, Isaï) Daltroff, b. 1764, d. 2 Jun 1808, Château-Salins, Moselle, France. She married (2) Godechaux Abraham, b. 1776, d. 24 May 1849.
56. Oury (Feisse) Samuel, b. 14 Apr 1776, Vantoux, Moselle, France. He married Rosette Jacob Morhange.
57. Rosette Jacob Morhange.
58. Raphaël Oury Hayem, b. Abt 1786, d. 26 Nov 1861, Vantoux, Moselle, France. He married Fleurette Francfort, 17 Feb 1813, in Vantoux, Moselle, France.
59. Fleurette Francfort, b. Abt 1784/1794, Vantoux, Moselle, France, d. Abt 1870.
60. Bernard Roubach, b. 1784, Hellimer, Moselle, France, d. 30 Mar 1866, Sarrebourg, Moselle, France. He married Babette Hesse.
61. Babette Hesse.
62. Alexandre Tsaüdike Lévy, b. 1802, Nancy, Meurthe-et-Moselle, France, d. 1887/1890, Nancy, Meurthe-et-Moselle, France. He married Marguerite Weiller.
63. Marguerite Weiller, d. Nancy, Meurthe-et-Moselle, France.

4th Great Grand Parents:

64. Kauffman Fribourg. He married Eve Lévy, 14 Mar 1736, in Boulay, Moselle, France.
65. Eve Lévy.
84. _____ Worms.
106. Louis Vormus. He married Nanette (Brunette) Lévy.
107. Nanette (Brunette) Lévy.

112. Wolf (Salomon) Samuel (Wolff), b. 1738, Mey, Moselle, France, d. 30 dec 1804, Vantoux, Moselle, France. He married Nanette (Jaket Anne) Bernard, 17 May 1767, in Metz, Moselle, France.
113. Nanette (Jaket Anne) Bernard, b. Abt 1738, Bionville, Meurthe/Moselle, France, d. 23 May 1812, Vantoux, Moselle, France.
114. Jacob Olry Morhange, b. Abt 1750. He married Guittelette Créhange, Bef 1777.
115. Guittelette Créhange, b. Abt 1755.
118. Samuel Francfort, b. Abt 1738, Vantoux, Moselle, France, d. 20 Oct 1820, Vantoux, Moselle, France. He married Eve (Hebeul) Fribourg, Abt 1783.
119. Eve (Hebeul) Fribourg, b. Abt 1747, d. 16 Feb 1823, Vantoux, Moselle, France.
122. _____ Hesse.
124. Daniel Lévy, b. 1772, Langatte, Moselle, France, d. 1844, Sarrebourg, Moselle, France.
126. _____ Weiller.

5th Great Grand Parents:

128. Isacq (Isaac) Fribourg, b. Abt 1674, Coume, Moselle, France. He married Calgen _____.
129. Calgen _____.
130. Hayem Lévy.
224. Louis Salomon, b. Abt 1710/1715, Vallières, Moselle, France. He married Madeleine Dalsace.
225. Madeleine Dalsace, b. Abt 1720, Metz, Moselle, France.
236. David Francfort, b. Abt 1710, Vantoux, Moselle, France, d. Abt 1757, Vantoux, Moselle, France. He married Anne David, 9 Jan 1735, in Metz, Moselle, France.
237. Anne David, b. 1715, d. Aft 1755.

6th Great Grand Parents:

448. Salomon Jacob, b. Abt 1680. He married Anne Mayer, Abt 1710.
449. Anne Mayer, b. Abt 1690.
472. Lazard Francfort, b. Abt 1670, Vantoux, Moselle, France, d. Apr 1726, Vantoux, Moselle, France. He married Sara (Dalsace) Lévy, Abt 1694, in Metz, Moselle, France.
473. Sara (Dalsace) Lévy, b. 1675, d. Aft 1742.
474. Alexandre David, b. Abt 1685, Lahnstein, Germany. He married Guittelet Bernkastel.
475. Guittelet Bernkastel, b. Abt 1690.

7th Great Grand Parents:

944. Samuel Francfort, b. Abt 1640, Frankfurt-am-Main, Germany, d. Apr 1715, Vantoux, Moselle, France. He married Merlet Samuel, Bef 1670, in Metz, Moselle, France.
945. Merlet Samuel, b. Abt 1650.

CLAUDE'S ANCESTORS

1. Claudia Georgette Brunschwig, b. 7 Aug 1936, Ixelles, Bruxelles, Belgium. She married Henry August Fribourg, 12 Aug 1956, in Homestead Hotel, Kew Gardens, NYC, USA, b. 10 Mar 1929, Paris 2, Seine, France.

Parents:

2. Max Rudolph Brunschwig, b. 19 May 1905, Basel, Switzerland, d. 23 Oct 1976, Kew Gardens, Queens, New York, NY, buried: Montefiore, Anse Sholom, New, Pinelawn, L.I. He married Simone Caroline Lévi, 10 Oct 1935, in Haguenau, Bas-Rhin, France.
3. Simone Caroline Lévi, b. 11 Mar 1912, Haguenau, Bas-Rhin, France, d. 4 Nov 1982, Jefferson House, Newington, CT, USA, buried: Montefiore, Anse Sholom, New, Pinelawn, L.I.

Grand Parents:

4. Gustav Brunschwig, b. 11 Mar 1869, Durmenach, Haut-Rhin, France, d. 4 Nov 1916, Basel, Switzerland, buried: Basel, Switzerland. He married Marie Nordmann, Abt 1896.
5. Marie Nordmann, b. 28 Aug 1873, Liestal, Basel, Switzerland, d. 3 Jun 1937, Basel, Switzerland, buried: Basel, Switzerland.
6. Léopold Lévi, b. 1872, Haguenau, Bas-Rhin, France, d. 1941, Lyon, Rhône, France, buried: Lyon, Rhône, France. He married Mathilde Wolff, 28 Apr 1907, in Niederbronn, Bas-Rhin, occupied France.
7. Mathilde Wolff, b. 3 Feb 1885, Sarreguemines, Moselle, France, d. 2 May 1969, Croissy-sur-Seine, Yvelines, 78 France, buried: Passy, Paris, Seine, France.

Great Grand Parents:

8. Isaac Brunschwig, b. 29 May 1839, Durmenach, Haut-Rhin, France, d. 19 Jul 1907, Basel, Switzerland, buried: Basel, Switzerland. He married Sarah Meyer.
9. Sarah Meyer, b. 26 Jun 1839, Durmenach, Haut-Rhin, France, d. 19 Jun 1912, Basel, Switzerland, buried: Basel, Switzerland.
10. Emanuel Nordmann, b. 1841, Liestal, Basel, Switzerland, d. 6 Jan 1933, Basel, Switzerland. He married Jeannette Dreyfus.
11. Jeannette Dreyfus, b. 1 Mar 1843, Niederhagenthal, Haut-Rhin, France, d. Basel, Switzerland.
12. _____ Lévy. He married Estelle (Esther) Roth, 1871.
13. Estelle (Esther) Roth, b. 1843, d. 1915.
14. Benjamin Wolff, b. 5 Dec 1844, Sarre-Union, Bas-Rhin, France, d. 1 Feb 1909, Sarre-Union, Bas-Rhin, France. He married (1) Caroline Roth, 1870, b. 1847, Niederbronn, Bas-Rhin, France, d. 23 Nov 1887. He married (2) Léonie Roth, b. 15 May 1848, Niederbronn, Bas-Rhin, France, d. 12 Feb 1926.
15. Caroline Roth, b. 1847, Niederbronn, Bas-Rhin, France, d. 23 Nov 1887.

Great Great Grand Parents:

16. Marcus (Marx) Brunschwig, b. 22 Nov 1806, Durmenach, Haut-Rhin, France, d. 18 Jun 1879. He married Claire (Clearly) (Weill) Weil, 19 Mar 1834, in Neu-Lengnal.
17. Claire (Clearly) (Weill) Weil, b. 24 Dec 1812, Lengnau, Aargau, Switzerland, d. 10 Feb 1874, Durmenach, Haut-Rhin, France.
18. Léopold Meyer, b. 11 Nov 1811, Durmenach, Haut-Rhin, France, d. 25 Oct 1878, Durmenach, Haut-Rhin, France. He married Babette (Pessel) Picard.
19. Babette (Pessel) Picard, b. Abt 1809, Blotzheim, Haut-Rhin, France, d. 1 Sep 1862, Durmenach, Haut-Rhin, France.
20. Bernard (Berle) Nordmann, b. 15 Aug 1808, Hégenheim, Haut-Rhin, France, d. 15 Jan 1888, Paris 10, Seine, France.

He married Joséphine Schwob, 29 Jun 1835, in Hégenheim, Haut-Rhin, France.
21. Joséphine Schwob, b. 19 Apr 1810, Hégenheim, Haut-Rhin, France.
22. Léopold Dreyfus, b. 25 Nov 1796, Niederhagenthal, Haut-Rhin, France. He married Rosine Rueff, 20 Dec 1825, in Niederhagenthal, Haut-Rhin, France.
23. Rosine Rueff, b. 22 Jan 1808, Niederhagenthal, Haut-Rhin, France.
24. Léopold Lévy, b. 1790, d. 1852.
26. Isaï Fesaias Roth, b. 1809, buried: Gunderschoffen, Bas-Rhin, France. He married Jeanette Bernadette Rosenwald.
27. Jeanette Bernadette Rosenwald, b. 1813, Sarre-Union, Bas-Rhin, France, d. 1867, buried: Gunderschoffen, Bas-Rhin, France.
28. Moïse Wolff, b. 20 May 1809, Sarre-Union, Bas-Rhin, France, d. 5 Aug 1886, Sarralbe, Moselle, France. He married Léa Kraemer.
29. Léa Kraemer, b. 1816, d. 19 Dec 1868.
30. Isaï Fesaias Roth, (see same person above in generation 5) b. 1809, buried: Gunderschoffen, Bas-Rhin, France. He married Jeanette Bernadette Rosenwald.
31. Jeanette Bernadette Rosenwald, (see same person above in generation 5) b. 1813, Sarre-Union, Bas-Rhin, France, d. 1867, buried: Gunderschoffen, Bas-Rhin, France.

3rd Great Grand Parents:

32. Moyse Koschel (Gaspard) Brunschwig, b. 1780, Durmenach, Haut-Rhin, France, d. 12 Feb 1814, Durmenach, Haut-Rhin, France. He married Anne (Jeanne, Hanna) Hauser, 5 mar 1798, in Durmenach, Haut-Rhin, France.
33. Anne (Jeanne, Hanna) Hauser, b. 1768, Durmenach, Haut-Rhin, France, d. 28 Jan 1845, Durmenach, Haut-Rhin, France.
34. Marx Isaac Weil, b. 7 Sep 1773, Lengnau, Aargau, Switzerland, d. 3 Jan 1852. He married Frometta Dreyfus, 7 Jul 1805, in Lengnau, Aargau, Switzerland.

I GAVE YOU LIFE TWICE

35. Frometta Dreyfus, b. 25 Mar 1787, Endingen, Aargau, Switzerland, d. 11 Oct 1865, Lengnau, Aargau, Switzerland.
36. Alexandre Meyer, b. 1780, Durmenach, Haut-Rhin, France, d. 30 Apr 1846, Durmenach, Haut-Rhin, France. He married Sara (Sorette, Sorlen) Ducas.
37. Sara (Sorette, Sorlen) Ducas, b. 16 Jul 1781-87, Hattstatt, Haut-Rhin, France, d. 13 May 1836, Durmenach, Haut-Rhin, France.
38. Raphaël Picard, d. 11 Apr 1852, Blotzheim, Haut-Rhin, France. He married Reisele (Rosalie) Lévy.
39. Reisele (Rosalie) Lévy, d. 13 Apr 1852, Blotzheim, Haut-Rhin, France.
40. Benjamin Nordmann, b. 7 Mar 1780, Hégenheim, Haut-Rhin, France, d. 19 Jan 1851, Hégenheim, Haut-Rhin, France. He married Marguerithe (Malka) Didisheim, 3 May 1798, in Hégenheim, Haut-Rhin, France.
41. Marguerithe (Malka) Didisheim, b. 8 Jul 1774, Hégenheim, Haut-Rhin, France, d. 29 Nov 1836, Hégenheim, Haut-Rhin, France.
42. Isaac Schwob. He married Françoise (Fromet) Schmole, 18 Aug 1805, in Hégenheim, Haut-Rhin, France.
43. Françoise (Fromet) Schmole.
44. Meyer Dreyfus, b. 1756, Niederhagenthal, Haut-Rhin, France, d. 27 Feb 1800, Niederhagenthal, Haut-Rhin, France. He married Sara Dreyfus.
45. Sara Dreyfus, b. 1760, Rixheim, Haut-Rhin, France, d. 4 Mar 1814, Niederhagenthal, Haut-Rhin, France.
46. Adam Rueff. He married Marie (Marian) Goetschel (Lévy), 20 Dec 1825, in Niederhagenthal, Haut-Rhin, France.
47. Marie (Marian) Goetschel (Lévy).
56. Jacques Wolff, b. 1783, Metting, Moselle, France, d. Sarre-Union, Bas-Rhin, France, buried: Sarre-Union, Bas-Rhin, France. He married Adelaïde Aron.
57. Adelaïde Aron.
58. Abraham Kraemer, b. Sarre-Union, Bas-Rhin, France. He married Annie Freund.
59. Annie Freund, b. Sarre-Union, Bas-Rhin, France.

Henry Fribourg

4th Great Grand Parents:

64. Marx Mordekhay Brunschwig, b. Blotzheim, Haut-Rhin, France, d. Abt 1806, Blotzheim, Haut-Rhin, France. He married Mariam (Maria Anna, Mariani) Brunschwig, 8 Feb 1762, in Blotzheim, Haut-Rhin, France.
65. Mariam (Maria Anna, Mariani) Brunschwig, b. Blotzheim, Haut-Rhin, France, d. Blotzheim, Haut-Rhin, France.
66. Alexandre Sender Hauser, b. Abt 1705, Durmenach, Haut-Rhin, France, d. 28 Sep 1788, Durmenach, Haut-Rhin, France. He married (1) _____ _____. He married (2) Guitel (Gitta) Jos Hess (Adler), b. Puttelange, Moselle, France, d. 1799, Durmenach, Haut-Rhin, France.
67. Guitel (Gitta) Jos Hess (Adler), b. Puttelange, Moselle, France, d. 1799, Durmenach, Haut-Rhin, France. She married (1) Salomon Aron, b. Phalsbourg, Moselle, France. She married (2) Alexandre Sender Hauser, b. Abt 1705, Durmenach, Haut-Rhin, France, d. 28 Sep 1788, Durmenach, Haut-Rhin, France.
68. Isaac Leman Weil, b. 29 Jan 1738, Lengnau, Aargau, Switzerland, d. 19 Feb 1823. He married Sara Meyer Moos, 14 Nov 1756.
69. Sara Meyer Moos, b. 6 Jul 1740, Hohenems, Vorarlberg, Austria, d. 2 Nov 1824, Lengnau, Aargau, Switzerland.
70. Marx Dreifuss, b. 17 May 1768, d. 19 Aug 1794, Endingen, Aargau, Switzerland. He married Hanna Alexander, 4 Feb 1786.
71. Hanna Alexander, b. 28 Jul 1769, Durmenach, Haut-Rhin, France, d. Endingen, Aargau, Switzerland.
72. Léopold Meyer, b. Bef 1784, d. Abt 1808, Durmenach, Haut-Rhin, France. He married Sara Lévy, Abt 1784.
73. Sara Lévy.
74. Aron (Dockes) Ducas, b. 14 Mar 1755, Hattstatt, Haut-Rhin, France, d. Aft 1799, Hattstatt, Haut-Rhin, France. He married Keyle (Keilen) Lehmann, 28 Jul 1773, in Hattstatt, Haut-Rhin, France.
75. Keyle (Keilen) Lehmann, b. Bef 1773, Niederhagenthal, Haut-Rhin, France, d. Aft 1773.

I GAVE YOU LIFE TWICE

76. Thodor Picard.
80. Joseph Nordmann, b. 25 Jul 1730, Hégenheim, Haut-Rhin, France, d. 19 Jul 1812, Nîmes, Gard, France. He married (1) Zerline Sara Günzburger, 13 Feb 1756, in Hégenheim, Haut-Rhin, France, b. 16 Jul 1735, Zillisheim, Haut-Rhin, France, d. 12 Dec 1802, Hégenheim, Haut-Rhin, France. He married (2) Fayele Ella _____.
81. Zerline Sara Günzburger, b. 16 Jul 1735, Zillisheim, Haut-Rhin, France, d. 12 Dec 1802, Hégenheim, Haut-Rhin, France.
82. Aron Didisheim, b. Abt 1744, Hégenheim, Haut-Rhin, France, d. 28 Jul 1814, Hégenheim, Haut-Rhin, France. He married (1) Sara (Sorlen) Lévy, 1 Jul 1773, in Hégenheim, Haut-Rhin, France, b. 10 Sep 1750, Froeningen, Haut-Rhin, France, d. 17 Mar 1784. He married (2) Barbe (Brendelé) Bloch, 4 Jun 1784, in Hégenheim, Haut-Rhin, France, b. Abt 1763, Mülheim, Grand Duchy of Baden, Germany, d. 10 Mar 1842, Hégenheim, Haut-Rhin, France.
83. Sara (Sorlen) Lévy, b. 10 Sep 1750, Froeningen, Haut-Rhin, France, d. 17 Mar 1784.
112. Abraham Wolff, b. 1738, Metting, Moselle, France.

5th Great Grand Parents:

128. Jacob Jacques Brunschwig. He married Judith Lévy.
129. Judith Lévy.
130. Mechoulam Salomon.
132. Daniel Hauser, b. 1680, d. 1731, Durmenach, Haut-Rhin, France.
134. Mendel Michel Hess, b. Puttelange, Moselle, France. He married Hanna Alexandre.
135. Hanna Alexandre.
138. Maier Moos, d. 1777, Hohenems, Vorarlberg, Austria. He married _____ Hendel.
139. _____ Hendel, b. 1712, d. 1799, Hohenems, Vorarlberg, Austria.
140. Wolf Dreifuss, b. 17 Aug 1742, d. 22 Sep 1808, Endingen, Aargau, Switzerland. He married Lea Moos, 24 Oct 1766.

141. Lea Moos, b. 29 Jun 1745, Hohenems, Vorarlberg, Austria, d. 3 Sep 1820, Endingen, Aargau, Switzerland.
148. Judas Leib Dockes. He married Vogel _____.
149. Vogel _____.
150. Lehmann Eliezer.
160. Jacob (Iekel) Nordmann, d. Hégenheim, Haut-Rhin, France. He married Fayele Ella _____.
161. Fayele Ella _____. She married (1) Joseph Nordmann, b. 25 Jul 1730, Hégenheim, Haut-Rhin, France, d. 19 Jul 1812, Nîmes, Gard, France. She married (2) Jacob (Iekel) Nordmann, d. Hégenheim, Haut-Rhin, France.
162. Mosche Güntzburger, b. Zillisheim, Haut-Rhin, France. He married Breinel (Brune) Bernheim.
163. Breinel (Brune) Bernheim.
164. Bernard (Bär Issachar) Diedisheim, d. 10 Dec 1789. He married (1) Madel Reinau, Aft 23 Aug 1745, in Habsheim, Haut-Rhin, France, b. Soultz, Haut-Rhin, France, d. 25 Jun 1773. He married (2) Bessel Lévy, Aft 9 Oct 1774, in Hégenheim, Haut-Rhin, France, b. Niederhagenthal, Haut-Rhin, France. He married (3) Reichelé Bloch, Bef Oct 1784.
165. Madel Reinau, b. Soultz, Haut-Rhin, France, d. 25 Jun 1773.
166. Jitzhok Itzig Lévy, b. Froeningen, Haut-Rhin, France.

6th Great Grand Parents:

256. Salomon Brunschwig, b. Blotzheim, Haut-Rhin, France, d. Blotzheim, Haut-Rhin, France.
260. Nesanel Zalmen.
264. David? Hauser.
276. Albrecht Gumper Moos, d. Abt 1769, Hohenems, Vorarlberg, Austria.
280. Michel Dreifuss, b. 24 Aug 1721, d. 25 Oct 1806, Endingen, Aargau, Switzerland. He married Hanna Wolf, 22 Mar 1740.
281. Hanna Wolf, b. 9 May 1713, d. 18 May 1814, Alt Breisach, Baden, Germany.
296. Eliezer Dockes.
320. Hetz (Nephtali) Nordmann, d. 1717, Hégenheim, Haut-Rhin, France.326. Benjamin Bernheim.

328. Aaron Diedisheim, d. 1735, Hégenheim, Haut-Rhin, France. He married Malka ____.
329. Malka ____, d. 1722.
330. Jekel Reinau.

7th Great Grand Parents:

512. Nesanel Samuel Brunschwig.
552. Moses Koschel Moos, d. Hohenems, Vorarlberg, Austria.
560. Getsch Dreifuss, b. Endingen, Aargau, Switzerland.
562. ____ Wolf, b. Alt Breisach, Baden, Germany.
640. Jeckel Nordmann, d. Apr 1693, Hégenheim, Haut-Rhin, France. He married Zerla ____.
641. Zerla ____, d. 1711.
656. Bernard Diedisheim. He married Miriam ____.
657. Miriam ____, d. 1721.

8th Great Grand Parents:

1024. Raphaël Brunschwig, b. 1675, Blotzheim, Haut-Rhin, France, d. 1745, Blotzheim, Haut-Rhin, France.
1280. Nephtali Nordmann.

זכרונם לברכה
(Zichronam Livrachah)

MAY THEIR MEMORIES BE A BLESSING

At the same time as I was searching documentary evidence for my genealogical endeavors in the 1990s, I contacted many living relatives whose whereabouts had become known to me. It was then that I realized the enormity of the impact that the Holocaust had had on Claude's and my family. I now list the names of all those known in both families to have been murdered by the Third Reich.

Murdered at Auschwitz

Roland Bercovici
Moïse Besman
Eugène Bloch
Jeanne Brunschwig
Marie-Anne Didisheim
Gilberte Ditisheim
Mathilde Dreyfus
Lucie Ach Fribourg
Marc Haguenau
Maurice Hauser
Caroline Lévy
René Lévy
Léon Samuel
Claude Salomon Samuel
Armand Simon
Gabrielle Clara Simon
Raymond Strauss
Lucie Wertheimer
Germaine Bernard
Henri Blatt
Eugène Fernand Blum
Esther Eva Cahen
Léon Diedisheim
Marguerite Dreyfus
Odette Elina
Judith Goldenstein
Léopold Achille Hauser
Hélène Kahn
Claude Lévy
Hélène Nordman
Claude Samuel
Madeleine Joseph Samuel
Berthe Irma Simon
Johanna Simon
Arthur Joseph Weill
Jean Wimphen

Henry Fribourg

Deported to unknown destination
    Lucien Blum   Gustave Cohen
    Jean Cohen   Robert David
    Jeanne Diedisheim   Albert Dreyfus
    Pierre Dreyfus   Pauline Hirtz
    Pélagie Kahn   René Libman
    ____ Weil   Jean Weiller
    Jules Wolff   Rolande ____

Murdered somewhere in Crimea
    Marousia Bezman and three brothers

Murdered at Birkenau
    Jean Wimphen

Murdered at Buchenwald
    Henri Hirsch

Murdered at Sobibor
    Simone (Adèle) Levaillant   Pierre Nordmann

Murdered at Kaunas, Lithuania
    Simon Pierre Dreyfus

Killed in Action
    Paul Georges David   ____Diamant-Berger
    Rolland Silva

Member of French Resistance, tortured and shot
    Edmond Bloch

TRAVELING THE WORLD FOR AGRONOMY AND FOR ME

    Many of the trips I have taken were reimbursed partly or entirely by my employer when attending professional meetings or consulting overseas. During these trips, I may have taken some days of accumulated leave time to do some sightseeing. In later years, Claude accompanied me on many of these trips, naturally at our expense. We also did some traveling not connected to professional activities, sometimes before or after a meeting, or during vacations with the family or after I retired.

    One of the aims in writing about these numerous trips is to illustrate for future generations the extent to which our lives in the second half of the 20th century have been so different from those of our own grandparents and their ancestors. I cannot dismiss the thought that what we deem extensive travels in our age may be considered parochial and insignificant by future generations. I will show that, in our age, it became commonplace to travel all over the world for play and work. This is in contrast to my grandparents' travels. They hardly ever ventured beyond the frontiers of France, although in their younger years my maternal grandparents Oury did live in Vienna, and Grand-Père Lucien Oury had gone to Great Britain for an apprenticeship in his youth. I remember conversations between my parents and grandparents when allusions were made to the upheaval that followed the defeat of France by the Germans in the War of 1870-71, resulting in the Boches forcibly annexing Alsace and Lorraine. Within a decade or two, my great-grandparents left their ancestral homes in Lorraine and Alsace to establish residence in France. As far as I am aware, though, this westward move of 150 to 250 km (90 to 160 miles) was the furthest they ever had or would travel. Their parents, my great-great-grandparents, probably never ventured beyond a day's ride from their home, except for those men who volunteered for or were pressed into military service.

Claude and Henry, 40 years married

NORTH AMERICA

When Daniel and Renée were young, we camped all over the continent. From unsolicited statements that each one has made over the years since then, it is clear that they enjoyed these trips and remember them fondly. At first, we carried a tent and other equipment in a small utility trailer in the rear of which I had built a "kitchen." We camped in many national forests and parks, mostly in the Appalachian Mountains. We particularly enjoyed the magnificent trees of the Joyce Kilmer Forest and the higher elevations of the Great Smoky Mountains. In 1967, we went to the Montreal Expo and camped in a mosquito-infested meadow on the outskirts of town. A couple of years later, we camped all the way around the Gaspé Peninsula, a beautiful area, and observed the high tides of the Bay of Fundy. On another trip to Canada, we went to Hudson Bay and Moosinee.

Daniel and Renée tent camping in the Joyce Kilmer Forest, 1967

In 1970, the American Society of Agronomy held its annual meeting at the University of Arizona in Tucson. We rented a small pop-up tent trailer and camped our way to the Rocky Mountains with our new Oldsmobile 88, the first car we ever had with air conditioning. After topping the pass, we headed in extremely hot weather toward what later became Dinosaur Park. We visited the Great Salt Lake and its Tabernacle, Mesa Verde and its cliff dwellings, Four Corners and the Navajo reservation, Glen Canyon Lake and the Grand Canyon, El Paso and Ciudad Juarez. In that city, I bargained for and purchased the large Mexican copper sun tray that adorns our living room.

I have been able to visit many places in the United States, either in connection with meetings or during vacations, and I have been at least once in each of the fifty states. My favorites are rural New England in summer, San Francisco in the spring, New Orleans in wintertime. The Pacific Northwest is very nice, and Claude and I enjoyed a 3-week tour of Alaska in June 1996. A helicopter overview of Denali Park and the two days we visited there will be remembered with pleasure. Driving trips to Seward and Homer were memorable, as well as the train ride from Skagway up to Dead Horse Gulch on the route up to the Yukon gold fields, and the 3-day cruise from Juneau to Glacier Bay. On the way to Homer, we stopped at Anchor Point, where I was successful in locating my 1948 roommate in Madison, Wisconsin. Ed Liebenthal had been a Pacific theater veteran from an impoverished Wisconsin family of many children. He used the G.I. Bill to learn about scientific agriculture and after graduation, homesteaded in Alaska. He had also worked as an agricultural county agent—his territory included the Kenai Peninsula and the entire Aleutian island chain! We had a very nice visit with him at his homesteaded farm, and with his son and his daughter-in-law.

Claude and I have traveled the Gulf Coast from southern Texas to Key West, the Atlantic coast from Miami to Maine, the Pacific coast in Washington, Oregon, and Big Sur, and many places in between. In 1994, while on our way to a professional meeting, we visited Seattle, a beautiful city, the spectacular Columbia River valley, and the very impressive post-eruption Mt. St. Helens. In 1990, on our return from an autumn meeting in the very attractive city of San Antonio, we spent several days in Cajun country, staying in French-speaking bed-and-breakfast homes.

We have also enjoyed several Elderhostels which provided one- to two-week educational experiences in relaxed environments, such as on Tybee Island near Savannah; on St. Simon Island, where John Wesley determined he liked the Indians and the mosquitoes less than the comforts of 17th century England; at Whispering Pines, Eisenhower's retreat in the wilds of Rhode Island not far from Newport; and at a dude ranch in the Davis Mountains of West Texas in December 1993 - January 1994, providing us an excuse to visit the grandiose but arid Great Bend country. There is one thing of which we are certain: although we have enjoyed all our travels, it is always satisfying to return to the green hills and valleys of East Tennessee, our home.

In Canada, we have enjoyed our trips to Québec in 1956, 1967, and 1971, and our visit to the Maritime provinces in 1967. In 1971, when we camped in Ontario, in the woods north of Lake Superior, we all four had an eerie experience, hearing wild wolves baying at night. We also had a very nice week in 1992 when, after an animal science meeting in Spokane, Claude and I went to Calgary for a day at the Stampede, and then drove to Banff and Jasper. The spectacular Lake Louise, where we stayed at THE (expensive) hotel, we shall always remember, as well as driving and walking on glaciers on our way north to Jasper from there. In 1996, after our vacation in Alaska, we spent a week in Vancouver, British Columbia, at an American Forage and Grassland Council meeting. The city is beautiful and the surrounding area well cared for in an environmentally conscious and productive manner. I was pleased to observe that, for British Columbia was an area that I had considered investigating to obtain employment in the mid 1970s, before the American government finally abandoned its Vietnam war.

Although I did not participate in the demonstrations against the US involvement in Vietnam, I was unequivocally opposed to that ignominious activity foisted upon us by arrogant and misguided politicians ignorant of history, such as Lyndon Johnson, Robert McNamara, Richard Nixon and Henry Kissinger. I had resolved that, if the war appeared to continue beyond 1977, I would discuss with my family a move to Canada, so that our son Daniel would not be subject to being drafted for participation in that abomination. In June 1997, we attended the 18th IGC in Winnipeg, Manitoba, an interesting and clean city on the banks of the Red River. With friends, we drove through the limitless plains to the shores of Lake Winnipeg, and learned much about the settling of the area by people from numerous ethnic backgrounds.

LATIN AMERICA (mostly)

In 1965, the IXth IGC, held usually once every four years, was scheduled to occur in São Paulo. I went there to present a paper, and took the opportunity to visit several other countries in Latin America. At the IGC, I was able to arrange visits with several forage workers in other Brazilian states, or other countries: Porto Alegre and several places in Rio Grande do Sul; La Estanzuela, a large research ranch in Uruguay run by the FAO of the UN; research laboratories west of Buenos Aires (INTA) and the research station at Pergamino, in the pampa; several locations around Lima, Peru; and the Inter-American Institute of Agricultural Sciences at Turrialba near San José, Costa

Rica. Although this trip was enjoyable and instructive, I decided that extended trips in the future would, if at all possible, include my wife, for I was lonely for her company and knew she would like the travels as well as I did.

Claude and I have been several times to Puerto Rico. Following a forage conference in the late 1960s, we spent a week exploring the island by car, from the rain forest in the northeast to the phosphorescent bay nestled in the arid southwest. In 1977, the whole family stopped there for a short while on our way to a 1-week vacation in the US Virgin Islands. Claude and I returned to St. Croix on our first Earthwatch expedition, where we measured leatherback turtles as they came ashore at night to lay their eggs. We walked the beach all night to locate the animals, and usually found two to four of the females each night. If necessary, we relocated the nests so that the eggs would not be washed out by the tide, and prevented poaching by Puerto Ricans in search of powerful aphrodisiacs reputedly contained in the eggs.

We went on three other Earthwatch expeditions, finding these two-week periods of constructive activity in a novel environment preferable to idleness in a tourist mecca. In 1984, we participated in an archaeological expedition near Syracuse, NY, in the Mohawk Valley. We helped excavate several "big houses" of former Mohawk villages for an investigator attempting to trace the movement of white traders through the glass beads they sold or gave away, and relate these incursions to the advent of epidemics and devastating decreases in native populations. The next year, we lived in Woods Hole, on Cape Cod, for two weeks, helping characterize the fauna and flora of tidal marshes being affected by municipal pollution.

In the late 1980s, the dean of the Graduate School at UT had initiated a program of free courses for faculty members who wished to expand their foreign language skills. In 1995, Portuguese was offered for the first time. Although I had been to Brasil twice, and once to Portugal, I did not consider myself capable of articulating my thoughts correctly in Portuguese. I decided to take this course, meeting twice a week for a one- and-a-half hour conversational class each time. After a month, the 14 beginners were split off with another instructor. I had the advanced class all to myself with my teacher, Manolisa Vasconcelos, a native of Fortaleza, in the state of Ceará,

Brasil. As a recompense for my assiduous study and rapid progress, the dean offered to provide me with a round trip ticket to Brasil so that I could practice my new knowledge for at least three weeks. I bought a ticket for Claude, and we were off to Fortaleza. I attended a week-long meeting of the Animal Science Society of Brasil, and had my room and board expenses paid by a grant through the agricultural development corporation of Ceará. We had an interesting time in the city and vicinity, going to and admiring the frequenters of its beaches, and watching and listening to an August (winter) version of *carnaval*, rather than the real thing that is held in February.

In the fall of 2002, Claude and I participated in our first international Elderhostel, in Costa Rica. It was supposed to be a program for North Americans to learn the geography, history and culture of this beautiful country, a true democracy since shortly after World War II, when the Costa Ricans abolished their military and used the money thus saved exclusively for education. A group of a dozen of us, traveling in a van, had an outstanding trip throughout the country, visiting for two or three days each in the high plateau and the capital of San José and vicinity; going up to two volcanoes; spending some time in the sea-level rain forest and, in Claude's case, socializing with the monkeys while gliding on a seat hung from a cable strung between tree tops; and visiting small towns and observing rural landscapes and their beautiful birds.

At the end of the Elderhostel, Claude and I flew to Panama City to spend almost a week in that country. We took a trip in a 20-meter (65-ft) 75-passenger schooner for the entire length of the Panama Canal. Having earlier read the David McCullough book that recounts the entire history of the creation of the Panama Canal, including the difficulties encountered by the French and subsequently by the Americans in building this engineering marvel, we did appreciate the achievement. We took several other trips to visit historical sites. A notable excursion took us by dugout canoe to an Indian village in the rain forest, where we ate a lunch of fried fish and plaintain, and Claude joined our boat handler, clad in his beads and loin cloth, in a festive village dance.

Henry Fribourg

TURKEY

Starting in the late 1960s, I had been searching for opportunities to design a program that would allow me to develop professionally, expand my knowledge of international agriculture, and provide employment for up to a year away from Tennessee. The University of Tennessee has never had a sabbatical program. Although many people think all university professors can have these opportunities to learn and refresh themselves, in fact these programs are limited to a very few universities. At UT, we had to find and obtain our own individual sources of study and support. In late 1972, I learned that Atatürk Üniversitesi, in Erzurum, Turkey, was looking for an American crop ecologist to teach for one year. This position was to be under the aegis of the US/Turkey Fulbright program, directed from Ankara. I learned that the University of Nebraska had been instrumental in founding and helping organize the College of Agriculture (Ziraat Fakültesi) of Atatürk Üniversitesi from 1958 to 1968. Many of the Turkish faculty members had degrees from Nebraska. In March, I applied for the one-year Senior Fulbright Lectureship through the Washington, D.C. office of the Bilateral Commission on Cultural Exchanges. In mid-June, I was notified that I had been selected and was expected to be in Istanbul on September 1 for a 2-week orientation.

July was a busy month. We found a renter for our home, packed the more delicate objets d'art for storage, studied Turkish grammar and vocabulary, read up on Turkish history and culture, and bought a VW fastback car for delivery in Belgium. Our son Daniel had been studying all year in preparation for his *Bar Mitzvah*, which was scheduled for July 27. He had been looking forward to it, and his grandparents were planning to come for the ceremony. Claude and I were determined that nothing should interfere with the *Bar Mitzvah*, and nothing did.

Four days later, on August 1, the four of us left on our great adventure, flying to Bruxelles (Brussels). The children were very excited about this undertaking. Daniel was almost 13, and Renée almost 11, perfect ages for adventure and travel, without too many regrets about leaving friends at home, as older teenagers might have.

We picked up our bright yellow car in Belgium and spent August driving to Turkey via Paris, and Turino, Roma, Napoli, Bari in Italy. We stopped for a couple of days to become acquainted with Jean and Josette Samuel, their children Madeleine and Jean Michel, and his father André, my great uncle on my mother's side, in Le Cheylard (Ardèche). In Bari, we took the ferry to Petras, Greece, driving on to the Isthmus of Corinth, Athens, Thessaloniki (Salonika), and finally Istanbul. In Istanbul, the half-dozen Fulbright lecturers starting out that fall, and their families, had Turkish language instruction every morning, and learned about history, culture, etc...by on-site visits in the afternoon. In mid-September, we drove to Ankara where we spent a week.

Part of the week was spent in discovering our way around the capital city and learning much about Turkey in an orientation process at the Turkish Fulbright office. Hüsnü Bey (*bey* is a term of respect for a gentleman, used after the first name, and is not a last name), a retired Turkish Army lieutenant colonel, was the Secretary of the Turkish Fulbright Commission. He was widely read and traveled, and also was an inexhaustible fount of information about his country. He tried to prepare us for our forthcoming stay in the eastern, less advanced part of Turkey. About half of our stay in Ankara had to be spent by me in becoming acquainted with the Turkish government bureaucracy, navigating the innumerable offices that would authorize the temporary immigration of my car. Hüsnü Bey's secretary helped me, I could not possibly have been successful without her help. Eventually, we did get all 17 necessary documents bearing the 23 required signatures, including some indelibly entered in my personal passport! The latter entries would ensure that, when I wanted to leave the country, the car would accompany me—otherwise departure would be forbidden. The impetus for this inflexible rule was to deter the illegal smuggling of cars in the country, and the accompanying depletion of scarce resources of hard currency.

In late September, we drove to Sinop, on the shores of the Black Sea, where we visited at the home of a UT food science M.S. graduate involved in a poultry and egg operation. We then followed the shores of the Black Sea to Trabzon, where Jason reputedly searched for the Golden Fleece. Unfortunately, all we found was a two-star hotel where the toilets did not function. The drive from

Trabzon up a winding narrow dirt road to the Anatolian plateau (*Anadolu*) was scary, but we eventually reached Erzurum at its elevation of 2,300 meters (7,000 ft), at the eastern end of a lacustrine glacial 20 x 15 km (12 x 9 miles) valley surrounded by 3,700-m (11,000-ft) mountains. Erzurum had been one of the outposts of the Roman Empire, as implied in the name of the city. We did find an old Roman coin in a cave we explored in spring 1974. When we arrived in Erzurum, the quarter-million population was conservatively Sunni Islamic and many adults were illiterate. I learned later, however, that primary education was universal, even in the most remote villages.

The university campus, on the western outskirts of the city, was modern concrete and steel. We were housed comfortably on the second floor of one of the numerous 3-story apartment buildings constructed for the faculty. Sometimes, western and traditional values clashed. For example, during the *Kurban Bayram*, a holy day which commemorates the binding of Ishmaël by Abraham—the Muslim version of the Judaic binding of Isaac—it is customary for persons who can afford it to slaughter livestock ritually, giving the cooked meat away later on to poor neighbors. Imagine our surprise when, a month after we moved in to our apartment, our neighbors lifted a sheep on their shoulder, carrying the animal up to their third-floor apartment, to cut its throat in the bathtub!

After settling in, I reported for work at the Tarla Bitkileri Bölümü (Plant Science Department). Some of my new colleagues welcomed me warmly. Others, for political, ideological, or religious reasons, would have nothing to do with me, even to the extent of not talking to me during the extended morning and afternoon tea breaks, at least at first. After a while, I figured out some of the historical perspective that guided my hosts, but about which I had been ignorant. During the first ten years of the existence of the university, about 50 different University of Nebraska faculty members had each spent two or more years in Erzurum. Most of these were in the College of Agriculture and known to me either personally or through their professional activities. However, whenever I met a new Turkish colleague, inquiries as to whom I knew at Nebraska centered on only two individuals, always the same two. I was extremely puzzled by that, until I found out, through an offhand remark, that these two were the only ones who had made a conscious effort to learn Turkish history, culture and language. This knowledge motivated me even more than I already was in reading about Turkey and learning how to speak Turkish. It took some effort, but eventually I was able to converse haltingly with colleagues, farmers, waiters and hotel clerks. This illustrated to me how serious the arrogance and cultural insularity of some of my compatriots can be when engaged in work or play abroad. This arrogance was demonstrated when I read the report of a former head of the University of Nebraska contingent, where he had written, after spending four years in Erzurum: "We could have made much faster progress in building up the program if the Turks had learned English faster."

My counterpart, Çoskun Köycü, had obtained an M.S. at Nebraska. He spoke English quite well and acted as my interpreter, guide, and mentor. He was supposed to learn all he could from me, since after my departure, he would be responsible for teaching Crop Ecology. I delivered three lectures a week, one English sentence at a time, with Çoskun Bey's interpretation into Turkish following my enunciation. Students were handed copies of my notes, previously translated to Turkish. It took both of us all week to get this work done. I wrote an article in the Journal of Agronomic Education in which I presented my understanding and evaluation of the Turkish educational system.

We were determined to be good representatives of our country. Unless we were shut out by Turks for political reasons, we made many friends. We were able to communicate in English with about a third of the faculty members, and French or German were helpful with another third. Social interactions occurred in each other's apartments, or at the Faculty Club where, each Friday evening, there was a banquet and dance.

While we were in Erzurum, Claude was busy meeting with neighbors, doing some free tutoring for the faculty wives who had accompanied their husbands in Nebraska and wished to improve their English, and supervising our children's schooling. Every day, several hours were reserved for this activity. Both children were enrolled in the Calvert school system, a correspondence school that many American diplomats and other US persons working overseas employ for their children when local schools are not desired. Both Daniel and Renée had specified books to read, assignments to complete, and written examinations to send back to the States. Consequently, they were able to resume school in Knoxville without any problem after our return.

Whenever there was a vacation, we would go off on a trip. During our year in Turkey, we drove over 40,000 km (25,000 miles), omitting only the southeastern mountainous Kürdish area, where the roads were poor and the region deemed unsafe. We visited prehistoric sites, 10,000-year old ruins and an Armenian monastery near Van, 2,000-year old archaeological digs at Troy, Ephesus, and Antioch, Crusader castles along the Mediterranean coast, whirling dervishes at Konya, Orthodox Christian worshiping caves in Cappadoccia, the Opera House in Ankara, Topkap2 Palace and Ha ya Sophia (meaning Holy Wisdom, not Saint Sophie) in Istanbul, the precipitous hills of Gallipoli, Turkish tobacco and sunflower fields in European Turkey. We saw nomadic women picking up the cooking fuel for next month after their camels had passed by and defecated, 6-year old 200-kg (450-lb) starving cows, innumerable sheep and goats, young women in miniskirts accompanied by their mothers in traditional dresses and their grandmothers with gunny sacks over their heads. Daniel and Renée received an education not available in books. We all four will always remember this unique year in our family life.

Winter weather in Erzurum is severe, with night-time temperatures often reaching down to -30 C (-30 F). We used an electric light bulb at the end of a long (it had to reach from the second floor to the dirt area used for parking by the front door) extension cord to keep the car engine warm enough that it would start the next morning. I learned the hard way that the engine should be turned over every single day, whether or not a storm was blowing. The apartment buildings on campus were a few hundred meters apart, separated by bare ground on which rested huge mounds of soft coal for the heating furnaces in each basement. In the winter, wolves were attracted to the easy pickings in garbage cans. The night guards patrolling the grounds would constantly blow their whistles, to warn wolves and human intruders away, and to reassure each other of their colleagues' nearby presence. To escape these conditions during the month-long vacation between the fall and the spring semesters, I had arranged to be invited by the Fulbright Commission in Yugoslavia. One of my former students, Djurdjica Vasilj, was a corn breeder on the faculty of the University of Zagreb in Croatia.

YUGOSLAVIA

In late January, we drove from Erzurum to Ankara, Istanbul, and the Bulgarian border, en route to Beograd (Belgrade). After a thorough search of our car by border police, including the spare tire, we crossed into Bulgaria. After several attempts at obtaining a hotel room for the night, we understood that our visa allowed us only to cross the country along a specific highway. Only hotels directly on this highway were allowed to take us in. However, since this was not the tourist season, none of these hotels was open, and it was forbidden for us to stop at a hotel in a town just one or two km off the highway. We drove all night to traverse "hospitable" Bulgaria, and recovered the next day at a hostelry just over the border in Yugoslavia.

We spent a long weekend in Beograd, enjoying the gourmet food in the Old City, where only pedestrian traffic was allowed. The best restaurants all served Turkish food only! This practice dates back to the days of their subjugation in the Ottoman Empire. We also went to Friday evening services in the Grand Synagogue, where a minuscule remnant, less than twenty persons, of a once-vibrant community was trying a comeback. We were able to communicate because I could understand their Ladino language and they could understand my Spanish. The four of us were quite depressed after we left, for all the attendees were elderly and it appeared to us that it was unlikely that this congregation would regain its vitality. Such was the destruction of European Jewry wrought by the Germans. On Saturday, we went to the Opera, where we heard Boris Godunov sung in Russian. This was the first time our children had attended an opera performance, and they enjoyed it.

We were welcomed in Zagreb by Djurdjica and her husband. It was obvious that life was not easy in this semi-Communist country, both because of the ever-present police and informers and the numerous queues at food stores. I was kept busy lecturing on statistics and computers, and traveling to Novi Sad and Ljubljana in Slovenia. While in Zagreb, we went for a memorable 5-day trip to Wien (Vienna) where we found a bed-and-breakfast in the old city.

We had a coffee *mit schlag* at the Café Mozart, across from the opera, and then heard *The Magic Flute*, sung in German. To this day, Daniel speaks well of that musical performance, so different from the more modern music that he usually fancies. We visited the Spanish Stables, the Schönbrunn Palace, the banks of the Blue Danube (which was brown), Cathedral St. Stephens, and many other sights.

Upon return to Zagreb, we experienced La Bohème sung in Serbo-Croatian at the local opera house, and again the children enjoyed an opera. I must admit, however, that in later years, they have favored more loudly contemporaneous musical works. In late February, we drove along the vineyards overlooking the Adriatic on our way to Split and Dubrovnik. Little did we realize that just a few years later, these beautiful cities would be reduced to rubble by civil war. We then pushed on to Titograd and skirted Albania by driving to Skopje where we noted we had returned to the Islamic world. On this trip, in contrast with our earlier lightning visit to Athens, we stayed several days in this historic city. We climbed the Acropolis to visit the Parthenon and other remnants of the Greek civilization of two millennia ago.

At the end of the second semester, we left Erzurum to take a vacation trip on our way west to Izmir. We had a restful weekend in Pammukkale (cotton castle) where we enjoyed the warm spring waters at which the Romans had erected still-standing bath-houses. We took the ferry to Venezia (Venice) where we enjoyed several days of sightseeing, before driving to Paris. On the way, we spent a few days in Sion, Switzerland, with Gert Rothschild, his wife Marlyse, and their two daughters, sleeping at their vacation chalet and hiking in the Alps during the day. We then visited Alsace and Lorraine; unfortunately, we had not enough time to do the region justice and decided that we would have to return later. Nonetheless, we found the small hamlet of Fribourg not too far from Nancy (Meurthe-et-Moselle). It was only much later, during my genealogical research, that I determined there was no apparent link, at least during the last three and a half centuries, between this village name and my family name. We flew back home from Paris, the car following on a freighter to Jacksonville.

I GAVE YOU LIFE TWICE

Daniel, Renée, her friend Raggedy Ann, and me at entrance to village of Fribourg, near Nancy in Lorraine, 1975

VISITING FRIENDS IN JAPAN

After Renée had started grade school, Claude began teaching French at the private college preparatory Webb School in Knoxville, first on a part-time basis, and then full-time. A couple of years after our return from Turkey, not willing to put up with the continuing discipline problems and lack of interest of many of the male students, she became a teacher of English as a Second Language (ESL). In this capacity, she made many friends from numerous countries during their stay in Knoxville. When I learned in 1982 that the first IGC to be held in Asia was scheduled to convene in 1985 in Kyoto, Japan, I decided to try to learn enough Japanese to not be completely illiterate and dependent upon travel guides. Claude made arrangements to have us invited for home stays at her former students' homes in their country.

After three years of hard study, five one-hour classes a week, each accompanied by two to three hours of homework, I had learned enough Japanese to be the equivalent of a poor third or fourth grade student. I knew only about 800 *Kanji* (Chinese) characters, in addition to the two 135-character syllabaries. Fortunately, that was sufficient for us to be able to find our way, decipher some directional signs and identify some items on menus.

Before attending the Congress, Claude and I flew to Hong Kong. After a few days in that thriving metropolis, we joined a group of other grasslanders for a tour of southern China. We not only visited tourist attractions in Macao and Kwangtung (Guangdong) province and its capital city (Canton), such as Sun Yat-Sen's original home, but also were able to walk into several villages and observe agricultural operations from close up. Although I was familiar with dense throngs in cities such as New York, nothing had prepared me for the density of people in Chinese cities and, even more so, in rural landscapes such as the Pearl River delta.

After attending the IGC in Kyoto, we joined a professional tour of Hokkaido to observe this northernmost large island and its agriculture modeled by returning Japanese graduate students on that of Wisconsin, where they had studied. We also visited the *Aïnu* culture on the volcanic eastern side, a remnant of the inhabitants that preceded the current Japanese residents of the island. We then flew to Sendai on Honshu island where, from there on, we stayed for several days at each of Claude's friends at different places. We learned to sleep on *futon*s on the floor of 10- or 12-bamboo mat guestrooms, and to eat exclusively Japanese home and restaurant cooking. We spent several days each in Sendai, Tokyo, Osaka, Kobe, and in the outskirts of Fukuoka. Invariably, we were treated with consideration and much courtesy by our hosts who went out of their way to make our visits pleasant and instructive.

TEACHING IN FRANCE

In the early 1980s, contact between a private university-level agricultural school, the Institut Supérieur d'Agriculture (ISA) in Lille and UT had been established after a representative from the Université Catholique had visited the US in search of potential student and faculty exchanges. Eventually, sixteen of their students came to Knoxville to do research for six months each and write their senior theses. Two of their faculty members came for 3-month teaching stays. In 1986, I was invited to become a member of their instructional faculty in September through December. Although I knew the subject matter, teaching in French exclusively was a new, demanding but enjoyable challenge. Both students and faculty were surprised that an "American" could speak French without any noticeable foreign accent. However, I frequently had to remind them that, as an American-educated scientist, I did not think the same way that they did, and this diversity of approach became apparent in many lively discussions. They had been taught to follow the Cartesian philosophical approach, and often they would apply previously-determined principles to specific situations. In contrast, my approach was to consider each situation and, buttressing my arguments with fundamental principles, arrive at a conclusion applicable to the specific situation. All of us benefitted from these exchanges, and my success was reflected in the warm personal relationships that developed during our stay and during subsequent visits in both of our countries.

Claude and I lived in the house of a faculty member who was away for the year. We made many friends, and lived pretty much as the French did. We were treated extremely well by our colleagues and had many social interactions with them and their families during the week. I was able to purchase a used car with a loan from ISA. The loan was repaid when the automobile agency that sold me the used car bought it back, as agreed, a couple of days before our departure.

That transportation made it possible for us to explore France and Belgium during weekends and vacations. One weekend, we took a night sleeping train to Basel, to spend a couple of days in Gert and Marlyse Rothschild's home in Basel. We later had a great time visiting the Pas-de-Calais département and Dunkerque (Nord); Normandie and St. Malo (Ile-et-Vilaine); the *menhirs* (upright prehistoric stone monuments) in Brittany; the vineyards near Bordeaux; the snowy passes through the Pyrénées to Andorra; friends near Perpignan in the Roussillon; Nîmes; our cousins in Ardèche, Paris and Bruxelles; Fontainebleau; and a memorable trip to many of the châteaus along the Loire River. It was in this autumn of 1986 that I finally became acquainted with the country of my birth, at least its historical, geographical, and architectural heritage. It also became clear to me that, after all these years, I did not approach problems or think like a Frenchman, but indeed as an American (of European origin).

Henry Fribourg

HELPING SUB-SAHARAN COUNTRIES

In 1977, I was approached by a representative of a University of Michigan unit that was conducting development activities on behalf of the US Agency for International Development (AID). I was asked to be member of a 2-person team to evaluate an agricultural research, teaching, and development proposal in the République Populaire de la Guinée. I considered this offer as a great opportunity to become acquainted with sub-Saharan countries and agriculture, and to again satisfy the altruistic urges I had to help peoples less fortunate than I have been. I agreed to go to Guinea for about five weeks. The other member of the team was Jesse Williams, a dairy specialist from the University of Minnesota with considerable experience in underdeveloped countries such as India and Nepal, where he had worked for several years.

Our mission was to develop a plan that could be implemented by the Guineans with supervision and financing from the US. It was obviously a political lure for Ahmed Sékou Touré, the former postman who was the Communist despot in charge, to moderate his extreme left-leaning concepts. Our plans were to include the modernization of a large and essentially abandoned agricultural experiment station established and operated for many years by the French before they were expelled from the country in 1958. We were also to provide for an agricultural college and for an extension-demonstration farm. Our plans were accepted by the State Department for a projected cost of over seven million dollars. By the time the plans were mostly implemented, a decade or so later, inflation and graft had increased the project cost to 35 million dollars.

It was an unexpected revelation to me that the educated francophone agriculturists with whom I spoke privately clearly wanted to improve their country and lessen the misery of so many of their countrymen. They felt constrained by the political climate. Maybe later, after Ahmed Sékou Touré died, they were able to put some of their ideas into practice. I was impressed that they did not appear to desire mostly to advance their own personal status. This was clearly in contrast with the impressions I had received from many of the Turkish intellectuals I had met just a few years earlier, because of the different cultural system in which they had to survive. In

Turkey, the only way that a faculty member could receive any increase in pay was by being promoted to a higher faculty rank. As I understood the situation, research productivity and teaching merit carried considerably less weight than success in passing oral subjective promotion examinations and appropriate social cultivation of one's superiors.

Having seen the *favelas* (waterless hillside slums) of Rio de Janeiro and Lima, the *gecekondu* (similar slums "built overnight") of Ankara, the *köylar* (villages) of eastern Anatolia, and the sweltering villages of equatorial Africa, I thought I had seen the depths to which human misery could descend. Nonetheless, I was not prepared for the poverty and misery that I saw in the Republica Popular do Cabo Verde (Cape Verde). I was asked in 1990 to join four other persons to assess the progress of food research and watershed development programs financed by AID in this volcanic archipelago of some fifteen islands, one hour's flight west from Dakar in Senegal. The islands had been used by Portugal in earlier centuries as a way station for the slave trade. The population reflects its multiple origins from many parts of Africa and the few Portuguese overlords.

Physiographically, it is in the Sahel. During the month I spent there, fine sand from the Sahara was blowing constantly across my face and into my eyes. The dry climate, the torrential occasional rains, the unconsolidated volcanic ash that covers most islands, and the unrestrained population explosion, combine to form a clear disaster, alleviated only by emigration and the solace provided by the religious beliefs I saw expressed publicly when the Pope visited the country during my stay. Fortunately for the Cape Verdians, more of them live in Massachusetts and Rhode Island than in the archipelago. Consequently, as long as US senators and congressmen from New England seek reelection, sufficient funds will be appropriated for development and food aid programs in the islands.

OTHER TRIPS TO EUROPE

In 1986, I attended the 11th annual meeting of the EGF in Troia, near Setubal, Portugal. This was a good opportunity to meet European forage scientists, mostly from the U.K. and Holland, with some from France, Belgium, Scandinavia, Spain, Italy, and Portugal.

It also gave Claude and me a chance to tour the northern, mountainous part of the country and the Oporto region, famous for port wine, with a conference tour.

Following this, we rented a car and drove to Coimbra, and thence to southern Spain. We visited Sevilla, Córdoba, and Granada. We walked to the home of Maïmonides, and saw a replica of Columbus' ship floating on the Guadalquivir, not far from the famous bull ring. We visited the fortress of Málaga high above the Mediterranean, and saw the Rock of Gibraltar from the mainland. Driving north, I was surprised by the desolate flat landscape of La Mancha, understanding then why so many of the *conquistadores* had left this region to find more hospitable terrain. We were enchanted by the medieval remnants in Toledo. We stayed the nights in a *parador* (remodeled castle or other historical monument) across the river from the huge hill on which Toledo was built. The view was splendid, both at night and in the daytime.

A few years later, in December 1990, on our way to an Earthwatch archaeological expedition on the northern shore of Majorca, we had time to visit Madrid and the Prado. We then drove to the orange groves of Valencia and explored Catalonia for over a week. In Majorca, we helped excavate a prehistoric site not far from the cottage where Frédéric Chopin spent some time with George Sand.

In 1994, the EGF met in Wageningen, home of a famous agricultural university. Prior to taking the train from Oslo to Amsterdam, where we rented a car, Claude and I drove for about ten days getting acquainted with Norway, its mountains and glaciers, the birthplace of skiing, the Viking ships found in archaeological digs, and the incessant rain of the west coast. While cruising a fjord out of Bergen, we ran into my former Wisconsin roommate Phil Dodell and his wife Myra. Surprise, surprise! We stopped en route in København, our second visit to this beautiful city, and spent an evening in the outstanding Tivoli Gardens. From Amsterdam, we drove over most of Holland, both above and below sea level, and admired the great levees protecting the country from the North Sea.

After the meeting, we stopped at the Basel home of Joseph Raeber, a former schoolmate from Iowa State days. Joe and his wife Gudrun were extremely hospitable, and we had several good days visiting northern Switzerland with them, including an interesting day in Fribourg, with its well-preserved medieval section, even though my family name may have no connection with the name of this city, at least since the middle of the 17th century. We continued our trip along the Rhine and Lake Konstanz, passing by St. Gallen where my grandfather Lucien often went to consult with his employers. In the Tyrol, we spent a couple of days in the well-appointed village home of Joseph Schuller, another former schoolmate from Iowa State and former executive of a large agricultural chemical company, being treated to a concert by the local oom-pah-pah band that evening. After several days in the mountains, we pushed on to Salzburg, where we attended a Mozart concert in the *Schloss* (castle) and an unusual marionette opera. Continuing by train to Budapest, we visited that city and its surroundings during the most intense heat wave in several decades! Nevertheless, it was well worth the trip.

The 16th IGC was held in Nice in 1989. We could not pass up this chance to visit the *Côte d'Azur* (Riviera) and found it exceeded our expectations. I could now understand why my grandparents liked so much to spend a couple of months each winter in Nice, walking each day on the *Promenade des Anglais* along the Mediterranean beach. We visited some of the high pastures, dairy farms, and cottage cheese makers in the lower Alps. We had a real *bouillabaisse* (fish soup) with our cousins Jean (Jean and I are first cousins, once removed) and Josette Samuel. We also visited Monaco and Menton, and I tried unsuccessfully to locate the hotel, not far from former (pre-war) Prime Minister Flandin's home, where our family had spent a vacation in the late 1930s on the Cap Ferrat peninsula.

When 1999 arrived, I had been working fairly steadily, in my spare time, at the family genealogical research and had initiated correspondence with a number of knowledgeable experts in France, notably Micheline Guttman and André Blum, both distantly related to my wife. So Claude and I took a trip of almost two months for the express purposes of getting acquainted or re-acquainted with our surviving European relatives, and to visit the locales where our ancestors had lived, primarily in Alsace and Lorraine, but also in Switzerland, Belgium, Champagne, and Burgundy. It was very satisfying to actually see these places, many of which up to that time were only names that we had heard our parents or grandparents mention. We found also that some of our relatives were still practicing Orthodox Judaism, some were members of Progressive congregations, some were irreligious, and some were practicing Catholics! The latter occurred either due to mixed marriages or to attempts to escape official racial persecutions. In general, we found it most politic to not engage in conversations on religious or political topics, for we "American cousins" thought quite differently from most of them. To them, the Holocaust and the hidden endemic antisemitism surviving in European societies were even more real than to us.

Almost invariably, though, when we were taking our leave, after having been received very hospitably, we were asked "When are you coming back?" I would indicate that it was up to them now to come and see us. In all but a very few cases, the answer to that was "Oh, but you know, America, it is so far away!" Sometimes, I could not help but mention that the distance was no different for them than it had been for us, only the initial direction! Quite a contrast with the freedom and ease of many Americans, who travel without fear (most of the time and most places, although this has been changing since September 11, 2001) and overlook distances.

I have often wondered why Claude and I, children of Europe and of Europeans, are so different from many Europeans in this regard. I have always enjoyed both traveling and returning home. Professionally, I have wanted from time to time to live up to the expectations inculcated into me from my earliest days as a Cub Scout: to do at least one good turn each day. I suppose that is the reason why I have been willing to travel to many places where other persons might not want to go. In addition, as a crop ecologist, I owed it to myself and my altruistic instincts, and to my students, to become as knowledgeable as possible, from direct observation, about most agriculturally-significant climatic and ecological niches of the world. I know that, when I created a graduate course in Crop Climatology, I was able to enrich my teaching immensely by drawing upon my experiences and the colored slides I had accumulated during my travels. Actually, even trips that most persons might consider as vacations were only partially so, as Claude can attest. Whenever a new agricultural or ecological situation appears during our travels, I cannot resist the impulse to investigate and photograph.

THE ANTIPODES

Other travels have been the result of the desire to increase professional competence, and sometimes have also led to networking for joint research. A case in point has been my involvement with New Zealand scientists. The 17th IGC was convened first at Massey University in Palmerston North, New Zealand, in January 1993, and reconvened two weeks later in Rockhampton, New South Wales, Australia. Claude and I left Knoxville two weeks early, stopping first in Hawaii for a few days on the island of Maui. We enjoyed this first visit to Hawaii, especially when we could get away from the hordes of Asian tourists on the western part of the island. The slopes and massiveness of the volcano at the east end were very impressive as we drove to the crater, although its caldera is smaller than the 45-km (30-mile) wide caldera of Aso Yama south of Fukuoka on the island of Kyushu in Japan.

Once in New Zealand, we rented a car in Christchurch and toured the South Island for a week. Without a doubt, this is one of the most beautiful and hospitable countries we have visited. We saw the rain forests and mountains of the southwest, spent a night at the foot of Mt. Cook, trod the Tasman Glacier, unavoidably squashed myriads of rabbits hypnotized by car headlights, observed a kiwi bird in a special avian sanctuary, admired the agricultural richness of the Canterbury Plains, and navigated Cook Strait on the ferry to the North Island.

Contact was made with several NZ scientists, eventually resulting in friendships, and in joint research in Tennessee on tall fescue toxicosis. New Zealanders had been working diligently for many years to solve the problem caused by a fungus growing in perennial ryegrass, the mainstay plant of their forage-livestock industry. The tall fescue toxicosis in the United States is caused by a close relative of the fungus that infests ryegrass. So it was an almost inevitable serendipidty that led to US forage scientists' desire for joint investigations with New Zealanders. I was only one among many to engage in this international endeavor. To report on the joint work which followed, financed in part by New Zealand, I was invited to return to that country in 1996 and 1999. During these trips, Claude and I visited Fiji and also some parts of New Zealand we had missed on our earlier trips.

In February 1993, we spent a few days in Brisbane (Queensland) on the east coast of Australia before heading north. After the Rockhampton meeting, we joined an IGC tour that wended its way toward Cairns. On the way, we visited a relatively small "station" west of Townsville operated by an older couple and their son. They maintained about 7,000 head of cattle plus (or should I say, in spite of) innumerable kangaroos. It had not rained for a couple of years, and our hosts thought they might have to sell half their herd very soon!

From Cairns, we took a ship to the Great Barrier Reef for a day of swimming and snorkeling while admiring the colors of corals and fishes. We then flew to Alice Springs (Northern Territory) in central Australia, where we both learned to do the Australian wave (to scare off the innumerable flies from our faces) and where Claude climbed to the top of Ayers Rock. After a few more hours of flying over the Australian desert, we had a very nice visit with a colleague in Adelaide (South Australia) and vicinity. We then took a bus to a small motorboat ferry that took us on a wild and bumpy ride to Kangaroo Island. The wildlife experience provided by our hosts was outstanding, for we were able to observe numerous wild free-ranging animals, including seals, koala bears and kangaroos. Our trip continued as we drove to Melbourne (Victoria) on the south coast for a visit to this very beautiful city. We completed our Australian experience with several days in Sidney (New South Wales) which included both a tour and a concert in the Opera House.

WHY DID I WRITE ABOUT THESE TRAVELS?

I did not write about these travels to boast. Rather, I believe I have illustrated for future generations the extent to which the lives of my immediate family have been different from those of our own grandparents and their ancestors. Travel has been much more feasible and affordable for us than it was for them, and required much less stamina. We have also observed first-hand the common threads that unite humanity and noted that, if we tried to blend in, or at least learn properly a few words of the local dialect or language, we were treated warmly and hospitably almost everywhere.

At the same time, I have endeavored to determine the extent of the genealogical histories of our family as far back as feasible, and I hope that my descendants will continue to maintain uninterrupted this thread to our ancestral roots and beliefs. I mentioned earlier that our son Daniel had become a *Bar Mitzvah* the week before our family left for Turkey. Two years later, our daughter Renée became a *Bat Mitzvah* and, when a high school junior, was confirmed at Temple Beth El. Claude and I were most pleased when our grandson Bryan, after having followed a similar course of religious instruction, was confirmed at our Temple in 1998.

Continuing the family tradition: my grandson Bryan was confirmed at Temple Beth El, Knoxville where his father Daniel, Claude and I proudly attended the ceremony

OUR CABIN ON THE LAKE

In 1982, after my mother-in-law Simone died, Claude and I decided to invest the funds from the inheritance into a vacation home that we would build at some short distance from our home in Knoxville. After investigating many areas and possibilities, we bought seven hilly wooded acres in spring 1984 on the southern shore of Douglas Lake. Claude and I spent the summer of 1984 with hand tools removing the grapevines, honeysuckle, brambles and poison ivy that infested the area, while noting the topography and deciding where the house would stand. I used a transit to survey where the access road would be constructed, and removed all the trees with my chainsaw. I also cleared the house and septic field sites.

After we had started clearing the land, Claude and I spent most Saturdays and Sundays at Buck Horn, having consciously decided that, if we were ever to finish our construction, we had to labor conscientiously and continuously until the task was completed. That winter, we laid out and dug trenches for the footings, and formed the ditches with second-hand plywood, to insure that we would have substantial concrete footings resting directly on the vertically-tilted layers of shale bedrock. We poured the footings on Memorial Day 1985. That summer, my friend and colleague Vernon Reich, Claude and I built the full basement cinder block walls. The logs were delivered on site in spring 1986 and erected that spring and summer. Vern continued to help us and I hired a local mountaineer carpenter, Chuck Quigley, to work with us. His strength, knowledge and good spirit were much appreciated throughout the entire construction project, and his rates were reasonable. In addition, I hired graduate students on a daily basis to do the heavier work. My graduate student Wayne Thompson in particular was very helpful throughout. In fall 1986, I hired a local contractor with a team of carpenters to erect the roof so that the structure would be in the dry by the time winter arrived.

Once the shingles were nailed onto the roof, I thought the biggest job was over. Little did I know! The construction of rooms, balcony, partitions, the plumbing of bathrooms and kitchen, the laying of electrical wiring and mounting of lights, the building of cabinets and vanities, the painting and varnishing, inside and outside, was going to take another six years of weekends to complete! When we finally were finished, though, we had a real feeling of accomplishment and pride.

Our log cabin is a pleasant place for us to come and spend most weekends, at all seasons of the year. We like to come here for the quiet, the view of the lake in summer and of the Smoky Mountains in winter, even though the view is obscured in warm weather by the noxious pollution emanating from tourists' automobiles in Pigeon Forge and Gatlinburg. It is restful to spend a couple of days here each week, for we feel liberated of artificial constraints. The large balcony overlooking nature, and indoors, the 6.5-meter (20-ft) ceiling over the living room, impart much spaciousness.

During the twelve years that elapsed from land acquisition to cabin completion, there were a few interruptions, such as our trips to France and to Japan. More serious was the week in November 1988 when, after complaining to my physician of a slight muscular shoulder pain that I thought had been caused by lifting heavy sandstone slabs that I was erecting as facing for the basement walls, I was diagnosed as requiring immediate coronary bypass surgery. In fact, the cardiologist identified four blockages (one 90%, two 95%, and one 100%). November 16, 1988, when the diagnosis was made, was also the day when I smoked my last pipeful. Early in the morning of the next day, I underwent surgery. I had a normal convalescence, going back to work on a half-time basis in January. I returned to laying the sandstone blocks in March, and have been reasonably healthy since, although I had to have a stent inserted in one of the grafts in 1999. I must admit, however, that not smoking at all was a struggle for me for several years. Now, though, I find the smell of tobacco smoke so distasteful that it revolts me.

The four coronary bypass grafts certainly constituted the most life-threatening medical episode in my life. Prior to that, I had undergone prostate surgery (TUR = transurethral resection), a double hernia repair, and several hammer-toe straightenings. The most painful (in medical terms of the day: *causing the most discomfort*) medical repair I have had, however, was the total knee replacement done on December 19, 1995. A portion of my knee cartilage had torn off. After those portions had been removed by arthroscopy in 1994, there was not enough cartilage remaining for pain-free standing and walking. Some day perhaps, the cause of osteoarthritis will be known, and more effective and benign remedies will be available which do not demand one or more hours a day of physical therapy for from six months to two years in duration.

Although in the summer of 1997 I could walk well for about one kilometer on level ground, it was obvious that my days of hiking 6 to 25 km (4 to 15 miles) a day in the Great Smoky Mountains were over. A yeast infection, originally diagnosed in my knee prosthesis a year earlier, was in remission but it flared up in late August 1997. Consequently, the prosthesis was removed on September 3 at Vanderbilt Medical Hospital in Nashville, a different hospital than the one in Knoxville where the infection had been contracted during the first surgery. After almost six months of antifungal therapy to eliminate the infection, when I was not allowed to place any weight on my right leg, and the tibia and the femur were kept apart by a cement spacer, a new total knee replacement was installed early in 1998. The many months of painful physical therapy paid off, for this second knee has been able to "hold its weight up," at least until now (2003).

FAMILY INHERITANCES—
PAST AND FUTURE

It was not until some years after my coronary surgery that I recognized that I had been at risk of hereditary heart disease. Both my parents died of strokes. When my father died of a massive stroke in January 1975, he had been in a nursing home in California for about six months, following several smaller strokes in New York City. Since these episodes occurred while I was in Turkey, my mother took my father to Los Angeles, where my brother Sylvain was a physician. My mother hoped that Sylvain's proximity and connection to the medical professions would be helpful to my father, but the inevitable could not be prevented.

Upon my return to the US from Turkey, I went to visit my parents in L.A. It was heart-rending to see my father, who used to be so quick-witted and knowledgeable, and possessed of an incisive and logical mind, reduced to a wheelchair-bound hulk that recognized me but could not express himself clearly. I shall always treasure the gold pocket watch that he left me in his will, for whenever I wear it I think of him even more than usual. Although he was not the original owner of this watch, he owned it for many years before his death. The construction of this watch was started in December 1900, nine months before my father was born, and completed in June 1906. I hope that my son Daniel will take good care of this precious memento.

Claude and I are really proud of our son Daniel. He possesses an extraordinary memory, recalling details of places we have visited when we have forgotten we ever were there. He is able to recall specific portions of books that he has read, and he has read many. He can tell the title of a movie he saw years ago after watching it again for just a minute or two. He taught himself how to read when he was about three years old, looking at the newspaper over my shoulder. He is a voracious reader, and has taught himself in many areas, such as medieval literature and history, through his reading. Being such a "quick read" made it difficult for him to attend school, because he was usually well ahead of the instructor and bored by repetition. While in his early twenties, he obtained a job as an all-around helper in a podiatric office. It was while in this employment that he realized his disposition for caring for patients. In spite of his dislike for uninspiring teachers, he persevered enough for several years in nursing studies at Walters State College, while fully employed, to become a Registered Nurse. In his current employment, he is responsible for the physical well-being of many mentally challenged patients. This kind of work might exhaust the patience and solicitude of some other people, but he does it well and with great caring and thoughtfulness. We admire his dedication to the welfare of his patients, who are not able to care for themselves.

After my father's death, my mother moved to Knoxville and resided for three years in her own apartment at Shannondale Retirement Homes. During that time, we would visit or go out to various cultural and other events on a weekly basis whenever possible, and kept in touch by telephone on a daily basis. My mother then fell and broke her hip, and had to be moved to the Nursing Home after surgery.

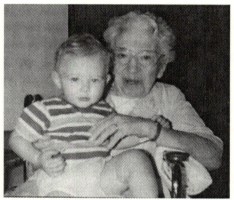

Great-grandmother Yvonne Fribourg and Bryan

For about two years, she lived in her room. One of her great pleasures, while confined to a wheelchair, was to be able to hold her great-grandson Bryan, Daniel' son, thereby knowing the Fribourg family would continue on for at least three more generations. She then had some strokes more severe than the small ones she had suffered earlier, causing her to lapse into a three-year coma. It was very difficult for me to come to the realization that my visits and ministrations were to no avail for many years, and that the primary reason for continuing daily visits was solely for the purpose of ensuring that the staff was taking proper care of her on a constant basis. I carry on the small finger of my left hand a 2.5-carat brilliant cut diamond mounted in platinum which was dear to her, a beautiful ring. I hope that my daughter Renée will take good care of this precious keepsake.

Renée had a difficult late adolescence. After completing her high school studies, she was unsure of what she wanted to do, and spent several years as a server in a succession of Knoxville restaurants. She eventually decided to attend the University of Tennessee, and obtained a B.S. degree in Ornamental Horticulture and Landscape Design. Following that she switched to the Department of Botany and earned an M.S. degree conducting research in cell culture. While analyzing her research data and writing her thesis on a personal computer, she became proficient in the use of a number of software programs. Upon graduation, recognizing that employment opportunities in her field were limited in Knoxville, she moved to Atlanta where, after a few temporary positions, she found her vocation. She has now been employed for several years as an electronic commerce network analyst, receiving promotions and accolades on a regular basis. We are as proud of her accomplishments as she is of her success.

Since I am writing about mementoes, I want my grandson Bryan to have and wear the solid gold ring with my initials which I have worn on my right hand since 1974, when I had it carved for me in Erzurum, Turkey. We hope that he will in the near future find his vocation. After completing his high school studies, he decided to work for a while, rather than continue on to college. He is enjoying being a clerk in a clothing store, and has also refined his acrobatic techniques in skateboarding.

It is good that the cabin was finished before my knee prosthesis afflicted me. I can now sit on the porch or in the air-conditioned spacious living room, and get satiated with the view, as I read a good book or write on my laptop computer. Alternatively, I can get my little jet boat running over Douglas Lake and feel the breeze in my face. When the weather is too hot, too wet, or too cold, I can go inside and work on the family genealogy or write the draft of my next manuscript.

I am glad that I started to write this tale, and grateful that I lived long enough to bring it to this state. I hope the readers will have gathered some of the flavor that events created in my life and that my descendants will understand better their ancestral roots. I hope that these descendants will be living in freedom, glad that some of us were fortunate enough to escape the Holocaust, and continue to follow the principles of a modern and moral Judaism.

THE FOXTROT IS NOT OVER YET!

APPENDIX I
NOTES ON THE DESCENDANTS OF BERNARD DIEDISHEIM AND THE NORDMANNS

Researched and written by André Blum,
26 chemin du Grand Buisson, 25000 Besançon, France
Edited and translated from the French by Henry Fribourg

[*The following are the prefaces to two exhaustive genealogical trees drawn up by my wife's fourth cousin, once removed, André Blum. His work, unselfishly shared with us, has been invaluable in developing Claude's genealogy on her father's side. I have included this appendix to provide the reader with an understanding of the painstaking research required for the construction of genealogical trees.*]

"At the beginning of my genealogical investigations, I met a not-too-distant cousin, Raymond Didisheim, from Lausanne, Switzerland, who gave me a copy of a genealogical tree of the descendants of Bernard Diedisheim, who had lived in Héguenheim in about 1700. This genealogical tree had been drawn up in April 1894 by M. Herrmann Günzberger, Secretary of the Héguenheim Jewish cemetery. The tree included only those descendants bearing the same surname, with the related families being recognized only by the spouses' names.

Among the spouses were many Nordmanns. It then occurred to me that these might all be related and I became interested in their genealogy. I used the telephone book to locate and contact the French Nordmanns, and was thus able to begin my investigations into this family. I was able to use the results of the research conducted by Simone Levaillant, attorney in St. Etienne, Loire, who unfortunately died after being deported. She had already found much information about the first Nordmanns settled in Héguenheim. She probably was familiar with the 1910 book of Dr. Achille Nordmann of Basel (*Author's note: Claude remembers having met him when he visited her parents in Kew Gardens and his hair was all white*) about the Héguenheim cemetery and the inter-connections among the inhabitants of southern Alsace, the Swiss, and the other inhabitants of their region.

In 1690, in Allschwyl, near Basel, Switzerland lived a head of household named Berlé Deidesheim. It is probable that he or his parents had come from Deidesheim in Rhenish Bavaria. This family later went to live in Héguenheim in southern Alsace and the name Deidesheim got transformed into Diedesheim.

....

The genealogy for both families was developed by taking the old records of the Jewish Cemetery of Héguenheim as a point of departure. These records go back to 1690 and are believed to be correct. The records used were certified as being true copies of the original by the Secretary of the Jewish Cemetery, M. Herrmann Günzberger, of Héguenheim, in April 1894.....................They encompassed seven generations.......................I added to them information from the following documents:

- the compilation of marriage contracts in Alsace between 1700 and 1789 established by Salomon Picard
- the work "Mémoire Juive en Alsace" by A.A. Fraenckel— (Marriage contracts in Alsace during the 18th century)
- the "General Census of the Jews who are tolerated in the province of Alsace, as per the carrying out of letters patent of His Majesty, under the Regulation order of July 10, 1794"
- the records of declaration of adoption of surnames by the Jews in compliance with the imperial decree of July 20, 1808
- the population censuses carried out in Héguenheim and neighboring townships in 1836, 1841, 1846 and 1851
- the records of civil status from Héguenheim and neighboring townships, for the period between 1789 and 1890
- the information kindly provided me by members of the family interested in this research

- the Dreyfus file, scrupulously developed by Dr. Mars d'Issoire
- the Hauser genealogy gathered by Me. Micheline Guttmann
- the writings of M. Chipaux on the Jews of Besançon
- the writings of Dr. Simon of Nîmes on the Jewish families of Nîmes and the Comtat Venaissin

This endeavor is in constant flux, and will be added to as I obtain additional information, either from my own efforts or from contributions from others. The results are available to all descendants of our common ancestors. They may contain numerous errors and I thank in advance those who can point them out to me. This is a collaborative study with the goal of allowing all of us to learn more about our ancestors and our cousins."

APPENDIX II
SPEECH GIVEN BY CHARLES WOLFF ON THE CENTENNIAL OF THE MAISON WOLFF ON SEPTEMBER 19, 1948

Translated from the French by Henry A. Fribourg

[*My wife Claude's grandmother, on her mother's side, was born Mathilde Wolff. I have reproduced this speech by Charles Wolff, her elder brother, to illustrate the strong roots that this family, as so many other French Jewish families, had in Alsace and Lorraine. The speech, delivered after a family reunion dinner in Strasbourg, is followed by the translation of several sets of handwritten notes by Charles Wolff on the fate of most members of his family during the Retreat and the German occupation of France until the Libération, 1940 - 1944.*]

"I shall take the liberty to say a few words and tell you why the whole family is gathered here today. Well! It is to celebrate the one hundredth anniversary of the Maison Wolff [Wolff Hardware Company] of Sarre-Union. This anniversary also comes at the right time for us to fulfill a wish that each one of us had, to find ourselves again all together, if not in our town, at least in our native Alsace.

In this year of 1948, it is exactly one hundred years ago that the Maison Wolff of Sarre-Union was founded by our grandfather under the name "Moïse Wolff," to deal in ironmongery and stoves. You still can find today, in the countryside around Sarre-Union, stoves in use with the brand "Moïse Wolff" stamped in the slit above the fire-door. Even up until this last war we were stocking spare parts that customers came to buy from us to repair their stove.

In 1870 our fathers became partners and, with their courage and hard work, they were able to improve their business each year with increasing success. Later when we had grown up some, we were enlisted in the same work. Starting in 1886, my sister Lucie and I were the first salespersons of the partnership and, thanks to our efforts, the business increased some more. And when my brothers and other sisters reached the age of 14, they too shared the load, helping to sell hardware, cooking utensils, etc...on market days. Let me just give you an example to demonstrate to you that we were well liked by the customers. When my sister Lucie got married and moved to Diemeringen, the customers did not inquire about her husband, but rather they said "we are going to Lucie's place". The children as well as their parents went to Lucie's for their purchases and my brother-in-law Salomon could leave the store to visit his customers in the countryside without any worry.

Eventually, one after the other, my brothers and sisters got married. In 1907 my brother Jules and I took over the management of the Sarre-Union business and my brother Sylvain that of the one at Sarralbe. We were so intricately linked together that every week, either the car from Diemeringen or our car from Sarre-Union was going somewhere to replenish stocks, so that our clientele could be served without waiting for materials lacking at one or the other place. At present, my nephew Georges manages alone the Sarre-Union business, following the tragic disappearance of my brother Jules deported by the Germans. I ask you, my dear ones, to please stand and observe a minute of silence in memory of all our dear ones who have disappeared, of whom we shall keep an eternal memory.

The one hundredth anniversary of the founding of our ancestors' firm is especially worthy of being celebrated. There certainly are few businesses in the region that, over a century and encompassing four generations, have remained within a single family.

Still, how many obstacles our business surmounted over the years! Created in the middle of a revolution, it has withstood three wars. But throughout, the Wolffs always remained at their station and, when circumstances forced them, as they did during the last war, to leave the Sarre-Union business temporarily, they always returned as soon as it was possible to renew and expand the work of their predecessors.

It is not only during exceptional conditions that the Wolffs showed themselves to be worthy, but also every day, through their unremitting work, earning the confidence of their customers. The proof of this exists in the fact that most of today's customers belong to the fourth or fifth generation of the initial customers.

By coming so numerous to this Reunion, you have not only wished to demonstrate that these virtues, to which you are paying homage, are also yours, you have also wanted to emphasize the closeness that has never failed to unify our family: this Union, that our mother Aunt Léonie begged us to maintain toward and against all comers in the wonderful testament that she left us. The happiness of being all together does not overshadow the thoughts we have of those who are absent. Those are my sister Mathilde who is too far from us, George Simon, Marthe Wimphen and her husband, Louise, Denise, Pierre and André Coblentz. And finally I do not want to forget to pay my respects to our old manservant Albert Muller who is here among us and who, for the last 48 years, has been in the employ of the Maison Wolff. He can be counted as a member of the family, he has witnessed the births of all the young ones in the family.

To conclude, I want to wish much luck and prosperity to all the young ones in their endeavors. May God watch over them and give them health to bring up their children well, and may they maintain the good qualities that their ancestors bequeathed to them. Engrave well in your memory that today, September 19, 1948, you, the young generation, have helped us, the older generation, celebrate the centennial of the Maison Wolff."

P.S. 1. COMMENTARY ON THE 1941-1945 EVENTS, AS OF THE END OF FEBRUARY 1945

With the encouragement of the [German] army of occupation, the French government introduced the racial laws in France. At the end of 1941 the Germans began the persecutions of Jews which, because of the brutality of the means employed and the cruelty of the Gestapo, have taken their place in history. There followed a very painful period for all the members of the family remaining in the occupied zone. In November 1942, after the landing of the Allied armies in North Africa, the Germans occupied all of France and intensified their efforts for the extermination of Jews—we use here the exact word used in their speeches and in the German and collaborationist French presses. The following is a description of the circumstances of each descendant of the Moïse Wolff progeny from 1940 until the Libération.

Albert Lévy and Blanche went to Marseille, where he was President of the General Union of the Jews of France (U.G.I.F.). After the landing in 1942, they went to Switzerland and he became seriously ill. He escaped deportation.

Marcelle Wolff went to Lyon with her daughter Fernande Birgé and later to Savoy. Her husband Armand was in New York.

Charles Wolff, with his oldest daughter and his son-in-law Pierre Lévy, traveled to Le Blanc (Indre) and held out until the latter was arrested on May 16, 1944. After then, they hid at Marembert (Indre) until the Libération.

Jules Wolff and Anna with their three daughters and Jean Michel went to St. Ouen-lès-Paray (Vosges) where they lived peacefully until the arrest of Jules on May 10, 1943. At first, he was in a guarded camp at Ecrouves (Meurthe-et-Moselle). He was then transferred to Drancy and deported as early as July. Since then, the family has had no news. On March 24, 1944, it was his daughters Paulette and Jacqueline who were arrested. They went through the camp at Ecrouves, then were transferred to Drancy and deported to Germany in early May 1944. They were able to send news out in May from near Hannover where they were in a special camp for prisoners' wives. It was lucky for Jacqueline to have been able to masquerade as a prisoner's wife, thus being able to stay with her sister. Their sister Louise had gone to Vichy France (the so-called Free Zone, *i.e.*, unoccupied France) as early as 1940 in Cannes, then Agen. In the meantime, Anna Wolff, whose health had deteriorated steadily because of these events, died all alone, with only M. Maréchal, the mayor and his family, in attendance.

Sylvain Wolff and Elise. He was arrested on December 12, 1941 by the Gestapo, and suffered terribly in a succession of concentration camps at Compiègne, Drancy, Pithiviers, Beaune-lès-Dames, La Rolande, and again Drancy. Thanks to the perseverance of his Aryan wife, he was liberated on October 28, 1942 and survived in Paris until the Libération.

Henri Wimphen and Augusta, having gone at first to Souillac (Lot) and later to St. Gervais d'Auvergne (Puy-de-Dôme) were not bothered and stayed with Mathilde Lévi who traveled with them. She had been at the beginning of the war at Plombières (Vosges). After the 1940 debacle, she went to Beaune (Côte d'Or) and then to Lyon where her husband Léopold died in 1941. After having spent some time at Brive-la-Gaillarde (Corrèze) with her daughter Simone [*my mother-in-law*], she settled at St. Gervais for the duration.

P.S. 2. SEPTEMBER 15, 1945.

Still no news of Jules Wolff and Mour Hirsch. Paulette and Jacqueline Wolff returned safe and sound from the Bergen-Belsen camp. Jean Wimphen died in February at Auschwitz. Henri Hirsch was gassed and burned at Buchenwald. No additional commentary about these camps is necessary, future Wolff generations will learn the terrible truth from history.

P.S. 3. WRITTEN AT LE BLANC ON FEBRUARY 11, 1945, 9 months after the landing of the Allied Armed Forces near Caen on June 6, 1944, and at the time when the German armies have been pushed back to the Rhine River in the West and to the Oder River in the East.

André Coblentz and family went first to Cannes. André then worked at the U.G.I.F. in Nice while his wife and children were in Haute-Savoie; later, they went to Genève.

Pierre Coblentz and Denise left as early as 1940 for the United States and live in New York.

Charles Malvy and Denise with their children were first at Souillac (Lot) then at Lyon and in Savoie. Charles was a captain in the French Resistance Army and in the army led by de Lattre de Tassigny.

Serge Birgé and Fernande went to Lyon and later to Savoie.

Max Simon and family went to New York. His son Arnold is an officer in the US Navy.

Edgard Simon and family were at La Châtre (Indre) with his parents. Hid for several months in 1944 with his family at Tijon (Indre) using false papers. Barely escaped being shot by the Germans on July 16, 1944.

Georges Simon and Jacqueline went to Bourganeuf (Creuse) after he was sent home from prisoner-of-war camp as a nurse-sergeant. Was an interpreter at the E.M.F.F.I., Creuse.

Pierre Lévy and Jeanne were with Charles Wolff at Le Blanc (Indre). He was arrested on May 16, 1944 by the French and delivered to the Compulsory Work Service of the Mixed Franco-German Commission. He was sent to Cherbourg and incarcerated at the Naval Prison as soon as he arrived. A lucky set of happenstances allowed him to escape on June 18, 1944. He returned to Le Blanc after walking for 18 days and 3 nights.

Marius Lubetzki and Germaine with their son, bound for Sào Paulo, boarded a ship at Cádiz on June 28, 1941.

Louise Cohn and her son first went to Cannes and then to Agen (Lot-et-Garonne). She obtained her divorce in 1944.

Georges Wolff was at Bergerac (Dordogne) after his escape. It is there he married Jeanne Cerf in 1942. A son, Daniel, the first of his generation with the Wolff name, was born to them in 1943. Georges is a lieutenant in the French Resistance Army.

Paulette Kahn was arrested by the Gestapo at St. Ouen-lès-Paray (Vosges) and deported with her sister Jacqueline Wolff. The latter was engaged to René Kahn from Woerth (Bas-Rhin).

Jacques Wolff and Leïlah went to Nice and later to Le Marembert (Indre). He was arrested on May 16, 1944 for the same reason as Pierre Lévy and suffered the same fate after having been his cellmate at the Naval Prison in Cherbourg.

Janine Wolff remained in Paris with her mother while awaiting for her father to be freed.

Pierre Blum with Marthe and the children first went to Souillac (Lot) and later to Clermont-Ferrand. He hid with his family near St. Gervais d'Auvergne (Puy-de-Dôme) using false papers and returned to Clermont-Ferrand after the Libération.

Jean Wimphen was engaged to Yvette Itzrowitz from Paris. He was employed by the U.G.I.F. at Sisteron (Alpes-Maritimes) where he was arrested by the Gestapo in September 1944. He was deported after going through the camp at Drancy. The family has no news.

Claude Wimphen was in Lyon after being mustered out in 1941. He hid to escape the Compulsory Work Service. At the time of the Libération he was a sergeant in the French Resistance Army.

Henri Lévi married Yvette Chupin on November 11, 1942 in Marseille, the day the Germans occupied the city. A son, Francis, was born in 1943. Henri was at the U.G.I.F. at Moiran (Isère). After the Libération he returned to his position as Mine Engineer at Bédarieux (Hérault).

Max Brunschwig and Simone with the children [*my wife-to-be and her sister*] went to Brive-la-Gaillarde (Corrèze). Since he was a Swiss citizen, he could obtain visas for the United States for his family and, as early as May 1941 *(Author's note: this date should be September 1941)* they boarded a ship bound for New York.

In remembrance. Cousin Henry Hirsch from Liège with his wife Thérèse went to Cannes, they were arrested in September 1943 by the Gestapo, and deported even though he was 75 years old. The family has no news. Their sons Lucien and Jacques, Belgian prisoners of war, escaped. Lucien went to Valence (Drôme) with false papers. Jacques got to England through Switzerland and came back after the Libération as a British officer.

APPENDIX III
SELECTED PROFESSIONAL
PUBLICATIONS[1]

Wells, G.R., H.A. Fribourg, S.E. Schlarbaum, J.T. Ammons, and D.G. Hodges. 2003. Alternate land uses for marginal soils.J. Soil Water Conserv. 58:73-81.

Fribourg, H., J. Waller, G. Latch, L. Fletcher, H. Easton, and A. Stratton. 2002. Evaluation under grazing of *Festuca arundinacea* cultivars infected with nontoxic endophytes. Proc. 19th Gen. Meet. European Grassland Fed., 27-30 May, La Rochelle, France.pp. 530-531.

Fribourg, H.A., J.C. Waller, K.D. Gwinn, and R.J. Carlisle. 2002. Changes in endophyte infestation in tall fescue pastures due to different stocking densities. http://www.agriculture.utk.edu/ansci/annualreports.htm

Fribourg, H.A., and J.C. Waller. 2002. Tall fescue and tall fescue toxicosis (web page). http://ohld.ag.utk.edu/pss/fescue/ (This is likely to change in future, please contact jwaller@utk.edu for correct address).

Waller, J.C., H.A. Fribourg, A.E. Fisher, M.A. Pavao-Zuckerman and T. Ingle. 2002. Methane emissions by *Bos taurus* grazing tall fescue pastures. Proc. 19th Gen. Meet. European Grassland Fed., 27-30 May, La Rochelle, France.pp. 748-749.

Fribourg, H.A., J.C. Waller, A.E. Schultze, B.W. Rohrbach and J.W. Oliver. 2001. Grazing endophyte infested tall fescue and changes in bovine blood components and gain. Proc. XIX

---

[1] *Abbreviations of journal names*: Agric. Systems = Agricultural Systems; Agron. J. = Agronomy Journal; Anim. Feed Sci. Technol. = Animal Feed Science Technology; Crop Sci. = Crop Science; J. Anim. Sci. = Journal of Animal Science; J. Dairy Sci. = Journal of Dairy Science; J. Agron. Educ.= Journal of Agronomic Education; J. Enviro. Qual. = Journal of Environmental Quality; J. Prod. Agric. = Journal of Production Agriculture; J. Soil Water Conserv. = Journal of Soil and Water Conservation; J. Tennessee Acad. Sci. = Journal of the Tennessee Academy of Sciences; Soil Sci. Soc. Amer. Proc. = Soil Science Society of America Proceedings.

Intern. Grassland Cong., Sào Pedro, Sào Paulo, Brasil. Feb.pp. 609-610.

Waller, J.C., H.A. Fribourg, C. Dixon, A.E. Fisher, and B.V. Conger. 2001. Orchardgrass pastures for early weaned beef calves. Proc. XIX Intern. Grassland Cong., Sào Pedro, Sào Paulo, Brasil. Feb.pp. 839-840.

Fribourg, H.A. and J.C. Waller. 2000. Summer annual grasses. [a revised web page] http://forages.orst.edu/topics/species/sumanngra/

Oliver, J.W., A.E. Schultze, B.W. Rohrbach, H.A. Fribourg, T. Ingle, and J.C. Waller. 2000. Alterations in hemograms and serum biochemical analytes of steers after prolonged consumption of endophyte-infected tall fescue.J. Anim. Sci: 78:1029-1035.

Oliver, J., J. Waller, H. Fribourg, K. Gwinn, M. Cottrell, and S. Cox. 2000. Aminoacidemia in cattle grazed on endophyte-infected tall fescue. Proc. IV Intern. *Neoptyphodium*/Grass Interactions Symposium 27-29 Sept., Soest, Germany.pp. 66, 241-244.

Waller, J., H. Fribourg, R. Carlisle, G. Latch, L. Fletcher, R. Hay, H. Easton, and B. Tapper. 2000. Tall fescues with novel endophytes in Tennessee. Proc. IV Intern. *Neotyphodium*/Grass Interactions Symposium 27-29 Sept., Soest, Germany.p. 142.

Pavao-Zuckerman, M.A., J.C. Waller, T. Ingle, and H.A. Fribourg. 1999. Methane emissions of beef cattle grazing tall fescue pastures at three levels of endophyte infestation.J. Enviro. Qual. 28:1963-1969.

Schultze, A.E., B.W. Rohrbach, H.A. Fribourg, J.C. Waller, and J.W. Oliver. 1999. Alterations in bovine serum biochemistry profiles associated with prolonged consumption of endophyte infected tall fescue. Veterinary & Human Toxicology 41:133-139.

Gwinn, K.D., H.A. Fribourg, J.C. Waller, A.M. Saxton, and M. Smith. 1998. Changes in *Neotyphodium coenophialum* infestation levels in tall fescue pastures due to different grazing pressures. Crop Sci. 38:201-204.

Oliver, J.W., J.R. Strickland, J.C. Waller, H.A. Fribourg, R.D. Linnabary, and L.K. Abney. 1998. Endophytic fungal toxin effect on adrenergic receptors in lateral saphenous veins (cranial branch) of cattle grazing tall fescue.J. Anim. Sci. 76:2853-2856.

Carter, J.D., O.J.-P. Ball, K.D. Gwinn, and H.A. Fribourg. 1997. Immunological detection of the *Neotyphodium*-like endophyte of annual ryegrass. Proc. 3rd. Intern. Symposium on *Acremonium*/Grass Interactions, Athens, GA, 28-31 May.

Batzer, J.C., K.D. Gwinn, and H.A. Fribourg. 1997. Effects of germinative events on endophyte-mediated resistance to *Pythium aphanidermatum*. Proc. 3rd. Intern. Symposium on *Acremonium*/Grass Interactions, Athens, GA, 28-31 May.

Fribourg, H.A. 1997. Fescue. *In* Encyclopedia of Science & Technology. 8th.ed.vol.7:99. McGraw-Hill, New York.

Fribourg, H.A., and J.C. Waller. 1997. Environmental quality and production efficiency of beef cattle in tall fescue pasture systems. Proc. XVIII Intern. Grassland Cong., Winnipeg, Manitoba, Canada, 8-19 June.p. 11-11 to 11-12.

Fribourg, H.A., and J.C. Waller. 1997. Native and other warm season perennial grasses in Tennessee. Tennessee Agric. Exp. Sta. Res. Rpt. 97-12. 13 pp.

Waller, J.C., and H.A. Fribourg, H.A. 1997. Strategies for improving efficiency of beef cattle in tall fescue pasture systems. Proc. XVIII Intern. Grassland Cong., Winnipeg, Manitoba, Canada, 8-19 June.p. 11-9 to 11-10.

Coley, A.B., H.A. Fribourg, M.R. Pelton, and K.D. Gwinn. 1995. Effects of tall fescue endophyte infestation on small mammal abundance.J. Environ. Qual. 24:472-475.

Fribourg, H.A. 1995. Summer annual forages. Chapter 37, pp. 463-472. *In* R.F. Barnes, D.E. Miller, and C.J. Nelson (ed.) Forages. vol I: An Introduction to Grassland Agriculture, 5th ed. Iowa State Univ. Press. Ames, Iowa.

Maxwell, T.J., H.A. Fribourg, et al. 1995. Program Review of Pasture Systems and Watershed Management Research Laboratory, USDA-ARS. Scientific/Technical Panel Report. 12-13 February 1995. PSWMRL, Curlin Rd., University Park, PA 16801. 27 pp.

Fribourg, H.A., J.C. Waller, R.W. Thompson, and W.L. Sanders. 1994. Mixed models for combined analysis of grazing studies.

Workshop Proc. 15th. European Grassland Federation, Wageningen, The Netherlands.pp. 10-13. 6-9 June.

Fribourg, H.A. 1993. Toxicoses in animals and management strategies to reduce the effects of endophyte toxins—[invited] Facilitator's comments. *In* D.E. Hume, G.C.M. Latch, and H.S. Easton (ed) Proc. 2nd. Intern. Symposium on *Acremonium*/Grass Interactions (Plenary papers), Palmerston North, New Zealand. pp. 123-127. ISSN # 1052-5181.

Fribourg, H.A., R.W. Thompson, J.C. Waller, and W.L. Sanders. 1993. Inference space choices in combined mixed model analyses of discrete grazing trials. Proc. XVII Intern. Grassland Congress, Palmerston North, New Zealand, 8-21 Feb. vol. I:762-763.

Thompson, R.W., H.A. Fribourg, J.C. Waller, W.L. Sanders, J.H. Reynolds, J.M. Phillips, S.P. Schmidt, R.J. Crawford, Jr., V.G. Allen, D.B. Faulkner, C.S. Hoveland, J.P. Fontenot, R.J. Carlisle, and P.P. Hunter. 1993. Combined analysis of tall fescue steer grazing studies in the eastern United States.J. Anim. Sci. 71:1940-1947.

Waller, J.C., H.A. Fribourg, R.W. Thompson, and A.B. Chestnut. 1993. Steer performance from tall fescue pastures with three levels of *Acremonium coenophialum* infestation. Proc. XVII Intern. Grassland Congress, Hamilton, New Zealand, 13-16 Feb.vol. II:1377-1378.

Chestnut, A.B., P.D. Anderson, M.A. Cochran, H.A. Fribourg, and K.D. Gwinn. 1992. Effects of hydrated sodium calcium aluminosilicate on fescue toxicosis and mineral absorption.J. Anim. Sci. 70:2838-2846.

Chestnut, A.B., H.A. Fribourg, D.O. Onks, J.B. McLaren, K.D. Gwinn, and M.A. Mueller. 1992. Performance of cows and calves with continuous or rotational stocking of endophyte infested tall fescue-clover pastures.J. Prod. Agric. 5:405-408.

Forage and Grazing Terminology Committee. 1992. Terminology for grazing lands and grazing animals.V.G. Allen (ed.) and 31 authors including H.A. Fribourg.J. Prod. Agric. 5:191-201.

Fribourg, H.A., K.D. Gwinn, and C.L. Schardl. 1992. Glossary of Tall Fescue Toxicosis Terminology.J. Prod. Agric. 5:189-190.

Wells, G.R., and H.A. Fribourg. 1992. Sustainable biomass production on marginal agricultural land.p. 17-26. *In* J.S. Cundiff (ed.) Liquid Fuels from Renewable Resources. Proc. Amer. Soc. Agric. Engrs., 14-15 Dec., Nashville TN.

Chestnut, A.B., H.A. Fribourg, K.D. Gwinn, P.D. Anderson, and M.A. Cochran. 1991. Effect of ammoniation on toxicity of *Acremonium coenophialum* infested tall fescue. Anim. Feed Sci. Technol. 35:227-236.

Chestnut, A.B., H.A. Fribourg, J.B. McLaren, D.G. Keltner, B.B. Reddick, R.J. Carlisle, and M.C. Smith. 1991. Effects of *Acremonium coenophialum* infestation, bermudagrass, and nitrogen or clover on steers grazing tall fescue pastures.J. Prod. Agric. 4:208-213.

Fribourg, H.A., A.B. Chestnut, R.W. Thompson, J.B. McLaren, R.J. Carlisle, K.D. Gwinn, M.C. Dixon, and M.C. Smith. 1991. Steer performance in fescue pastures with different levels of endophyte infestation. Agron.J. 83:777-781.

Fribourg, H.A., C.S. Hoveland, and P. Codron. 1991. La fétuque élevée et l'*Acremonium coenophialum*—Aperçu de la situation aux Etats Unis [Tall fescue and *Acremonium coenophialum*—Review of current situation in the United States]. Fourrages, la Revue de l'Association Française pour la Production Fourragère 126:209-223.

Chestnut, A.B., H.A. Fribourg, M.A. Cochran, and P.D. Anderson. 1990. Effects of ammoniating *Acremonium coenophialum* infested fescue hay on signs of fescue toxicosis in sheep. *In* S.S. Quisenberry and R.E. Joost (ed.) Baton Rouge, LA. Proc. Intern. Symposium *Acremonium*/Grass Interactions. New Orleans LA, November 5-7, 1990. p. 212-215.

Fribourg, H.A., A.B. Chestnut, R.W. Thompson, J.B. McLaren, R.J. Carlisle, K.D. Gwinn, M.C. Dixon, and M.C. Smith. 1990. *Acremonium coenophialum* infestation levels in *Festuca arundinacea* pastures and steer performance. *In* S.S. Quisenberry and R.E. Joost (ed.) Baton Rouge, LA. Proc. Intern. Symposium *Acremonium*/Grass Interactions. New Orleans LA, November 5-7, 1990. p. 221-224.

Fribourg, H.A., J. Meier, G.P. Owens, V. Lopes, and J. Hodson. 1990. Final Evaluations of the Food Crops Research Project (655-

0011) and the Watershed Development Project (655-0013), and the PL 480 Title 206 Program and Design Recommendations for a Consolidated Project. Prepared for US Agency for International Development, Praia, Cape Verde, under REDSO/WCA Indefinite Quantity Contract No. 624-0510-I-00-9039-00, by Experience, Inc., Washington, DC.

Fribourg, H.A., A.S. Wattenbarger, J.D. Burns, and J.L. Kazda. 1990. Revegetation and beautification of roadsides in Tennessee. USDA, Soil Conservation Service and Institute of Agriculture, University of Tennessee. SP 162, 2nd.rev.

Savary, B.J., K.D. Gwinn, J.W. Oliver, A.B. Chestnut, R.D. Linnabary, J.B. McLaren, and H.A. Fribourg. 1990. Analysis of ergopeptine alkaloids in bovine serum. *In* S. Quisenberry and R.E. Joost (ed.) Baton Rouge, LA. Proc. Intern. Symposium *Acremonium*/Grass Interactions. New Orleans LA, November 5-7, 1990. p. 263-266.

Chestnut, A.B., B.H. Erickson, P.P. McKenzie, H.A. Fribourg, J.B. McLaren, and J.C. Waller. 1989. Effect of differing levels of fungal (*Acremonium coenophialum*) infection of tall fescue (*Festuca arundinacea*) on bovine serum prolactin. Proc. XVI Intern. Grassland Congress, Nice, France, Oct. 1989(1):701-702.

Fribourg, H.A., C.R. Graves, G.N. Rhodes, Jr., J.F. Bradley, E.C. Bernard, G.M. Lessman, M.A. Mueller, R.B. Graves, M.L. Thornton, B.A. Latka, and A.M. Plouy. 1989. Rapeseed - A potential new crop. Tennessee Agric. Exp. Sta. Bull. 669.

Fribourg, H.A., J.B. McLaren, A.B. Chestnut, and J.C. Waller. 1989. Recent effects of *Acremonium coenophialum* Morgan-Jones & Gams on the performance of beef cattle grazing *Festuca arundinacea* Schreb. Proc. XVI Intern. Grassland Congress, Nice, France, Oct. 1989(1):705-706.

Fribourg, H.A., M.C. Smith, and R.J. Carlisle. 1989. Forage productivity on adjacent soils in the loessial plain of West Tennessee.J. Prod. Agric. 2:305-308.

Fribourg, H.A., G.R. Wells, H. Calonne, E. Dujardin, D.D. Tyler, J.T. Ammons, R.M. Evans, A. Houston, M.C. Smith, M.E. Timpson, and G.G. Percell. 1989. Forage and tree production on marginal soils in Tennessee.J. Prod. Agric. 2:262-268.

Graveel, J.G., H.A. Fribourg, J.R. Overton, F.F. Bell, and W.L. Sanders. 1989. Response of corn to soil variation in West Tennessee, 1957-1980. J. Prod. Agric. 2:300:305.

Thompson, R.W., H.A. Fribourg, and B.B. Reddick. 1989. Sampling intensity and timing for detecting incidence of *Acremonium coenophialum* in fescue pastures. Agron.J. 81:966-971.

Waller, J.C., J.B. McLaren, H.A. Fribourg, A.B. Chestnut, and D.G. Keltner. 1989. Effects of *Acremonium coenophialum* infected *Festuca arundinacea* Schreb.on cow-calf production. Proc. XVI Intern. Grassland Congress, Nice, France, Oct. 1989(2):1193-1194.

Zanzalari, K.P., R.N. Heitmann, J.B. McLaren, and H.A. Fribourg. 1989. Effects of endophyte infected fescue and cimetidine on respiration rates, rectal temperatures, and hepatic mixed function oxidase activity as measured by hepatic antipyrine metabolism in sheep.J. Anim. Sci. 68:3370-3378.

Fribourg, H.A., S.R. Wilkinson, and G.N. Rhodes, Jr. 1988. Switching from fungus infested to fungus free tall fescue pastures.J. Prod. Agric. 1:122-127.

Gudlin, M.J., R.W. Dimmick, and H.A. Fribourg. 1988. Acceptability of hyacinth bean as food for bobwhite quail.J. Tennessee Acad. Sci. 63:79-81.

Waller, J.C., J.C. Forcherio, H.A. Fribourg, M.D. Vaught, M.C. Smith, and R.J. Carlisle. 1988. Performance of fall calving cows and their calves grazing fescue-based forage systems.J. Prod. Agr. 1:338-342.

Graveel, J.G., and H.A. Fribourg. 1987. Using reading grade level to assess readability of selected plant and soil science textbooks.J. Agron. Educ. 16:24-29.

Fribourg, H.A., D.G. Keltner, and J.B. McLaren. 1986. Effects of *Acremonium coenophialum* on forage intake and beef production from tall fescue pastures. *In* F.M. Borba and J.M. Abreu (ed.) Proc. 11th. Meet. European Grassland Fed., Troia, Portugal, 4-9 May, Soc. Portug. Past. Forr., P.O. Box 67351, Elvas, Portugal.p.489-493.

Mitchell, R.L., H.A. Fribourg, and J.B. McLaren. 1986. Validation of the Species Composition Index. Agric. Systems 20:269-279.

Mitchell, R.L., J.B. McLaren, and H.A. Fribourg. 1986. Forage growth, consumption, and performance of steers grazing bermudagrass and fescue mixtures. Agron.J. 78:675-680.

Fribourg, H.A. 1985. Summer annual forages.p. 278-286. *In* M.E. Heath, D.S. Metcalfe, and R.F. Barnes (ed.) Forages. 4th ed. Iowa State Univ. Press. Ames, Iowa.

Fribourg, H.A., and J.B. McLaren. 1985. The Species Composition Index: A tool for explaining variability in grazing experiments. Proc. XV Intern. Grassland Congress, Kyoto, Japan: 666-668.

Fribourg, H.A., and K.W. Bell. 1984. Yield and composition of tall fescue stockpiled for different periods. Agron.J. 76:929-934.

Fribourg, H.A., R.J. Carlisle, and J.B. McLaren. 1984. Bermudagrass, tall fescue and orchardgrass pasture combinations with clover or N fertilization for grazing steers. II. The species composition index and variability in forage growth and consumption, and animal performance. Agron.J. 76:615-619.

Fribourg, H.A., J.R. Overton, W.W. McNeill, E.W. Culvahouse, M.J. Montgomery, M. Smith, R.J. Carlisle, and N.W. Robinson. 1984. Evaluations of the potential of hyacinth bean as an annual warm- season forage in the Mid-South. Agron.J. 76: 905:910.

Hannaway, D.B., D. Fuhrer, and H.A. Fribourg. 1983. An interactive computer program for plotting bar and line graphs. Agron.J. 75:844-845.

McLaren, J.B., R.J. Carlisle, H.A. Fribourg, and J.M. Bryan. 1983. Bermudagrass, tall fescue and orchardgrass pasture combinations with clover or N fertilization for grazing steers.I. Forage growth and consumption, and animal performance. Agron.J. 75:587-592.

Barth, K.M., J.B. McLaren, H.A. Fribourg, and L.A. Carver. 1982. Crude protein content of forage consumed by steers grazing nitrogen-fertilized bermudagrass and orchardgrass-ladino clover pastures.J. Anim. Sci. 55:1008-1014.

Fribourg, H.A., R.J. Carlisle, and V.H. Reich. 1982. Warm- and cool-season forage crop yields on adjacent soils. Agron.J. 74:664-667.

Fribourg, H.A., J.B. McLaren, and R.J. Carlisle. 1982. Increasing productivity and extending grazing season of *Cynodon* pastures for steers with N and overseedings of *Trifolium* and *Festuca* in the southeastern U.S. In J.A. Smith and V.H. Hays (ed.) Proc. XIV Inter. Grassland Congress:714-715.

Creel, R.J., and H.A. Fribourg. 1981. Interactions between forage sorghum cultivars and defoliation managements. Agron.J. 73:463-469.

Fribourg, H.A., and R.J. Carlisle. 1981. Teaching statistical methods with the Statistical Analysis System (SAS). J. Agron. Educ. 10:19-23.

Fribourg, H.A., and R.J. Creel. 1981. Selection of concomitant variables affecting regrowth, yield and digestibility in forage sorghums. Agron.J. 73:443-445.

Fribourg, H.A., C.H. Jent, S. Maher, J.D. Burns, and J.H. Paugh. 1981. Guide to revegetation of surface coal-mined areas in Tennessee. USDA, SCS, and UT, Inst. Agric., SP-248. 27 pp.

Fribourg, H.A., K.M. Barth, J.B. McLaren, L.A. Carver, J.T. Connell, and J.M. Bryan. 1979. Seasonal trends of in vitro dry matter digestibility of N-fertilized bermudagrass and of orchardgrass-ladino pastures. Agron.J. 71:117-120.

Fribourg, H.A., B.F. Headden, J.D. Burns, and D. Henry. 1979. Revegetation and beautification of roadsides in Tennessee with grasses, legumes and other selected plants. USDA, SCS, and UT Inst. Agric., SP-162 (Rev.).

Fribourg, H.A., J.B. McLaren, K.M. Barth, J.M. Bryan, and J.T. Connell. 1979. Productivity and quality of bermudagrass and orchardgrass-ladino clover pastures for beef steers. Agron.J. 71:315-320.

Fribourg, H.A., and J.R. Overton. 1979. Persistence and productivity of tall fescue in bermudagrass sods subjected to different clipping managements. Agron.J. 71:620-624.

Carver, L.A., K.M. Barth, J.B. McLaren, H.A. Fribourg, J.T. Connell, and J.M. Bryan. 1978. Total digestible nutrient content of consumed forage and total digestible nutrient consumption by yearling beef steers grazing nitrogen-fertilized bermudagrass and orchardgrass-ladino clover pastures.J. Animal Sci. 47:699-707.

Carver, L.A., K.M. Barth, J.B. McLaren, H.A. Fribourg, J.T. Connell, and J.M. Bryan. 1978. Plasma urea nitrogen levels in beef steers grazing nitrogen-fertilized bermudagrass and orchardgrass-ladino pastures.J. Anim. Sci. 47:927-934.

Chamberlain, C.C., K.M. Barth, and H.A. Fribourg. 1978. Corn silage maturity and beef heifer performance. Tennessee Agric. Exp. Station Bul. 583.

Fribourg, H.A., and D.L. Ingram. 1978. Probability of low and high temperatures in Tennessee. NOAA Tech. Memo EDS 23.

Fribourg, H.A., and R.W. Loveland. 1978. Seasonal production, perloline content, and quality of fescue after N fertilization. Agron.J. 70:741-745.

Fribourg, H.A., and R.W. Loveland. 1978. Production, digestibility, and perloline content of fescue stockpiled and harvested at different seasons. Agron.J. 70:745-747.

Ingram, D.L., and H.A. Fribourg. 1978. Heating and cooling degree days for Tennessee. NOAA Tech. Memo EDS 24.

Fribourg, H.A., and J.B. Williams. 1977. Guinea agricultural production capacity and training project—Final report. Center for Research on Economic Development. Univ. Michigan, Ann Arbor. AID Project 675-11-130-0201, AFR/DR/SFWAP. 377 pp.

Fribourg, H.A. 1976. Food for survival? Ethics, food and people. Phi Kappa Phi Journal 56(2):10-16.

Fribourg, H.A. 1976. Agronomic education in Turkish universities—Implications for foreign graduate student programs in the USA.J. Agron. Educ. 5:48-52.

Fribourg, H.A., W.E. Bryan, G.M. Lessman, and D.M. Manning. 1976. Nutrient uptake by corn and grain sorghum silage as affected by soil type, planting date, and moisture regime. Agron.J. 68:260-263.

Fribourg, H.A., B.N. Duck, and E.M. Culvahouse. 1976. Forage sorghum yield components and their in-vivo digestibility. Agron.J. 68:361-365.

Fribourg, H.A., D.B. Hannaway, and V.K. Patterson. 1976. A versatile generalized computer program for generating CALCOMP plots of data points, histograms, and functions. Agron.J. 68:829-830.

Fribourg, H.A., W.E. Bryan, F.F. Bell, and G.J. Buntley. 1975. Performance of selected silage and summer annual grass crops as affected by soil type, planting date, and moisture regime. Agron.J. 67:643-647.

Fribourg, H.A., J.R. Overton, and J.A. Mullins. 1975. Wheel traffic on regrowth and production of summer annual grasses. Agron.J. 67:423-426.

Fribourg, H.A. 1974. Fertilization of summer annual grasses and silage crops.p. 189-211. In D.A. Mays (ed.) Forage Fertilization. Amer. Soc. Agron. Madison, WI.

Fribourg, H.A. 1974. Tarım ve sorunları (Problems of Modern Agriculture). (In Turkish) Bitki 1(2):246-256.

Montgomery, M.J., H.A. Fribourg, J.R. Overton, and W.M. Hopper. 1974. Effect of maturity of corn on silage quality and milk production.J. Dairy Sci. 57:698-703.

Safley, Jr., J.M., H.A. Fribourg, J.V. Vaiksnoras, and R.H. Strand. 1974. Probability of sequences of wet and dry days for Tennessee. NOAA Tech. Memo. EDS 22.

Tabor, R.L., F.F. Bell, G.J. Buntley, H.A. Fribourg, and M.E. Springer. 1974. Agronomic productivity of the landscapes of three soil associations in Maury County, Tennessee: An analysis.J. Soil & Water Conserv. 29:272-275.

Fribourg, H.A. 1973. Summer annual grasses and cereals for forage.p. 344-357. In M.E. Heath, D.S. Metcalfe, and R.F. Barnes (ed.) Forages. 3rd ed. Iowa State Univ. Press. Ames, Iowa.

Fribourg, H.A., and J.R. Overton. 1973. Forage production on bermudagrass sods overseeded with tall fescue and winter annual grasses. Agron.J. 65:295-298.

Fribourg, H.A., and R.H. Strand. 1973. Influence of seeding dates and methods on establishment of small-seeded legumes. Agron.J. 65:804-807.

Fribourg, H.A., R.H. Strand, and J.V. Vaiksnoras. 1973. Precipitation probabilities for West Tennessee. Tennessee Agric. Exp. Station Bul. 510.

Fribourg, H.A., R.H. Strand, J.V. Vaiksnoras, and J.M. Safley, Jr. 1973. Precipitation probabilities for East Tennessee. Tennessee Agric. Exp. Station Bul. 512.

Fribourg, H.A., R.H. Strand, J.V. Vaiksnoras, and W.L. Sanders. 1973. Relationship between the empirically-estimated parameters of the incomplete gamma function used in calculating precipitation probabilities and climatic variation in Tennessee. NOAA Tech. Memo. CLIMAT-2, Environmental Data Service Series.

Kilgore, W.L., B.L. Bledsoe, H.A. Fribourg, J.B. McLaren, J.M. Bryan, and J.T. Connell. 1973. Performance of three hay packaging and handling systems as affected by hay moisture content. Proc. Assoc. South. Agric. Workers:30.

Strand, R.H., and H.A. Fribourg. 1973. Relationships between seeding dates and some concomitant environmental variables, seeding methods, and establishment of small-seeded legumes. Agron.J. 65:807-810.

Strand, R.H., H.A. Fribourg, and J.V. Vaiksnoras. 1973. Precipitation probabilities for Middle Tennessee. Tennessee Agric. Exp. Station Bul. 511.

Fribourg, H.A. 1972. Quantification of the aspect parameter in ecological site characterizations. Ecology 53:977-979.

Strand, R.H., and H.A. Fribourg. 1972. A computerized personal bibliographic reference system. Agron.J. 64:845-847.

Chamberlain, C.C., H.A. Fribourg, K.M. Barth, J.H. Felts, and J.M. Anderson. 1971. Effect of maturity of corn silage at harvest on the performance of feeder heifers.J. Anim. Sci. 33:161-166.

Edwards, N.C., Jr., H.A. Fribourg, and M.J. Montgomery. 1971. Cutting management effects on growth and regrowth after cutting and on dry matter digestibility of the sorghum-sudangrass cultivar Sudax SX-11. Agron.J. 63:267-271.

Fribourg, H.A., N.C. Edwards, Jr., and K.M. Barth. 1971. *In vitro* dry matter digestibility of 'Midland' bermudagrass grown at several levels of nitrogen fertilization. Agron.J. 63:786-788.

Benson, J.A., E. Gray, and H.A. Fribourg. 1969. Relation of hydrocyanic acid potential of leaf samples to that of whole plants of sorghum. Agron.J. 61:223-224.

Fribourg, H.A., D.K. Springer, J.D. Burns, K.E. Graetz, C.H. Jent, and C.M. Henninger. 1969. Roadside revegetation and beautification in Tennessee. USDA, SCS and Inst. Agric., Univ. Tennessee SP-162. Rev.

Beuerlein, J.E., H.A. Fribourg, and F.F. Bell. 1968. Effects of environment and cutting on the regrowth of a sorghum-sudangrass hybrid. Crop Sci. 8:152-155.

Fribourg, H.A., R.H. Brown, G.M. Prine, and T.H. Taylor. 1967. Aspects of the microclimate at five locations in the southeastern United States. South. Reg. Series Bul. 124.

Fribourg, H.A. 1966. Performance of summer annual grasses for grazing and green-chopping, 1955-1966. Tennessee Agric. Exp. Station Bul. 413:78-85.

Springer, D.K., H.A. Fribourg, J.D. Burns, and K. Graetz. 1966. Roadside revegetation and beautification—grasses, legumes and other plants for roadside revegetation and beautification in Tennessee. Tennessee Agric. Exp. Station, Tennessee Agric. Ext. Service, and USDA, Soil Conservation Service, Bul. SP-162.

Fribourg, H.A. 1965. Summer annual grasses for Tennessee. Tennessee Agric. Exp. Station Bul. 373 (Rev.).

Fribourg, H.A. 1965. Performance of summer annual grasses for grazing and green-chopping—1965. Tennessee Agric. Exp. Station Bul. 396:63-70.

Fribourg, H.A. 1965. Performance of summer annual grasses for grazing and green-chopping. Tennessee Agric. Exp. Station Bul. 384:51-58.

Fribourg, H.A. 1965. The effect of morphology and defoliation intensity on the tillering, regrowth and leafiness of pearlmillet, *Pennisetum typhoides* (Burm.) Stapf. & C.E. Hubb. Proc. IX Intern. Grassland Congress:489-491.

Fribourg, H.A. 1963. Performance of some forage crop varieties, 1945-1962. Tennessee Agric. Exp. Station Bul. 371.

Fribourg, H.A. 1963. Summer annual forage grasses for Tennessee. Tennessee Agric. Exp. Station Bul. 373.

Fribourg, H.A., and V.K. McCombs. 1963. Programs for computing agronomic forage data using electronic data processing techniques. Agron.J. 55:405-407.

Fribourg, H.A., and W.W. Stanley. 1960. The effect of heptachlor and toxaphene on stand of ladino clover. Econ. Entom. 53:1134-1135.

Broyles, K.R., and H.A. Fribourg. 1959. Nitrogen fertilization and cutting management of sudangrass and millets. Agron.J. 51:277-279.

Johnson, L.F., E.A. Curl, J.H. Bond, and H.A. Fribourg. 1959. Methods of studying soil microflora-plant disease relationships. Burgess Pub. Co., Minneapolis, Minn. 178 pp.

Fribourg, H.A., and W.V. Bartholomew. 1956. Availability of nitrogen from crop residues during the first and second seasons after application. Soil Sci. Soc. Amer. Proc. 20:505-508.

Fribourg, H.A., and I.J. Johnson. 1955. Dry matter and nitrogen yields of legume tops and roots in the fall of the seeding year. Agron.J. 47:73-77.

Fribourg, H.A., and I.J. Johnson. 1955. Response of soybean strains to 2,4-D and 2,4,5-T. Agron.J. 47:171-174.

Fribourg, H.A. 1953. A rapid method for washing roots. Agron.J. 45: 334-335.

Fribourg, H.A., and W.K. Kennedy. 1953. The effect of rates of seeding on the yield and survival of alfalfa in meadow mixtures. Agron.J. 45:251-257.

ABOUT THE AUTHOR

Born in Paris in 1929, Henry Fribourg escaped the Holocaust with his family in January 1942, taking refuge in Cuba. In 1945, his family arrived in the United States and became US citizens in 1951. He earned degrees from the University of Wisconsin, Cornell University and Iowa State College, prior to serving in the US Army during the Korean conflict. In 1956, he married Claude Brunschwig; they have two children, Daniel and Renée. Shortly after his marriage, he joined the faculty of the University of Tennessee, serving for forty-six years as a Professor of Forage Crops Ecology. Henry has been active in Temple Beth El, a Reform synagogue, serving for many years on its Board of Directors and as President of the congregation. He retired in 2001 and has been reading and writing while continuing to reside within the view of the Great Smoky Mountains in Knoxville, Tennessee.

Printed in the United States
75839LV00005B/65